THE CLASSICS
OF WESTERN
SPIRITUALITY

George A. Maloney, S.J. — Director, John XXIII Ecumenical Center, Fordham University, Bronx, N.Y.

Bernard McGinn — Associate Professor of Historical Theology and History of Christianity, University of Chicago Divinity School, Chicago, Ill.

John Meyendorff — Professor of Patristics and Church History, St. Vladimir's Seminary, Tuckahoe, N.Y.

Seyyed Hossein Nasr — President, Imperial Iranian Academy of Philosophy, Teheran, Iran.

Heiko A. Oberman — Director, Institute fuer Spaetmittelalter und Reformation, Universitaet Tuebingen, West Germany.

Alfonso Ortiz — Professor of Anthropology, University of New Mexico, Albuquerque, N. Mex.; Fellow, The Center for Advanced Study, Stanford, Calif.

Raimundo Panikkar — Professor, Department of Religious Studies, University of California at Santa Barbara, Calif.

Fazlar Rahman — Professor of Islamic Thought, Department of Near Eastern Languages and Civilization, University of Chicago, Chicago, Ill.

Sandra M. Schneiders — Assistant Professor of New Testament Studies and Spirituality, Jesuit School of Theology, Berkeley, Calif.

Huston Smith — Thomas J. Watson Professor of Religion, Adjunct Professor of Philosophy, Syracuse University, Syracuse, N.Y.

John R. Sommerfeldt — Director, The Center for Contemplative Studies, Western Michigan University, Kalamazoo, Mich.

David Steindl-Rast — Monk of Mount Savior Monastery, Pine City, N.Y.

William C. Sturtevant — General Editor, Handbook of North American Indians, Smithsonian Institution, Washington, D.C.

Isaiah Tishby — Professor of Medieval Literature, Hebrew University, Jerusalem, Israel

David Tracy — Professor of Theology, University of Chicago Divinity School, Chicago, Ill.

Victor Turner — William B. Kenan Professor in Anthropology, The Center for Advanced Study, University of Virginia, Charlottesville, Va.

Kallistos Ware — Fellow of Pembroke College, Oxford; Spaulding Lecturer in Eastern Orthodox Studies, Oxford University, England.

NAHMAN
OF
BRATSLAV
THE TALES

TRANSLATION, INTRODUCTION AND COMMENTARIES
BY
ARNOLD J. BAND

PREFACE
BY
JOSEPH DAN

PAULIST PRESS
NEW YORK • RAMSEY • TORONTO

Cover Art:
The artist, POMONA HALLENBECK is a native of the southwest who now lives in New York City and teaches at schools and workshops in New York, Texas, New Mexico and Canada. She also does textile designs and multimedia education materials. Of her cover for Nahman of Bratslav, *The Tales*, she says: "Nahman was a teller of tales . . . a guardian of folklore . . . a communicator of direct insights through the medium of symbolisms. His tales became the avenue for fusing fantasy and spiritual truths as he perceived them.

"The symbolic imagery therefore is represented here with visual shapes expressed through symbolic use of color. The areas of white represent light, innocence, joy, purity, glory. The whiteness of the princess is that purity for which one searches; the whiteness of Nahman's face reveals his search . . . for the Lost Princess . . . or the attributes of whiteness. The lightness and brightness are equated with superior spirituality, intelligence, and are suggestive of God's Presence. The blue-whiteness of the castle indicates the ethereal quality of the search . . . that element of the unknown for which one must take risks. The use of gold suggests solar and illuminated truth, truth removed from un-awareness. The horse becomes consciousness. . . . the instrument of transportation to the castle . . . through the elements of un-knowing, to full realization . . . illumination . . . to En-lightenment."

Design: Barbini Pesce & Noble, Inc.

Library of Congress
Catalog Card Number: 78-53433

ISBN: 0-8091-0238-2 (Paper)
ISBN: 0-8091-2103-4 (Cloth)

Published by Paulist Press
Editorial Office: 1865 Broadway, New York, N.Y. 10023
Business Office: 545 Island Road, Ramsey, N.J. 07446

Printed and bound in the
United States of America

PREFACE

CONTENTS

The Editors of this Volume:

ARNOLD J. BAND is Professor of Hebrew and Comparative Literature at U.C.L.A. Having completed his Ph.D. in Comparative Literature at Harvard University he went on for further study at Hebrew University, Jerusalem, and the University of Paris. He is a Past President of the Association for Jewish Studies (1973-75) and has held visiting Professorships at the University of Indiana, Hebrew University, Tel Aviv University, Harvard University, the University of Judaism, and Hebrew Union College.

Dr. Band has published many scholarly articles in both Hebrew and English as well as a volume of Hebrew poetry. His books include *Nostalgia and Nightmare: A Study in the Fiction of S.Y. Agnon* (University of California Press, 1968).

Professor Band has been Chairman of the Comparative Literature Program at U.C.L.A. since 1969.

JOSEPH DAN was born in Bratislava, Czechoslovakia in 1935 and immigrated to Jerusalem, Israel in 1938. Since 1974 he has been Professor of Kabbalah in the Department of Jewish Thought at Hebrew University in Jerusalem and is currently the Taubman Visiting Professor of Judaic Studies at the University of California at Berkeley. Professor Dan is the author of approximately one hundred scholarly articles and papers and nine books including *The Hasidic Novel* (1966), *The Hebrew Story in the Middle Ages* (1974), and *The Hasidic Story* (1975).

Hasidic literature—unlike Hasidic theology—is a very conservative literature in everything concerning its form. The teachers of Hasidism, the Zadikim, chose as their main means of expression the form of homiletics, which was a central vehicle for expressing Jewish religious ideas for nearly two millennia and became the dominant literary form in Eastern Europe in the centuries preceding the appearance of Hasidic literature late in the eighteenth century. This choice cannot be attributed to accident alone: it is quite natural for an innovative, revolutionary movement to emphasize its adherence to tradition rather than to emphasize its new departures; and homiletics, by nature, tends to magnify the element of continuity. Though the Hasidim popularized new ideas, mainly the new concept of the role of the Zadik as an intermediary between man and God, it did that, with the assistance of the basic rules of homiletics, as if this idea and others are just another layer in the infinite meanings of Biblical verses and Talmudic passages, quoting extensively medieval and early modern Jewish scholars in the field of ethics and Kabbalah, thus creating the image of continuous religious evolution rather than a new departure.

Rabbi Nahman of Bratslav was no exception. His main ideas were expressed in his massive *Likkute Moharan*, a collection of sermons and homilies written down by his faithful disciple, Rabbi Nathan. Other Bratslavic literary works, like *Sefer ha-Midot* and *Likkute Ezot*, collections of ethical advice arranged according to subject and alphabetically, also follow accepted Jewish literary norms. When viewing the very large literary production of Rabbi Nahman's school, one does not notice any new literary element which differs from the similar production of other Hasidic schools or even pre-Hasidic Jewish ethical and homiletical groups—that is, until one arrives at the tales of Rabbi Nahman, given here for the first time in a complete translation to English. These tales present a unique phenomenon, completely dissimilar to any previous Jewish mystical expression.

A unique literary phenomenon of this kind is certainly of some interest to the historian of religion, of mysticism and of literature. The question to be discussed here is: Does this phenomenon convey any message which would be of contemporary interest to the reader of literature? Do Rabbi Nahman's tales present to the twentieth century anything more than an unusual literary riddle?

The popularity of these tales today seems to prove that an affirmative answer to these questions is possible. But formulation of such an answer is very difficult; it seems that some of the answers given to this question in this century cannot be accepted. The suggestion, for instance, that by these tales Rabbi Nahman popularized his own mystical, Kabbalistic theology and presented it in a form which could be understood by the masses (a suggestion made by S.A. Horodetzki) is proved wrong by the simple fact that the tales are much more difficult than Rabbi Nahman's homiletical works. Even the closest disciples of Rabbi Nahman who wrote commentaries on these tales—Rabbi Nathan of Nemirov and Rabbi Nahman of Tcherin—claim that they do not understand many elements in these tales. The many different interpretations offered to these tales tend to demonstrate how confusing they are, from a theological point of view, rather than didactic, especially if one remembers that Rabbi Nahman was an accomplished teacher, his didactic power revealed in his sermons. Another possibility (suggested by Martin Buber), that these tales serve as exempla for moral and ethical behavior, rests upon introducing changes into the tales, cutting passages from their context and presenting interpretations which often have no basis in the text. If there was any didactic purpose to these stories, they should be regarded as an attempt which had failed completely. The history of these tales and the mounting interest in them prove clearly that this is not the case. The answer should be found in their literary characteristics, rather than in any particular ethical or theological message which they supposedly carry.

It was the late Professor Joseph Weiss of London who pointed out the intense personal nature of these tales (his work being continued today by other scholars, most notably M. Piekarz of Jerusalem), and it seems that only if we follow this element can we arrive at an understanding of both the tales themselves and their impact upon our generation. Examined as a form of personal expression, these tales require literary study, rather than a mystical or religious approach, though of course their intense religiosity and mysticism should not be minimized; these elements should be taken into account as expression, of Rabbi Nahman's personal, unique religious and mystical experience, rather than a propaganda pamphlet for certain Hasidic, Kabbalistic or ethical norms. Only in this way can the personal impact that these tales often carry, the deep impression that they sometimes have on the reader, be explained. In short, both telling these tales and reading them is primarily a literary experience.

It is not enough, however, to contend that Rabbi Nahman's tales should be read as literature, even though this is highly unusual in the history of Jewish mysticism; the question is whether these tales have any special literary merit, which would allow us to include them among the best literary works created within the framework of a religious movement. This question can be answered only if we do not regard the religious and mystical elements in the tales as separated from the personal experiences of Rabbi Nahman, but see all the elements that combined to create the tales as one, an intense spiritual autobiography presented in the guise of popular tales. This attitude (first suggested by Joseph Weiss twenty years ago) would enable us to understand the literary characteristics of the tales as well as to evaluate their place in the history of nineteenth-century narrative fiction.

When Rabbi Nahman departed from the accepted Jewish literary norms, which prevailed within the Hasidic movement and governed his own literary work until 1806, he was motivated by the feeling that some experiences cannot be conveyed by these traditional means. This starting point—which should be regarded as nothing less than revolutionary (for instance, no other Hasidic author wrote a major book without relying on Biblical verses or Talmudic passages)—is the basic starting point of literary fiction: things that can be expressed in another form, such as essays or factual manuals, should not and need not be expressed in the form of fiction. Fiction becomes a necessary means only when other systems of communication and expression have been proven to be inadequate; otherwise, fiction is superfluous. It seems that the intense emotions evoked in Rabbi Nahman by various events in 1806 (studied in detail by M. Piekarz) caused Rabbi Nahman to seek a new way to express himself, first and foremost for his own sake, and he employed all the literary materials he could command to serve this purpose.

The process of creating the stories expressed the change

in Rabbi Nahman's attitude toward his religious and Kabbalistic background. Whereas his theology, expressed in his homiletical works, is based on the teachings of the Kabbalah, especially the Zohar and the Lurianic Kabbalah (developed by Rabbi Isaak Luria in sixteenth-century Safed), his stories are based only on his own personal experience. Still, we do find major Kabbalistic elements, especially the Lurianic concepts of mythological cosmic history and mystical redemption, serving as major motifs within the tales. But there is a basic difference between "using" Kabbalistic ideas and "expressing" them in the tales: those elements which are present in the tales ceased to be building blocks of a mystical theology and became chapters in the mystical biography of Rabbi Nahman's soul. It is as if the whole enormous Lurianic mythology, which describes cosmic history as a continuous battle between the powers of God against the powers of Satan, became identified with the battle going on in Rabbi Nahman's soul. The Lurianic epic of the upheavals and catastrophes which mark the early history of the world became personal memories of earlier experiences of Rabbi Nahman's soul. The most important element — the Kabbalistic concept of messianic redemption as formulated in the generations after Luria became the essential purpose of Rabbi Nahman's soul. Everything that was happening in the earthly and celestial worlds became a part of Rabbi Nahman's personal experience—past, present and future.

This process of identification in a deep spiritual way with cosmic developments is rare, but not impossible, in both mystical and literary creative work. (It should be mentioned that a somewhat similar process is described by Rabbi Hayim Vital, the great disciple of Luria, who tells in his "Book of Visions" in great detail the migrations of his own soul—which he believed to be the soul of the messiah from generation to generation throughout history until it reached his own body. According to Vital, the information concerning this process was supplied to him by his teacher, Rabbi Isaak Luria.) It always includes a process of selection and change, for the author will not accept the external system as his own experience without personalizing the major elements in that system before they became immanent in his innermost being. Because of that, a detailed comparison between Lurianic theology and Rabbi Nahman's tales cannot result in detailed identification between the various elements, for once this process has begun, personal and biographic elements are completely identified with cosmic events and become something new, a cosmic-autobiographical experience which escapes systematic, exhaustive interpretation. The sufferings of the messiah in Jewish mythology and the sufferings of Rabbi Nahman because of the controversy raging around him or the death of his young son, or the frustrations which accompanied his messianic activities—all these become one and the same experience when described in his tales in the guise of folk-tale events. There is no meaning, for instance, to the question as to which character in the tale represents the author, for, as in all great works of literature, every character would represent some part of the author's experience, and all of them together represent his basic attitudes and the various shades of his experience. This unity between the author and the work of fiction, involving the complete transformation of every external element into a personal, intense biographic element, is both a basic requirement and the sign of success of every major literary work.

Rabbi Nahman's relationship with Lurianic Kabbalah can be compared to Tolstoy's attitude toward the Napoleonic wars. Tolstoy did not set out to write an objective history of Napoleon's impact on Russia; he experienced, in a very intense way, this enormous historical upheaval, and expressed it by the description of his various characters and their relationship to that upheaval. Rabbi Nahman did not set out to explain Lurianic myths; he expressed the deep identification between his own experience and this myth with the help of his various folk-tale characters. The objective, external nature of the Napoleonic wars is not denied by Tolstoy; it is irrelevant to his novel, for only those aspects of it which were internalized by the author contributed to the creation of the great novel, when they were mingled and identified with his other experiences. Rabbi Nahman certainly does not deny the objective truth of messianic, Lurianic Kabbalistic myths, but the relevant part of them which has any bearing on his tales is that which Rabbi Nahman internalized and completely identified with all his other experiences to create the tales.

Rabbi Nahman's tales should be regarded as a great literary accomplishment of a mystical author who achieved complete identification and unity between external and internal elements and expressed them in a unified spiritual autobiography, in the guise of folk-tales. Such achievements are very rare in the history of religious literature, and as one such rare example it should be read in the twentieth century.

Joseph Dan
The University of California, Berkeley
January 1978

FOREWORD

O F the thousands of Hasidic tales circulated in the past two centuries, few have earned the veneration and affection of the thirteen Tales of Nahman of Bratslav told by the master to his disciples in the Ukraine between 1806 and 1810. Still studied by Bratslav Hasidim as scripture, these tales have attracted a varied audience intrigued by the remarkable blend of intense Kabbalistic faith and narrative artistry. Recited in Yiddish but recorded in both Hebrew and Yiddish, these tales are usually printed in bilingual editions—Hebrew above and Yiddish below—each language version considered both holy and authentic.

In this current English translation I have tried to capture the ambience of both language-texts at the same time: the oral familiarity and charm of the Yiddish and the metaphysical rigor and grandeur of the Hebrew. To each of the tales I have prefaced a brief Editor's Prologue to set the tone and direction of the reading. At the end of the volume I have appended a fuller commentary on each tale which the reader may consult after his encounter with the text of each tale. These commentaries cover many of the main points of each tale, but cannot possibly explain everything since even Nahman's closest disciples would not pretend to understand all the allusions of the master. A general introduction on Nahman of Bratslav, his biography and theory of spiritual literature, precedes the thirteen canonical tales so that the reader may better understand the lyrical yearning, the shared symbolism, and the shrewd satire which fuse in each tale. A selected bibliography has been appended so that the reader can study the scholarly sources used in the preparation of this volume.

While I had long been dimly aware of the importance and problematics of these texts, I was inspired to render them intelligible and available to a wide audience after struggling with them in a graduate seminar I held on the Hasidic tale at U.C.L.A. in 1973-74. In the slow, tedious preparation of the translations and commentaries, I was assisted by six women: Haya Kleen, who prepared an experimental translation of some of the tales from their Hebrew source; Diana Pfeffer, who did a preliminary translation of two of the longer stories from their Yiddish source; Carol Himmelman-Christopher, Linda Paulson, and Luminita Niculescu, who typed and edited my own versions, draft after draft, as I sought the proper tone and idiom; and my wife, Ora Band, for accompanying me through the desert of doubt and frustration through which one must wander to translate and understand a difficult classical text. If, to these six women, I could have added the Lost Princess, my labors would have been totally unneccessary.

My greatest debt is owed, of course, to another seventh figure, the Seventh Beggar, the marvelous legless dancer who never appeared at the wedding feast, but whom we all still await. To him I dedicate this volume.

Arnold J. Band

INTRODUCTION

I. NAHMAN OF BRATSLAV:
A BIOGRAPHY

THE reputation of Nahman of Bratslav (1772-1810), both as charismatic religious leader and intriguing author of enigmatic tales, is inevitably associated with Hasidism, the religious and social movement which has embraced and revitalized much of Jewish spiritual life from the mid-18th century until today. Though a problematic figure in his lifetime and even after his death, Nahman has usually been accorded the title "zadik" reserved only for those saintly leaders who have succeeded in attracting large or small sects of devout adherents. Nahman never attracted large numbers of followers; yet his self-image as zadik, his concept of his role in the tradition of saintly figures throughout Jewish history and in Hasidism in particular, provide the most direct access to an understanding of this unique religious leader who emerged in a fairly backward province of Czarist Russia precisely at the threshold of the great industrial and political revolutions of the modern period.

Jewish history, to be sure, has never lacked for pious worshipers and exceptional men of deep faith and erudition. Often, in the centuries of Diasporan existence, religious praxis and belief were suffused with a longing for redemption from the bondage of exile, for a messianic age that fired the imagination by the infinite richness of its possibilities: the renewed harmony of existence, the elimination of war and deprivation, the resurrection of the dead, the return to the ancestral homeland. Hasidic (the word means "pious") leaders of the 18th century did not diverge from these traditional norms and aspirations which had shaped Jewish life. Though several generations of intense research into the origins of the Hasidic movement have produced a host of contradictory theories regarding the nature and purpose of the original sects which appeared in the southwestern Ukraine in the early decades of the 18th century, several uncontestable facts have emerged. During these decades, there appeared a variety of individual groups led by forceful, pious men, many of whom did not fit the mould of traditional rabbinical leadership which prided itself as the interpreter of the sacred law. While some of these new leaders were prodigiously learned, others were not; some adhered strictly to the traditional rabbinical norms of authoritarianism, but others indulged in charismatic practices including faith healing; some stressed asceticism while others preached service of the Lord through joy and ecstasy. Their followers also varied: Some were learned and wealthy; others were ignorant and poor.

Within these divergent currents, two religious phenomena seem to be constant. Each group developed an extraordinary allegiance to its specific leader, whose authority derived more from personal charisma than formally ordained traditional practices. This new allegiance slowly replaced the traditional structures of Jewish communal life, which had rapidly disintegrated during the wars and social upheavals in Eastern Europe during the latter half of the 17th century. And though these new leaders did not preach reform or even outwardly challenge the status quo in both praxis and belief, they did convey, often in vastly popularized form, many of the basic notions of Lurianic mysticism which had developed in Palestine in the late 16th and early 17th centuries and had rapidly spread from the Ottoman Empire into the Kingdom of Poland with which it was contiguous.

The diluted mystical doctrines disseminated by these early zadikim were probably less revolutionary than the very fact of their dissemination among masses of Jews. Mysticism, or Kabbalah, was by no means an unknown phenomenon in the Jewish world and had, by the end of the 13th century, produced a sophisticated new myth of creation and redemption which found its fullest expression in the Zohar, attributed to Rabbi Simeon bar Yohai of the 2nd century A.D., but actually written by Moses de Leon in Provence in the last two decades of the 13th century. While not rejecting the Biblical narratives and prophecies embodying the traditional notions of creation, divine governance of the universe, and redemption, the Kabbalistic exegesis of the Biblical texts suggested a subtly alternative myth to explain in great detail an elaborate theosophy to be studied only by mature, erudite scholars. Central to this myth was the sefirotic structure in which ten emanatory spheres were postulated to explain the bridge between the transcendent, perfectly ineffable divinity and the very tangible, imperfect world in which we live our daily lives. Of greatest concern to humanity was, of course, the lowest sphere, the Shekhinah: exile, in general, was often considered an analogue of the exile of the Shekhinah itself, whereby this sphere was sundered from the system; and redemption is thus the analogue of the reunion of the Shekhinah with the other spheres of the sefirotic structure. The Shekhinah is often identified with the spirit of God, which dwells within the world or within the individual soul of the worshiper or with the corporate historical entity of the people of Israel. The destiny of the cosmos is thus intertwined with the fate of the people of Israel.

In Lurianic Kabbalah, many of the previous Kabbalistic elements are refined and energized. The creation of the world is described not as an emanatory process from an infinite source of power or light, but as an act of divine contraction (*tzimtzum*) whereby God contracts himself, thereby creating space for a created world. This act is described in detail as catastrophic, the violent tempestuous clash of a variety of forces within God himself, a rending apart called *shevirat hakelim* ("the breaking of the vessels") that can be mended by the process of *tikkun* (remedying or repairing) in which man can take part. Our presentation of the basic movements of the Lurianic system has been grossly simplified here, so that one can gather that Lurianism, even in its diluted form which was probably prevalent in most early Hasidic circles, could suffuse the most mundane acts of the simplest man with redemptive drama. Adam, in fact, or other great figures of the past, could have wrought this cosmic restoration, had they been endowed with the proper spiritual temper or perseverance. But since neither Adam nor Moses nor Rabbi Simeon bar Yohai himself had these requisite characteristics, the opportunity was still available for the individual, or for the Jewish people as a whole, or—more importantly—for the proper zadik, to effect this restoration of the primordial harmony. The way had been clearly delineated from the beginning of time in the Torah itself, but we mortals have not been able to achieve the proper degree of intense prayer, fervent praxis, or categorical belief necessary for the act.

The Lurianic portrayal of this process was dazzling in its complexity but even in its popularized versions sufficed to give the masses of downtrodden Jews, often recent exiles, some sense of the meaning of the world, an understanding of their repeated exiles, and hopes for redemption through prayer and praxis. It certainly helped prepare tens of thousands of Jews to accept the messianic claims of Shabbetai Zevi in 1666 and, despite the normative rabbinic reaction to all signs of messianic claims usually identified with Shabbateanism in the late 17th and early 18th centuries, it could infuse the early, often isolated groups of early Hasidim with religious ardor. This new ardor coupled with the comforting sense of belonging to a cohesive sect led by a self-assured, forceful religious leader contributes significantly to our understanding of the emergence of dozens of these groups in the southwestern Ukraine, specifically in Podolia, in the early decades of the 18th century.

By the third and fourth decades of the century, many of these groups coalesced under the charismatic leadership of Israel Baal Shem Tov (usually called "The Besht," 1700-1760), the zadik considered by all later Hasidim—and historians—as the founder of the movement. A popular though far from ignorant charismatic healer who employed amulets and magic spells, the Besht attracted masses of adherents who came to be cured and join him in ecstatic prayer, one of the special characteristics of his religious praxis. Precisely because of the dynamic relationship between the zadik and his follower, the term "Hasid," which formerly meant simply "pious," developed the connotation of "pious adherent of a certain charismatic leader, of a certain Rebbe or zadik." Both the Besht and his Hasidim clearly believed in his supernatural powers and visions, which were featured in a wealth of anecdotes narrated either by the master himself or by his Hasidim. The Hasidic tale, in fact, was one of the prominent literary genres spawned by the Hasidic movement as such, though it did not neglect more traditional genres such as exegesis and homily. By the time of his death in 1760, the Besht had left behind him a group of dedicated disciples and other, more tangential sects which were attracted to his charismatic posture, but had not yet adopted all his practices or the unquestioning adulation of his saintly figure.

During the twelve years following the death of the Besht, the movement was organized and shaped by his leading disciple, Dov Ber of Mezherich, which was farther north in the province of Volhynia. By 1772, the year of both the death of Dov Ber and the birth of Nahman of Bratslav, communities of Hasidim, each with its own zadik, were firmly entrenched throughout southwestern Russia and eastern Austria (Galicia) while some groups had penetrated Byelorussia, Lithuania, and even the Galilee in northern Ottoman Palestine. By 1772 the movement was powerful enough to be engaged in a bitter struggle with the traditional rabbinical authorities—called "mitnaggedim" ("opponents") by the Hasidim—involving rabbinic bans which proved to be virtually ineffectual. Nahman was thus born at the very beginning of the third generation of Hasidic masters, a generation marked by further rapid growth and nascent rivalry between the various Hasidic courts and dynasties. Obviously a sensitive child, reared in the heartland—he was born in Medzhibozh, the home of the Besht himself—of a dynamic new religious movement, Nahman could naturally aspire to the religious virtues that were to be expected of a zadik, a possible agent in the redemption of the world.

On various occasions in his life Nahman suggested that he was the fifth in the line of unique zadikim, each the great man of his times: Moses, Simeon bar Yohai, Isaac Luria, the Baal Shem Tov, Nahman of Bratslav. Any account of Nahman's concept of his role in the dynamics of history which informs his life's activities and his writings should begin with this list of paragons: conspicuously absent are the Patriarchs, Ezra, Akiba, Saadia, Maimonides, or Joseph Karo, names frequently featured in the catalogues of scholars and saints.

Nahman's catalogue embraces not great doctors of the law, but charismatic leaders, the mythic heroes of the Jewish mystical tradition. Moses, chosen to receive the Torah at Sinai, led his people through the desert to the promised land—a recurring Bratslav theme. Simeon bar Yohai, actually a 2nd-century (A.D.) rabbi, was adopted by the Kabbalists, primarily because of his centrality in the Zohar (13th century), as one of the inspired mentors of Jewish mysticism. Isaac Luria, the most seminal figure in Safedic mysticism of the 16th and 17th centuries, preached a new mythic system aiming to explain the chaos of our imperfect world and focusing upon its imminent redemption. The Baal Shem Tov, of course, was the progenitor of the Hasidic movement in the 18th century and the great-grandfather of Nahman himself. To identify himself as the fifth in this brief catalogue of giants of the spirit, Nahman had to have pretensions to a status not supported by existential facts: At no time in his life did he attract a sizable following or visibly quicken the process of redemption. In opposition to, or derogation of, the more successful zadikim of his period, he considered himself *the* zadik of the generation (*zadik hador*), just as Moses, Simeon bar Yohai, Isaac Luria, and the Besht were the zadikim of their generations. It is no accident that the *zadik hador* motif appears in many of his stories told between 1806 and 1810, after the failure of his most fervent personal dreams and his fierce clash with Rabbi Aryeh Leib of Shpole, a Hasidic leader in the same area of the Ukraine.

Nahman's family lineage certainly provided the basis for claims of distinction within the Hasidic world. His mother, Feige, was the granddaughter of the Besht; his uncle, Baruch of Medzhibozh (1750-1812), was the leading zadik among the lineal descendents of the Besht. His paternal grandfather, Nahman of Horodenka, had been a close colleague of the Besht. And yet, during the twelve years before Nahman's birth (April 4, 1772), the undisputed leader of the movement was Dov Ber, the Magid of Mezherich, a disciple but not a descendent of the Besht, who shifted the center of activity from Medzhibozh in Podolia to Mezherich in Volhynia by propagating the teachings of Hasidism and establishing autonomous congregations (*edot*) in many locations. Though respected as the scion of a distinguished family, Nahman could not escape the implications of the conflicting claims to leadership between the descendents of the Besht and the disciples of the Magid.

Though the Ukraine was only on the periphery of the intense international political activity of the latter half of the 18th century, a member of the literate intelligentsia could hardly be unaware of the rise of Russian imperialism, the disintegration of the Kingdom of Poland, the frequent shuffling of territories in the international games played by absolutist monarchs. The Ottoman Empire, furthermore, was not too far from the centers of Hasidism, and several Hasidic leaders, including Nahman of Horodenka, had made trips to the Holy Land or had actually settled there. Nahman of Bratslav himself barely escaped the Napoleonic armies in Acre during his visit to the Holy Land in 1798-1799. Napoleon's military exploits and what they implied regarding the overturn of traditional regimes and patterns of behavior were not unknown to the Jewish leaders of Eastern Europe and are reflected in Nahman's writings.

International politics, to be sure, were not the prime preoccupation of the Hasidic world devoted to devout piety and communion with God. While the average Hasid might not have been too learned, the zadikim and their closest disciples were often astonishingly sophisticated intellectuals, erudite both in the law and in the mystical literature, both Zoharic and Lurianic.

Reading through the extensive Bratslav literature, one is struck by the preponderance of speech over action even in the biographical-hagiographical writings of Nathan Sternhartz of Nemirow, Nahman's Boswell. Our attention is focused not upon what Nahman does—for he actually does very little—but upon what he says, his *sihot* (brief explications of reality in the light of Torah passages), or his *derashot* (his longer Torah homilies), or his stories. The contrast with the stories about the Besht in *Shivhe HaBesht* is illuminating: The Besht is always doing something, succoring the sick and needy, performing miracles, engaging in dramatic situations. Only two situations in Nahman's hagiography generate plot action: his enigmatic trip to the Holy Land and the last days of his life as he wasted away with consumption. J. Weiss, furthermore, has noted that what we do have of Nahman's biography does not follow the pattern of the biographies of zadikim which, in contradiction to those of great rabbinic scholars, require the sudden revelation of the zadik as a learned, charismatic leader after a lengthy period of ignorance and obscurity through adolescence and early manhood. Nahman, the scion of the Besht, could not be plausibly depicted as an obscure, ignorant simpleton.

This interest in what Nahman said rather than in what he did might explain why we actually know so little about the first twenty-six years of his life (1772-1798) until his journey to the Holy Land. Nahman, never a popular zadik, had very few Hasidim until his move to Bratslav in 1802. It wasn't until that period, in fact, that Nathan, the most proximate source of information about Nahman, accepted him as his zadik. When one considers the sanctity attributed by Bratslav Hasidim to every utterance or gesture of their zadik—an attitude clearly reflected in Nathan's writings—the reticence about the early period is remarkable. From the scanty and often ambiguous evidence emerges a picture of a sensitive young ascetic, given to intensive prayer and the visiting of graves of zadikim, obsessed by a sense of failure, of rejection by God, and sinful eroticism.

In 1775 Nahman married his first wife, Sosia, and moved, as was the custom, to her father's house in Usyatin, further east in the Ukraine. During these years, his closest friend and first disciple was Simeon Ber of Medvedevka, a neighboring town. Nahman's marriage does not seem to have diminished the sense of sinfulness aroused by sexuality, one of the pervasive themes of that period. After his mother-in-law's death and his father-in-law's remarriage, Nahman moved to Medvedevka (1790?), apparently because of a clash with his new mother-in-law. It is in Medvedevka that he began to attract Hasidim. Two features of the Bratslav Hasid-zadik relationship are apparent even in Medvedevka. Unlike his uncle Baruch, Nahman did not stand at the center of a large, princely court, but offered his Hasidim, at best, the model of an intensely devout, ascetic individual. And unlike most zadikim who were constantly attended by their Hasidim, Nahman would meet with his Hasidim on specific occasions only: on Rosh Hashanah (the New Year), on the Sabbath of Hannukah, and on Shavuot. (Later he would make two trips to neighboring villages on Shabbat Shirah and Shabbat Nahamu.) These sessions were occasions for prayer, song, dance, and, most important, the zadik's homily or, after 1806, his storytelling.

Nathan's account of Nahman's journey to the Holy Land (1798-1799) reads more like a Bratslav tale than a realistic travelogue: The plot is structured to cast into relief those enigmatic aspects of Nahman's behavior that have elicited abundant commentary both from Bratslav exegetes and modern scholars. Read as ordinary human activity or as a travel adventure, Nahman's behavior in this report is un-motivated. Our curiosity is engaged as we are forced to ask questions that the plot line simply does not answer: Why did Nahman make this trip? Had he planned it in advance, or impulsively decided upon it while visiting Medzhibozh in the spring of 1798? Why did he abandon his wife and three daughters with such insensitive statements? Why did he make the mysterious visit to Kamenitz-Podolsk, a city where no Jew could reside (they could trade there during the day)? What prompted him to act so childishly and churlishly in Istanbul? Why did he want to leave the Holy Land once he had landed there, in Haifa? What really happened between him and the young Arab in Haifa? What did Nahman do most of the time between the summer of 1798 and the spring of 1799? Why did he leave the country when he did? And why did he leave through the most dangerous port, Acre, then under siege by Napoleon's forces?

All these lacunae in the narrative cannot be attributed to the ignorance of the narrator. While it is true that it was

Simeon who had accompanied Nahman on this journey, and not Nathan who wrote the story, the narrative is too consistently enigmatic to be caused by ignorance of detail. The journey is presented as a rite of passage in which the hero seems to be aware of the various steps and their implications while the narrator considers them an enigma to be pondered. Arthur Green, in his biography of Nahman, elaborates ingeniously upon the traditional view of the journey and explains it as either a stage in Nahman's spiritual progress viewed within the Kabbalistic system or a valiant attempt to confront and master crisis situations. Green, furthermore, notes that the sequence of events takes the shape of a paradigmatic rite of passage with a dangerous ordeal, a journey to the center of the world, and a passage through water as a prelude to rebirth.

The journey has been regarded in Bratslav tradition as a turning point in Nahman's career, but it was hardly a prelude to the discovery of his role as zadik or his revelation to a larger following. Nahman returned from the Holy Land to Medvedevka where he resided for a bit more than a year before his move to Zlatopol—the cardinal tactical error of his life, for Zlatopol was considered the domain of one of the most popular and powerful of the Ukrainian zadikim, Aryeh Leib of Shpole, familiarly called "the Zeide" ("the Old Man"). Familiar with the structure and internal rivalries of Hasidic society, Nahman should have realized that an aspiring zadik cannot settle in a town considered the domain of a well-established popular zadik, particularly since Nahman did not ask permission to do so from the notables of the community. The move was unfortunate, for the old zadik, once a friend of Nahman's, became a ferocious foe and fought him through 1807. The conflict involved other zadikim and generated wild accusations on both sides: Nahman called the Zeide a false zadik, while the latter claimed that Nahman was arrogant, willful, even heretical. One cannot pretend that Nahman was naive; it was he, after all, who tried to have the venerable Zeide excommunicated in Berdichev in the summer of 1802. After this gambit failed, Nahman moved further west to Bratslav, outside the Zeide's domain. Within a year, however, Nahman was embroiled in a bitter quarrel—equally inexplicable—with his own uncle, Baruch, a zadik with enormous popular appeal. By the summer of 1803, Nahman's reputation and isolation were firmly established. Of the major zadikim, only Levi Isaac of Berdichev maintained a cordial relationship with him throughout the years.

The documents referring to the controversy are so hostile or cryptic that one cannot arrive at a clear picture of what really happened after 1802. It is clear that Nahman was rejected and vilified by representatives of the Hasidic leadership and his pride was characteristically undermined and intensified. His sense of paradox was validated by his intense personal experience. In his defeat, he regarded himself as the zadik of the generation (*zadik hador*), the only true zadik. Like that of Moses, his model, his inspired leadership was unappreciated; his personal isolation fed his paradoxical view of the universe. His sense of exile, furthermore, could be interpreted as an analogue of the exilic state of the Shekhinah as construed by Lurianic Kabbalah. Just as God is great precisely because he is doubted and his world is imperfect, so the true zadik is great because he is rejected. Perhaps this rejection corroborated his extremely radical view of his role as zadik which, in subsequent years, encompassed the role of the messiah. Nahman, after all, referred to his soul in messianic terms and demanded an allegiance from his Hasidim which surpassed that of any other zadik. While all zadikim insisted upon utter belief in God, Nahman extended this imperative to belief in himself as God's chosen zadik. Confession of sins, therefore, became one of the prominent features of Bratslav Hasidim, both upon initiation into the sect and at set periods during the Hasid's career. Finally, the political conflicts that beset Nahman in the last decade of his life certainly contributed not only to the intensification of his world view, but to the obliquity of Bratslav discourse: The truth must be veiled from the eyes of the scoffers who, in their perversity, think reality is what their experience has taught them. It is entirely possible that much of the enigmatic charm of the Bratslav tales, the main concern of this volume, derives from this same impulse. While the Torah of the zadik of the generation, his aspirations for the redemption of the cosmos and his understandings of the operation of the Godhead must all be told to a world thirsting for this knowledge—these great secrets must be conveyed in the enigmatic mode.

While the immediate causes of the rift between Nahman and his colleagues might have been personal and petty, by the time he moved to Bratslav there were pronounced and fixed differences between his religious position and that of some of the leading Hasidic thinkers of the period, particularly Shneour Zalman of Lyady (1745-1815), the leading theoretical disciple of Dov Ber of Mezherich, the Great Magid. In a seminal article on Hasidic religious typology, Y. Weiss differentiates between what he calls "the Hasidut of Mysticism" (that of the Magid and Shneour Zalman) and the "Hasidism of Faith" (that of Nahman of Bratslav, among others). While both types begin from essentially Lurianic positions, the Hasidut of Mysticism regarded God as immanent and impersonal, and thus emphasized God's dwelling in all being. The Hasidism of Faith was theistic and saw God as transcendent but personal, deeply involved in the major phases of history: creation, revelation, and redemption. The Hasidut of Mysticism somewhat softened the cataclysmic imagery of the Lurianic process of *tzimtzum* by formulating evil as dialectically related to good, a phase, as it were, in the process toward final *tikkun*. The Hasidism of Faith maintained all the violence of the initial cosmic cataclysm and posited evil as a threatening, demonic force.

Given such contrasting world views, the response of each group had to be radically different. The Hasidut of Mysticism stressed both contemplation and ecstasy in prayer since it is assumed that God is close and the worshiper loses personal identity in these acts of devotion. Bratslav Hasidism of Faith, assuming that God is distant and totally above reason, insisted on a religious attitude founded on complete paradoxical faith in which the personality of the worshiper is fully present and the awesome gap between him and the personal God is painfully unbridgeable for the average human being. Man's prayer is thus not a contemplative loss of self, but a personal dialogue with God over a gaping chasm. In the Bratslav Hasidism of Faith, therefore, one would suffuse prayer with personal requests for divine intervention in one's life or in the processes of history while in the Hasidut of Mysticism one never prayed for one's personal needs. If, in the Hasidut of Mysticism, God was omnipresent and sin had no real independent existence, man's basic view of life could be optimistic and the zadik, though important as a guide in life, did not need to assume supernatural qualities. The Hasid of Faith, on the other hand, was pessimistic, ridden with anxieties concerning sinfulness, and demanded a zadik whose theurgic powers were far beyond those of the average man, that is, he needed a *zadik hador*. His despair was as profound as his yearning for immediate messianic redemption. The Hasidut of Mysticism, argues Weiss, nullified eschatological tensions since it was, in general, less interested in the processes of history than was the Hasidism of Faith.

While we cannot determine how prominently these religious differences figured in the controversies that swirled about Nahman, it should be rather obvious that elements of the Hasidism of Faith paralleled some of his known personality traits and will contribute to an enrichment of our understanding of his tales.

Nahman's eight-year Bratslav period was an era of neither spiritual tranquility nor public acclaim. His political battles continued, he gathered few Hasidim, and his personal life was beset with tragedies: the death of his only son, for whom he had messianic expectations, in 1806; the death of his wife, Sosia, in 1807; and the inception of his tuberculosis also in 1807. Doubtless his greatest disappointment was the frustration of his messianic expectations, which had surfaced in 1803 or 1804 and intensified until their complete disappointment in the fall of 1806, for Nahman not only yearned for the coming of the messiah, but believed—according to his biographers—that he himself was messiah, son of Joseph, the messiah who would usher in the period of redemption. Though the evidence for Nahman's messianic career before 1806 is often veiled in typical Bratslav manner or interwoven with homiletical materials, the sheer quantity of the evidence is so overwhelming that there can be no doubt that he had both fervent pretensions and the inevitable profound disappointment.

Despite his personal anguish of 1806-1807, Nahman did not relinquish his messianic yearnings, but rather channeled them into the stories that he began to tell from the summer of 1806 through the spring of 1810, for each story, in one way or the other, deals with the problems of faith in redemption of the cosmos. Since Nahman did not reside steadily in Bratslav between the spring of 1807 and his death in Uman on October 15, 1810, the recording of the stories presents many bibliographic problems that will be discussed later.

Nahman's travels in the spring of 1807 are as puzzling as his trip to Palestine in 1798-1799 and as unexplainable as his visit to Kamenetz-Podolsk in 1798 or to Shargorod in 1805. Obviously despondent at the turn of events in late 1806, Nahman left Bratslav in early 1807 for Navritch, perhaps to escape the responsibilities of being the charismatic leader. Sometime in the spring he heard that his wife, who had remained in Bratslav, had contracted tuberculosis and he arranged to meet her in Ostrog where he knew a pious physician whom he could trust. They stayed there but a short period and traveled on to her family home in Zaslow where she died in June of that year. Shortly after her death, Nahman returned to Bratslav to resume his role as zadik while making plans for a second marriage, which took place three months after Sosia's death—a common practice in those days. During this period Nahman learned that he, too, had contracted tuberculosis, a fact that probably impelled him to settle in Lemberg for some eight months together with his faithful disciple Simeon, since Lemberg, the capital of Austrian Galicia, probably had the best doctors available. During this period, Nahman prepared the first volume of his collected sermons, *Likkute Moharan*, for publication not in Lemberg itself, which had many fine presses, but in Ostrog across the border in Czarist Russia. During this same period he instructed his disciples to burn one of the major esoteric manuscripts he had written; later entitled *HaSefer HaNisraf*, the manuscript was destroyed in the summer of 1808. By the end of that summer, we find him back in Bratslav where he spent the next two years of his life wasting away with his incurable disease yet preparing homilies and stories.

In May of 1810, Nahman removed to Uman, one of the leading cities in the Ukraine. His behavior in Uman, however, has become one of the more problematic chapters in his biography. Even if we assume that he felt his days were numbered, we really do not know why he selected Uman for his final residence. Medzhibozh, the home of the Besht and his own birthplace, would have been an equally logical choice. We do not understand his association with the various enlightened Jews of Uman, members of the Rapoport and Hurwitz families, well-known freethinkers whose views were an anathema to Nahman and his disciples. And we really do not know why he never troubled to appoint a successor, a truly bizarre act for a Hasidic zadik fully aware that his end is near and he has no male heir or outstanding disciple.

Nathan Sternhartz of Nemirow (1780-1845), Nahman's

scribe and secretary, preserved for us many of the master's homilies and stories and assumed the leadership of the sect — though not as zadik — after Nahman's death. While supplying us with much biographical material and ideological information, he has succeeded brilliantly in preserving the paradoxicality of his master's spiritual life, so sharply torn between absolute, almost presumptuous faith and abysmal doubts about his ability or worthiness to achieve such pure belief. Nathan obviously understood that the type of zadik embodied in Nahman, who demanded so much of himself and his Hasidim, was truly unique and any attempt at duplication was by definition absurd. At best, one could record and transmit as faithfully as possible the homilies, sayings, and — above all — the tales of the master, which contain the esoteric secrets of his soul and that of the cosmos. Bratslav Hasidim regard the literary heritage, and especially the stories, as the living presence of the master. It is the duty of the Hasid to ponder their secrets in order to purify his own soul and thus hasten the day of redemption.

II. THE BRATSLAV THEORY OF THE SACRED TALE

THE publication of *Kinder und Hausmaerchen* by Jacob and Wilhelm Grimm in 1812 and 1815 should serve as a convenient if oblique point of departure for our discussion of the folktale as practiced by the Hasidim and by Nahman of Bratslav in particular. During the same years, but about 1,000 miles east of Kassel and Goettingen where the Grimm brothers lived, the first two collections of Hasidic tales, *Shivhe HaBesht (In Praise of the Baal Shem Tov)* and *Sippure HaMaasiyot (The Tales)* of Nahman of Bratslav were being collected and edited. Just as there is no historical connection between the editorial activities in the West and those in the East (the identity of dates is purely accidental), so there is no similarity in the aims of the collectors. The Grimm brothers, as both scholars and romantic nationalists, were motivated by a desire to recover the authentic Germanic folk tradition. The two Hasidic editors, Dov Ber ben Samuel, the compiler of *Shivhe HaBesht*, and Nathan Sternhartz of Nemirow, Nahman of Bratslav's disciple and amanuensis, were both pious men anxious to present tales by or about their respective charismatic leaders, thus glorifying the name of the Lord and inspiring the Hasidim to emulate the ways of their masters. At issue here is the meaning of the term "modern": If we use the term generically, referring to a period of time—the last two centuries, for instance—all the above-mentioned collections are of the "modern" period. If "modernity," however, is measured by the secular, inquisitive, and historic spirit, the Grimm broth-

29

ers are modern while neither Dov Ber ben Samuel nor Nathan of Nemirow is. On the other hand, while these collections of Hasidic tales have not generally been included in histories of Modern Hebrew literature, the arguments Dov Sadan and others have proposed for their inclusion are quite convincing.

Both Yosef Dan and Mendel Piekarz contend that the Hasidim, certainly by 1780, had effected a radical change in the attitude toward the tale. Whereas the telling of tales had previously been frowned upon by Jewish authorities, it was regarded as a worthy pastime by Hasidic masters for a variety of reasons: Since God was immanent in this world, he could be present even in a seemingly idle tale which, upon examination, might contain a deep theological truth; the tale projected before the devout the image of the Hasidic hero, the zadik—more often than not the Besht himself; the tale was an effective means of communicating basic religious notions.

The Bratslav concept of the tale and its role was somewhat more complex and self-conscious. Apart from the Bratslav tales themselves, we have from the early 19th century three striking *theoretical* statements on the essence of the tale and its function in society: two sermons delivered by Rav Nahman himself at the end of 1806 and included in *Likkute Moharan*; and the first Introduction to Nahman's tales, *Sippure HaMaasiyot*, which was written by his disciple, Nathan of Nemirow, in 1814. Since Nathan's Introduction builds upon the sermons, we shall analyze the Introduction and later refer to the sermons. The composite theory of the tale is one of the most coherent and remarkable in the history of Hebrew literature.

Written about four years after Rav Nahman's death in 1810, the Introduction strikes a subtly balanced tone, fusing evangelic and apologetic overtones both couched in terms taken from Ecclesiastes, thereby suggesting the parallel between Rav Nahman and King Solomon, who, after all, "spoke in riddles and parables, and dressed the Torah in several garbs." The note is evangelic since it heralds the first publication of this new, sacred text, the formal publication of the great tales delivered "from his holy mouth," from the holy mouth of Rav Nahman, the "perfection of mankind, our honorable lord, teacher, and master, our glorious and mighty pride, the holy and awesome rabbi, the great light, the supernal light, the precious and holy light, blessed is his name, Rav Nahman (the memory of the zadik is a blessing), the great grandson of the holy, awesome, and god-like Rabbi, the Baal Shem Tov (the memory of the zadik is a blessing)." In these stories—authentic since actually heard from his holy mouth—the master "pondered, and sought out, and set in order many proverbs (Eccl. 12, 9) and garbed and hid lofty and mighty concepts in tales (*Sippure HaMaasiyot*) in marvelous and wondrous ways." Though new, the book followed the legitimizing precedent of the ancients who "would speak in riddles and parables and garb the Torah in several different garments when they wanted to talk of divine secrets." These sacred texts were being published primarily for the benefit of the faithful followers of Rav Nahman who wanted to know the precise text of these awesome tales since "our master has told us that every statement in these stories contains a potent meaning and he who changes one statement of these stories omits much of the meaning."

It is obvious from the first section of the Introduction that Nathan was fully conscious of the novelty and daring of this publication, since these tales are sacred scripture, "worthy to be expounded in public and told in the synagogues, and whosoever is expert in sacred texts, especially in the Zohar and the Lurianic writings can understand some of the allusions in this text." Nathan also realizes that much of the impact of the stories was due to the charisma of the story teller, Rav Nahman. "It should be clear to any intelligent person that he who hears statements from the very mouth of the sage is not like he who sees them in a book, especially in such allusory matters as those which cannot be understood without the movement of the limbs and the nodding of the head and the wink of the eye and the inclination of the hand etc." Ever conscious of his mission, Nathan brings as support of his project the striking statement of his master, Rav Nahman himself:

> Before he told the first tale of this book ("The Loss of Princess"), he said: "In the tales which other people tell are many secrets and lofty matters, but the tales have been ruined in that they are lacking much. They are confused and not told in the proper sequence: what belongs at the beginning they tell at the end and vice versa. Nevertheless, there are in these tales which other people tell lofty and hidden matters."

The "tales which other people tell" are obviously universal folktales culled from many sources, some even Gentile. Nathan is defensive about this point since he asserts several times that most of Rav Nahman's stories are original, that when he did use these stories of foreign provenance he added to, modified, and improved them. Normally, his stories are really original ideas "garbed" in story form. Time and again we encounter the three terms: *hasagah* = concept or idea; *maaseh* = the tale; and some form of the root *lbš* = to garb. The Bratslav story is supposed to be the garb in narrative terms of a theological concept. The mundane or Gentile origin of the story should not disqualify it for sacred usage once the material has been transmuted by the inspired master storyteller.

The following passage in the Introduction seems at first to be a digression to the source of historical legitimization, to the Besht, but, as Joseph Dan has pointed out, it forms with the first passage an integral theory of literary composition:

> And the Besht (may his holy memory be a blessing), could "unite unities" by means of tales. When he

saw that the upper conduits were ruined and he
could not repair them through prayer, he would repair and join them by means of a tale.

Basing his reasoning on the pervasive Lurianic terminology,
Dan explains the Bratslaver (a composite of Nahman and
Nathan's ideas) theory:

1. The "lofty and hidden concepts" found in tales
other people, be they Jews or Gentiles, tell are parallel to the "holy sparks" that fell into the created
world at the time of the cataclytic act of creation.

2. The tales themselves underwent a process similar
to the Lurianic "breaking of vessels" at the time of
creation; they are therefore confused, ruined, disor-
derly, and their original meaning has been lost.

3. The inspired zadikim, in this case the Besht, is
endowed with the power to reveal the holiness hidden in the stories by restructuring them according to
their original, proper order. In this sense the zadik
"repairs" the story.

4. Once the story has been repaired, it assumes
enormous religious, even theurgic power and a zadik
like the Besht can use the story to "unite the uni-
ties," that is, to reunite the *sefirot* (*tiferet* and *malkhut*), which had split asunder in the act of creation.

Dan's explanation derives from Rav Nahman's own
theory concerning the relationship between the telling of
stories and the details of sefirotic structure, a theory fully yet
circuitously expounded in the famous sermon "Patah Rabbi
Simeon" (*Likkute Moharan* I:60), a classical Bratslav homily
based on the introductory passage of the Idra Rabba of the
Zohar to *Parashat Naso* of the Book of Numbers (128). The gist
of this sermon is found in Nathan's Introduction to the *Sippure
HaMaasiyot*, which we have been analyzing. Nathan tells us
that his master turned to the telling of tales in a deliberate
attempt to achieve by this new method what he had failed to

achieve by more conventional methods: the repentance of his flock, their return to the Lord—as he, Rav Nahman, understood it.

> When our master, blessed be his memory, began to engage in the telling of tales, he stated explicitly as follows: "I am about to begin to tell tales," by which he meant that since he could not help them return to the Lord by means of Torah lessons or holy discourses . . . he is beginning to engage in tales. In the same period he delivered the sermon, "Patah Rabbi Simeon . . ." At the end of that sermon it is explained that by means of tales "the true zadik" awakens from their sleep those human beings who have fallen asleep and sleep away their days.

The sleep mentioned here is a specific spiritual sleep, the period of spiritual obtuseness when the true essence of one's soul, which should properly be connected to the upper world of *sefirot*, is dormant, hence disconnected from the source of illumination. The tale is a particularly convenient vehicle for the awakening of the soul from its dormancy since it is, by its very nature, a "garb" (*levush*) and can transmit the supernal illumination subtly, gradually, thus avoiding the risk of blinding the human being with the brilliant light from above.

Nathan's Introduction includes one more intriguing notion called from the sermon "Patah Rabbi Simeon": there are tales that are in the category of "in the midst of days" and there are tales in the category of "the years of antiquity." Nathan refers here to a threefold classification of tales found in the sermon: (a) standard tales with no specific sefirotic association; (b) tales classified as "in the midst of days," thus connected with the lower seven spheres; (c) tales classified as "of the years of antiquity," thus associated with the three upper spheres. Tales in the second group recount great acts of divine beneficence in the past, such as the stories of the Patriarchs or the exodus from Egypt; tales in the third group predict the great act of redemption in the future. Tales of the second group are connected with the lower spheres since they present accounts of incomplete redemption, a fact attested to by our experience of this imperfect world. Tales of the third, redemptive group are logically associated with the upper three spheres, but since the final redemption has not yet taken place and the messiah has not yet come, these stories are usually left unfinished, for example, "The Loss of the Princess" and "The Seven Beggars."

The Bratslav theory of literature, its concept of the utilization of folktales, would be incomplete without reference to the notion of the zadik, especially as it appears in the model sermon "Bo El Par'oh," also delivered toward the end of 1806. After two introductory paragraphs describing the Lurianic cosmogony—*tzimtzum*, *shevira*, and *tikkun*—and two types of heresy, Nahman approaches his main theme: the nature and function of the zadik. Nahman refers not to the zadik generically, but to "the Great Zadik of the category of Moses." (Those who know the secondary literature on Bratslav Hasidut are familiar with Yosef Weiss's now widely accepted contention that when Nahman speaks of "the Great Zadik" or "the Zadik of the Generation" he refers to himself. Weiss bases his argument both on the original texts and the commentary of Nahman of Cheryn, one of the leading 19th-century Bratslav exegetes.) The Great Zadik must investigate the words of the heretics who have fallen into the "empty space" opened up in the previously harmonious cosmos when the infinite God contracted himself in order to create the world we live in. Since the empty space implies total absence of all divine presence, it is the locus of all evil. As such, it is the domain of silence, particularly since its opposite, the created world, was brought into existence by divine speech. The letters of the Holy Tongue by which the world was created and in which divine law is revealed comprise the border between the created world and the empty space. The

Great Zadik, in that he belongs to the category of Moses, partakes of the paradoxical nature of Moses: He is both a great leader and "heavy of tongue," that is—interpreted by Nahman—a man of silence, hence the only man capable of descending to the realm of silence, the empty space, to redeem the souls that have fallen there. The zadik does this by means of the *nigun* (melody) or the *zemer* (the song) which is peculiar to him, a manifestation of his essence as a man of faith.

Though this sermon does not mention the telling of tales as such, the literary implications of this adaptation of the Lurianic myth are far-reaching. Our teller of tales, Rav Nahman, is the Great Zadik who, by his very nature, is distanced from his audience, his Hasidim. The gap between him and his audience, however, can be bridged through the telling of tales which are a garb of his divine concepts. The tales have a specific therapeutic, cosmic function: They redeem souls from the empty space. In this sense, the tales are marvelous and the telling of tales, a redemptive act. But, following the usual Bratslav sense of paradox, the tales are an impure mode of expression, and the telling of tales is a "descent of the Zadik" into a lesser realm of existence for, as Nahman and Nathan tell us, the master resorted to this medium of communication *after* he felt he had failed miserably in his other modes of communication: prayer, homilies, and Torah lessons.

The paradox inherent in the telling of tales is a reflex of the remarkable analogue Nahman repeatedly draws between the God's relationship to the created world and the zadik's relationship to his Hasidim. In both cases, the sense of vitality emanating from the source is so overwhelming, so far beyond the capacity of ordinary human beings, that special means are required for transmission of the illumination: In both cases "garb" must be used. God uses the letters of the Torah or the Shekhinah, the lowest sphere of the sefirotic system; the zadik uses his tales to talk to his Hasidim. The Torah of the zadik, like the Torah of the Creator of the universe, is garbed in tales since it would be impossible to transmit it as it is. For God, as for the zadik, the telling of tales, the contact with the created world, is a deliberate, willed act of descent motivated by compassion. It is no coincidence that one of the leitwoerter in the sermon "Bo El Par'oh" is *rahamanut* (compassion).

Nathan's claim that these stories are original even when they utilize "tales other people tell" is correct to the extent that the master's intention—and his audience's understanding—was the presentation of a theological message in a carefully contrived garb. Though one might assign motif-numbers taken from Stith Thompson's *Motif Index* to parts of these tales, one is dealing only with a garb. In this sense, the Bratslav tales differ radically from the Beshtean tales, for instance, which do not pretend to be a garb (though Nathan does introduce this notion) of a preconceived theological message. The Bratslav tales conform to the known pattern of allegory in that they embody an obvious and continuing reference to a system of ideas (or events). Behind the stories stands the elaborate system of the *sefirot* with all its dynamic, cosmic implications. Unlike Philo and many medieval interpretations of scriptures, the reader of the Bratslav tales—which are, indeed, scriptural—does not engage in allegorical interpretation because the plot and figurative languages of the text are embarrassingly frank and concrete, too much like the life of ordinary human beings as we know it. The reader of the Bratslav tale is presented an allegorically structured text. Within the conventional categories of modes of allegorical interpretation best summarized by Dante in the 10th Epistle to Can Grande, the meaning called for in the Bratslav tale is anagogic in that it illuminates the entire scheme of creation, the governance of the universe and—most important—of redemption.

Given the amazing self-awareness of Nahman and

Nathan concerning the nature of "garbing"—really the allegorical technique—it is surprising that they did not succumb to a mechanical equation of narrative and ideational systems. One can, perhaps, ascribe this deliverance from potentially tedious contrivance to several features unique to Rav Nahman, the teller of tales, who, as Yosef Weiss would argue, identified with the redemptive heroes of his own tales, be it the *mishneh lamelekh* or the *zadik emet.*, and thus suffused his tales with an anxious immediacy. Furthermore, Nahman, as we have stated, conceived of the telling of tales as an act analogous to the redemption of the cosmos by God at the end of days. This concept of narrative, coupled with his identification with his heroes, prevented the dissociation of sense from sensibility, of idea from image, which critics from Coleridge on have assailed so relentlessly. The narrative concretization of his ingenious concept of the narrative art is to be found in what we—parodying Frank Kermode—would like to call "the sense of a non-ending": When one tells a tale involving the third, redemptive group, those of "the years of antiquity," one does not finish the tale since the very act of fiction and the dynamics of the cosmos are concomitant. While we, today, often tend to glorify fiction as the consummate and characteristic human activity, Rav Nahman considered the proper telling of his tales of such cosmic import that only "the Zadik of the generation" or his authorized disciples should perform this act.

Whether or not the thirteen canonical Bratslav tales actually conform to the theory expressed in these three early and authentic Bratslav documents—and there is good reason to state that many of them don't—the very self-consciousness of the theoretical statements betrays an awareness of an implicit crossing of genre borders. Nathan knows that there is a difference between the telling of tales and traditional Torah literature, homilies, commentaries, and so forth; he also knows that there is a difference between traditional Torah literature, however sacred it might be, and these stories which were uttered "by the holy mouth" of the zadik of the generation. While these three genres are not at all similar to the three genres we have referred to earlier, we should at least share Nathan of Nemirow's consciousness that there are genres with their implicit assumptions even when the borderlines are blurred. Not all genre borders, finally, are equally distinct. The crossing of the border from folk literature to "literature" might raise serious problems of definition, but not grave concerns of intentionality. The crossing from folk literature or literature to scripture does raise the problem of intentionality; the scholar dismisses with peril to his perspective the notion that these utterances were regarded as scripture by their audience.

III. THE TEXT AND THE TRANSLATION

THOUGH universally recognized as one of the most central texts in both Modern Hebrew and Yiddish literature, the *Sippure HaMaasiyot shel Rabbi Nahman MiBratslav* (The Tales of Rabbi Nahman of Bratslav) are virtually unknown to readers who have no Hebrew or Yiddish. The volume presented first by Buber in German in 1906 is not a translation and does not claim to be one. Buber himself asserts: "I have not translated these stories of Rabbi Nahman, but retold them in all freedom, yet out of his spirit as it is present to me." Even a cursory glimpse at Buber's re-creation will convince the reader of the truth of this disclaimer: Buber has endowed the narrative with psychological qualities the original does not have and, in doing so, has deleted both the stark Kabbalistic allusions of the Hebrew and the numinous tone of both the Hebrew and the Yiddish.

Buber is not the only "translator" who has deliberately avoided linguistic accuracy. We find a similar technique employed by Meyer Levin in his *Classic Hassidic Tales* (1932, 1975); more recently, in Elie Wiesel's *Souls on Fire* (1972), the original Bratslav text is, at best, a source of inspiration. Even in Hebrew, one of the original languages of the first edition (1815/1816), we find attempts—most recently that of Yehudah Ya'ari—to recast the Bratslav tales in a more accessible style.

These repeated efforts to retell the Bratslav tales by avoiding their original linguistic medium reflects the ambiva-

43

lence of many non-Bratslav writers and critics. (Bratslav Hasidim consider these stories scripture and would neither think of tampering with them nor see any reason to do so since the precise words of their zadik, Rabbi Nahman of Bratslav, embody cosmic truths that could be lost in any other form.) While all the tales were ultimately recorded and transcribed by Nathan Sternhartz for the 1815 edition, the dating of first recitation and the attested audience is not simple. Piekarz has collated the following bibliographic information:

1. The Loss of the Princess   Summer 1806
2. The King and the Emperor   1806-1807
3. The Cripple   1806-1807
4. The King Who Decreed Conversion 1806-1807
5. The King Who Had No Children   1806-1807
6. The King and the Wise Man   1806-1807
7. The King Who Fought Many Wars 1806-1807
8. The Rabbi's Son   1806-1807
9. The *Hakham* and the *Tam*
   (The Clever Man and
   the Ordinary Man)   Spring 1809
10. The Burgher and the Pauper   Spring 1809
11. The King's Son and the Maidservant's
    Son Who Were Switched   Spring 1809
12. The Master of Prayer   Spring 1809
13. The Seven Beggars   Spring 1810

Of these 13 stories, Nathan Sternhartz heard only numbers 1, 11, 12, and 13 directly from the master. Other stories were conveyed through other disciples, usually Naftali. Since Nahman died several years before the stories were prepared for their first authorized bilingual edition—Hebrew on the top, Yiddish on the bottom—he certainly could not have approved of their final version as he did in the case of *Likkute Moharan*, Part I, which was published in 1808 in his lifetime.

Since these tales were considered sacred by Nahman's closest disciples and pregnant with Kabbalistic secrets which only their zadik understood properly, Nathan Sternhartz would have to have been a supreme confidence man to foist upon his colleagues falsified or garbled versions of these tales, even if he had been elected the zadik's legitimate heir—which was not the case.

While the tales are known to be of unusual historic importance, sacred to Bratslav Hasidim and either emulated or derogated by secular writers, they are, upon close examination, stylistically bizarre and thematically enigmatic. Reading both the Hebrew and Yiddish texts, one cannot escape the extreme paratactic structure with the mesmerizing repetition of the "and," or the predominance of leitwoerter culled from Kabbalistic terminology (more obvious in the Hebrew than in the Yiddish), or the childishly simplistic Yiddish or the pronouncedly Yiddishized Hebrew. The plots of many of the stories bear a strikingly superficial resemblance to dozens of folktales one has encountered elsewhere, but it is always obvious that these folk-plots, so rich in allusion, are only the vehicle for something else, for some personal or cosmic message.

The tales are a translator's nightmare and one can sympathize with the temptation to retell rather than translate. Unfortunately, retelling does not advance our understanding of the Bratslav tale, its message and poetics. I am not presenting the Bratslav tales merely as a possible source of reading entertainment or inspiration, though they certainly can provide both. I am treating them as serious literary documents that occupy a central position in two literary traditions, Hebrew and Yiddish, and raise a series of intriguing questions regarding the essence of a literary text and the legitimacy of interpretation.

The present translation was prepared from a simultaneous comparative reading of both the Hebrew and Yiddish texts as they are presented in the standard versions used by Bratslav Hasidim. Both the Hebrew and the Yiddish were first published in Ostrog in 1815/1816, five years after the death of their author in Uman in the Ukraine. Though it is obvious both from the testimony of the author's amanuensis, Rabbi Nathan, and the author's method of narration before the inner circle of his Hasidim that the stories were originally told in Yiddish, scholars have not agreed as to the original language of written composition. We know that Rabbi Nathan transcribed these stories, though he did not hear them all from the master's mouth when they were told between 1806 and 1810. We know that Rabbi Nahman himself probably edited a few of these tales, perhaps the earlier ones among them. But we don't know whether they were originally transcribed in Hebrew or in Yiddish since the Hebrew is so strikingly calqued by the Yiddish semantics and syntax that arguments as to original language are inconclusive. In working from both languages at the same time, one notices both the fidelity of translation—in whichever direction it actually did take place—and yet a difference in tone. The Yiddish is naturally more intimate and familiar since it was the normal language of discourse among Bratslav Hasidim while Hebrew was the language of prayer and study, which no one spoke as a natural language. The Hebrew, while often considered barbarous to the purist because of its adherence to Yiddish thought patterns and its disregard for sequence of tenses or agreement of person or genders, has a peculiar charm precisely because of its faithfulness to the colloquial Yiddish speech patterns.

The tales were preserved as holy text, as we are often told, originally uttered by the holy mouth of the rabbi whose message had the power to restore the wayward to faith in the Lord, to enhance the faith of the believer, and, in a deeply Kabbalistic sense, to contribute toward the restoration of this shattered world in which all mankind finds itself. The tale has the power of redemption; telling the tale is, in essence, a redemptive act. If one is to translate these tales in order to present them to a reader in English, one must make every effort to preserve those characteristics of the narrative technique which are essential to the scriptural, redemptive essence of the original text. The translation should adhere as closely as possible to the thought patterns of the original without disintegrating into garbled, awkward English. It must maintain the pervasive paratactic structure of many of the sentences which appear both in the Hebrew with its normative Biblical "waw" consecutive, and also in the Yiddish, which preserves a prominent "un" (and) wherever the Hebrew has the "waw"—or was it the other way? In either case, the result is a trance-inducing numinous style in which the tale seems to be recited in a dream that preserves the outlines but not the details of logical discourse. Any excessive reduction of this effect to please a westernized sensibility would lose one of the main features of the texture.

The Hebrew text, furthermore, conveys a dimension of connotations lost in the Yiddish. The Hebrew reader cannot escape the repeated usage of Kabbalistic terminology, images, and ideational patterns, which are blurred in the Yiddish unless the technical Hebrew Kabbalistic term is transferred untranslated from the Hebrew to the Yiddish. "Ilan" in Hebrew means a tree and is translated or appears as "boim" in the Yiddish, but the Hebrew "ilan" evokes associations with the Kabbalistic "tree of the spheres" (the world-tree in folklore and anthropology) while "boim" remains nothing but a tree. In this sense, the Hebrew text must be treated as the primary text first consulted by the translator and then compared with the Yiddish text, word for word, to see how the author understood the Hebrew word, how it was calqued in his mind by his normal language of discourse, Yiddish.

In doing so, one notices an elaborate network of leitwoerter in each story. Though many of these refer, either directly or indirectly, to Kabbalistic themes, others are simply literary devices that create the unity of the story by amplifying the plot line. In either case, some effort was made to retain the same translated word for each leitwort. Though these stories are open to multiple interpretations and have a long history of exegesis from the early 19th century to today, the precision of translation and the organization of the text into coherent paragraphs—the original pays little attention to this typographic feature—will provide a firm basis for an intelligent, grounded foray into the labyrinth of possible meanings.

The research done during the past generation in the history and ideology of the various Hasidic sects, and Bratslav Hasidism in particular, has established beyond doubt that these tales are structured by certain Kabbalistic notions and energized by the personal tensions of their author, Rabbi Nahman. With the emergence of Gershom Scholem and his disciples in Jerusalem, Hasidism was carefully analyzed and described as a major trend in Jewish mysticism, a sophisticated, variegated heir (even by opposition) of much of the Lurianic mysticism of the 16th and 17th centuries. Yosef Weiss, a Scholem disciple, has studied crucial aspects of Rabbi Nahman's personality and theology while Mendel Piekarz has examined many of the important historical and bibliographical issues that required clarification. The books of Weiss and Piekarz, coupled with the relevant chapters in recent surveys by Dan and Shmeruk and the doctoral dissertations of Elstein, Green, and Mantel, furnish us with reliable background information to the tales. Some of these tales are fully or partially explicated in these works and we shall refer to them in our commentaries. What emerges from the above is one of the most intriguing figures in modern literary history, paradoxically obsessed by self-doubt and messianic intimations at the same time, a brilliant homilist and teller of tales, a specialist in the enigmatic mode of discourse.

NAHMAN
OF
BRATSLAV
THE TALES

I. THE LOSS OF THE PRINCESS

Written in the spring of 1806 at the peak of Nahman's messianic yearnings, "The Loss of the Princess" is the narrative embodiment of the author's preoccupation with the problem of religious faith. By "faith" Nahman never meant the simple belief in the existence of a divine being, but rather the excruciating struggle the true man of faith must engage in to maintain his belief in certain specific instances of divine intervention in history, particularly in redemption. The hero of the story, the viceroy, volunteers to find the lost princess, but is repeatedly frustrated in his attempts because of a series of distractions. Only when he persists, despite the rebuffs of the giants he encounters in the desert, does he seem to make progress toward his elusive goal.

The search for the lost princess or the golden mountain or the pearly castle — motifs found in the folk literature of many nations — refers to the specific object of faith in this story. The unspecified wrath of the king and the enigmatic disappearance of the daughter are figurative representations of the Lurianic myth of creation in which the Lord contracts himself, thereby creating room for the universe to be created. The contraction precipitated a violent cataclysm involving the expulsion or exile from the presence of God of part of the divine spirit, usually the Shekhinah, here portrayed as the princess. It is the goal of the viceroy to restore the Shekhinah — the princess — to her home, thus restoring the primordial harmony of the cosmos. Who, then, is the viceroy? He may be any believer, or the zadik, or the "true zadik, Nahman," or even the historic people of Israel.

RAV Nahman answered and said: On the way, I told a tale (of such power) that whoever heard it had thoughts of repentance. This is it.

Once there was a king. The king had six sons and one daughter. The daughter was extremely important to him and he cherished her and enjoyed her company very much. Once, on a certain day when he was with her, he became enraged at her and from his mouth slipped the sentence: "May The Not-Good take you away." That night she went to her room, and in the morning no one knew where she was. Her father, the king, grieved deeply and he sent here and there searching for her.

Then the viceroy, seeing that the king was deeply grieved, rose and requested that a servant, a horse, and money (for expenses) be given to him. And he set out to search for her. And he searched for her for a very long time until he found her.

(Now Rav Nahman tells how he searched for her until he found her.)

He traveled for a long time, here and there, in deserts and fields and forests. And he searched for her for a very long time. While traveling in the desert, he saw a path off to the side and reflected: "Since I have been traveling such a long time in the desert and cannot find her, I shall follow this path—maybe I will come to a settled place." And he traveled for a long time. At last he saw a castle with many soldiers posted around it. The castle was very beautiful and the soldiers were standing around it in perfect order. And he feared that the soldiers would not let him in, but he reflected: "I shall attempt it."

He left his horse and walked to the castle. They let him pass and did not hinder him at all. He walked from room to room without hindrance and came to a hall where he saw a king sitting with his crown, many soldiers standing guard, and many musicians playing instruments in his presence. And it was lovely and beautiful there. Neither the king nor any other person asked him anything. He saw delicacies and fine foods there, and he stopped to eat and went to lie down in a corner to observe what was going on there. He observed that the king ordered that they bring the queen and they went to bring her. When they brought in the queen, there was a great tumult and great joy and the musicians played and sang mightily. They placed a throne for her next to the king. And she was the lost princess! And the viceroy recognized her. After a time, the queen glanced about and saw someone lying in the corner and recognized the viceroy. She rose from the throne and went there and touched him.

She asked him: "Do you recognize me?"

He answered: "Yes. I recognize you. You are the princess who has been lost." And he asked: "How did you get here?"

She answered: "Because that sentence slipped from my father's mouth. And this place is *The Not-Good.*"

He told her that her father was deeply grieved and that he had searched for her for many years. And he asked her: "How can I free you from here?"

She told him: "You cannot free me unless you choose a place and stay there for one whole year. During this entire year you must yearn for me, to free me from here. You will constantly yearn and search and hope to free me. And you will fast. On the last day of the year, you shall fast and not sleep from sunset to sunset."

And he went and did so. At the end of the year, on the last day, he fasted and did not sleep. He set out to go to the princess to free her. As he went, he saw a tree, and on it grew very fine apples. He craved them very much, and he went to eat from them. As soon as he ate from the apple, he fell over and sleep seized him. And he slept for a very long time. His servant shook him, but he did not wake up. After some time, he stirred from his sleep and asked the servant: "Where am I in the world?"

The servant told the viceroy the entire story: "You have been sleeping a very long time, several years, and I, in the meanwhile, have lived off the fruit." The viceroy grieved deeply and went to the castle and found the princess. And she wailed bitterly to him: "If you had only come on that day you would have freed me from here. Because of that one day, you have lost everything. It is true that not eating is very difficult, especially on the last day when the evil impulse waxes strong. And so, choose another place and stay there, too, for a whole year. On the last day you will be allowed to eat. Only do not sleep and do not drink wine so that you will not fall asleep, because the main thing is sleep."

He went and did so. On the last day he was walking back there and he saw a spring gushing forth and it looked red and smelled of wine. He asked the servant: "Do you see this spring? There should be water in it, but it looks reddish and smells of wine." And he went and tasted a bit from the spring. Immediately, he fell over and slept some seventy years. During this period many soldiers passed by with their baggage trains traveling behind them. And the servant hid from the soldiers. Afterwards, there passed a carriage and the princess was sitting in it. She stopped next to the viceroy and alighted and sat next to him and recognized him. She shook him vigorously, but he could not wake up. She began to wail about him, that all the labors performed and travails endured for so many years in order to free her were lost because of that one day when he could have freed her. She wept much about it:

"It's a great pity both for him and for me, because I have been here such a long time and cannot get out." Afterwards she took the kerchief off her head and wrote on it with her tears and left it next to him. She rose and sat in her carriage and rode off.

Later, he woke up and asked the servant: "Where am I in the world?" The servant told him the whole story, that many soldiers had passed by and that the carriage had been there and the princess had wept and cried out: "It's a great pity for you and for me!" In the meanwhile, the viceroy glanced about and saw that the kerchief was lying next to him. And he asked: "Where did this come from?" And the servant answered that the princess had left it after having written on it with her tears. The viceroy took it and raised it to the sun. He began to see the letters and read what was written there, all her lament and cry, that she was no longer in the former castle, but that he should search for a golden mountain and pearly castle. "There you shall find me!"

He left the servant behind and went on alone to search for her. And he traveled for several years searching for her. He reasoned that surely there is no golden mountain and pearly castle in a settled place because he was expert in the map of the world. And so (he concluded): "I shall go to the deserts." He went to search for her in the deserts for many and many a year. At last he saw a man so huge that his size was not human and he was carrying a tree so huge that no such tree is found in any settled place.

That giant asked him: "Who are you?"

The viceroy answered: "I am a human being."

The giant wondered and said: "I have been in the desert for a long time, but I have never seen a human being here."

The viceroy told him the whole story, and that he was searching for a golden mountain and a pearly castle. The giant said to him: "Surely it does not exist at all." He rebuffed him and told him that they had deluded his mind with nonsense, that it surely did not exist at all. And the viceroy began to weep bitterly and said: "It surely, definitely exists some- where." The wild man rebuffed him again saying that they surely had deluded him with nonsense. And the viceroy said that it surely exists.

The wild man said to the viceroy: "In my opinion, this is nonsense. But since you insist, I, who am in charge of all the animals, will do you a favor and summon them all. Since they roam throughout the entire world, one of them might know about that mountain and castle." And he summoned them all, from the smallest to the biggest, all kinds of animals. He asked them, but they answered that they had not seen anything of the sort. So he said to the viceroy: "See! They have deluded you with nonsense. If you listen to me, you will go back, because you will surely not find it since it does not exist anywhere in the world."

But the viceroy insisted vigorously and said that it surely, definitely exists. The wild man said to the viceroy: "Here, in the desert, I have a brother who is in charge of all the fowl. Perhaps they know since they fly high in the air. Perhaps they have seen that mountain and castle. Go to him and tell him that I have sent you." And the viceroy went on for many and many a year in search of him. Finally he again found a man as huge as the former one and he, too, carried a huge tree. And this giant asked the viceroy the same question. The viceroy told him the whole story adding that his brother had sent him. And he, too, rebuffed him saying that it surely does not exist. The viceroy insisted that it does. The giant said to the viceroy: "I am in charge of all the birds. I shall summon them—perhaps they know." He summoned all the birds and asked them all, from the smallest to the biggest, and they answered that they knew nothing about that mountain and castle. The man said to him: "You see that it surely does not exist anywhere in the world. If you listen to me, go back." But the viceroy insisted and said that it surely does exist somewhere in the world. The giant said: "Further in the desert you will find my brother who is in charge of all the winds. They roam throughout the whole world—perhaps they know."

The viceroy traveled and searched for many and many a year, and finally found a man as huge as the former one and he, too, carried a huge tree. This giant asked the viceroy the same question, and the viceroy told him the whole story. This giant, too, rebuffed him, but the viceroy insisted again. Finally, the third giant said to the viceroy that he would do him a favor and summon all the winds to come and he would ask them. He summoned them, and all the winds came and he asked them all. None of them knew anything about that mountain and castle. The giant said to the viceroy: "Don't you see that they have told you nonsense?" And the viceroy began to weep loudly and said: "I know that it surely must exist."

At that moment he saw that another wind had arrived. And the giant in charge of the winds was very angry with it: "Why are you late? Didn't I order all the winds to come? Why didn't you come with them?"

The wind answered him: "I was detained because I had to transport a princess to a golden mountain and a pearly castle."

And the viceroy was overjoyed to hear this.

The giant in charge asked the wind: "What is expensive there?"

The wind said: "Everything is very expensive there."

So the giant in charge of the winds told the viceroy: "Since you have been searching for her for such a long time and have performed so many labors, and money might now be an obstacle, I am giving you a purse, and whenever you put your hand in it you will draw money from it." And he ordered a wind to take him there. The storm wind came and carried him there and brought him up to the gate. The soldiers standing guard there would not let him enter the city, but he put his hand into the purse and took out the money and bribed them and entered the city. And it was a beautiful city. He went to a rich man and arranged for his board, knowing that he had to spend time there, because he had to employ intelligence and wisdom to free her.

(And how he freed her, Rav Nahman did not tell.)

And finally he did free her.

II. THE KING AND THE EMPEROR

Though the literary form of "The King and the Emperor" differs significantly from that of "The Loss of the Princess," the basic religious situation is similar. In both cases the hero or heroine (in this story, the emperor's daughter) must struggle through a series of episodes to a goal that implies the restoration of cosmic harmony. In this story, the emphasis is less on the psychological aspects of the struggle, the main theme of "The Loss of the Princess," than upon the cunning of the daughter, which seems to be a manifestation of a controlling destiny. The emperor had violated his pledge to marry his daughter to the king's son. The daughter—a narrative representation of the Shekhinah—undergoes exile several times, but by dint of her persistence and cunning regains her position of prominence and rediscovers her betrothed. The leitmotiv "to go home," so subtly suggested in each episode, becomes the triumphant pronouncement of the emperor's daughter to her rediscovered betrothed at the end of the story. The return from spiritual exile (first precipitated by the broken pledge and then repeated in the loss of the ring) is effected here, too, by persistence and ingenuity. Man lives in spiritual exile, in a fallen state, but the way home is open for those with the will, persistence, and cunning. The return of the individual home from exile is portrayed as analogous to the return of the Shekhinah, a part of the divine presence, back to her home.

ONCE there was an emperor who had no children. There was also a king who had no children. And the emperor set out throughout the world, searching for some advice or remedy so as to beget children. The king, too, set out like that, and they both chanced upon the same inn. And they did not know each other. But the emperor recognized that the king had royal bearing and he asked him, and the latter admitted that he was a king. The king, too, recognized that the emperor had royal bearing, and he, too, admitted that he was an emperor. And they told each other that they were traveling to get children, and they entered into an agreement that if, when they came home, their wives gave birth one to a male and the other to a female, they would match them.

The emperor traveled home and begot a daughter. The king traveled home and begot a son. And that match was forgotten. The emperor sent his daughter to study. The king, too, sent his son to study. And they both chanced upon the same teacher. They fell deeply in love, and agreed that they would marry each other. The king's son took a ring and put it on her hand and they married. Later, the emperor sent for his daughter and brought her home. The king, too, sent for his son, and brought him home.

And people proposed matches to the emperor's daughter, but she wanted no match because of that agreement with the king's son. And the king's son longed for her very much. The emperor's daughter, too, was always sad. And the emperor used to walk with her through his courts and halls and show her his greatness, but she was sad. The king's son longed for her so much that he became ill. And whenever they asked him: "Why are you ill?" he did not want to tell. So they asked his valet: "Perhaps you can explain it?" And the valet told them that he knew, because he had served him where he studied. And he told them the story.

Then, the king recalled that he had made a match with that emperor long ago, so he proceeded to write to the emperor to prepare himself for the wedding, because they had made this match long ago. And the emperor no longer wanted to, but he did not dare refuse, so he answered that the king should send him his son, and he would see whether he could govern countries. Then he would give him his daughter in marriage. The king sent him his son, and the emperor sat him in a room and gave him documents of state business to see if he could govern the country.

And the king's son longed very much to see the emperor's daughter, but he could not see her. Once, he walked near a mirrored wall and he caught sight of her and grew faint. She came to him and cheered him and told him she wanted no other match because of the attachment with him.

And he said to her: "What shall we do?—Your father does not want it."

And she said: "Nevertheless!"

After this, they decided to set out by sea, so they rented a ship and set out by sea. And they traveled upon the sea. After a time, they wanted to reach the shore. They reached the shore, and there was a forest there. They went there, the emperor's daughter took the ring and gave it to him. And she lay down to sleep. Later, the king's son saw that she would soon rise, and he placed the ring next to her. When they rose and went to the ship, she recalled that they had forgotten the ring, so she sent him for the ring. He went there, but could not find the place. And he went to another place and could not find the ring, so he went from place to place looking for the ring until he lost his way and could not return. She went to look for him, and lost her way, too.

And the further he walked the more he was lost. Then he saw a path and came into a settlement. And he could do nothing, so he became a servant. She, too, walked and lost her way. And she decided that she would dwell by the sea, so she went to the seashore. There were fruit trees there. And she dwelt there. During the day she went to the seashore, thinking perhaps she could find passers-by, and she lived off the fruit. At night she used to climb a tree to protect herself from the beasts.

2

And it came to pass that there was an immensely wealthy merchant, who had commerce throughout the entire world. And he had an only son. And the merchant was already old. Once the son said to his father: "Since you are already old and I am still young, and your agents pay no attention to me, when you die and I shall be left alone, I will not know what to do. So give me a ship with merchandise and I shall go to sea, to become experienced in commerce." And his father gave him a ship with merchandise. And he went to other countries and sold the merchandise and bought other merchandise and was very successful.

Meanwhile, while he was at sea he caught sight of the trees where the emperor's daughter was staying. The sailors thought that this was a settlement and wanted to go there. When they came closer they noticed that they were only trees and they wanted to return. At that moment, the merchant's son looked into the sea and saw a tree there and on top of it sat something like the image of a person. And he thought that he was mistaken, so he told the other men who were there and they looked and saw something like a person on top of the tree. And they decided to draw nearer, and they sent a man with a small boat there. And they looked into the sea to direct the messenger so that he would not stray from the way but would go directly to that tree. When the messenger went to that tree, he saw a person sitting there, and told them.

So the merchant's son went himself and saw that the emperor's daughter was sitting there, and told her to get down. And she told him she did not want to embark on the ship, unless he promised her he would not touch her until they came home and married legally. He promised her. When she embarked on his ship, he saw she could play musical instruments and she could speak several languages, and was glad that he chanced to meet her. Later, when they approached his home, she told him that it is proper that he go home to inform his father, his relatives, and all his good friends. Since he was bringing such an important woman, they should all come out to greet her. Afterwards, he would find out who she was. (Previously she had also stipulated that he must not ask her who she was until after the wedding. Only then he would know who she was.) And he agreed to this.

She also said to him: "It is also proper that you should make all the sailors who sail the ship drunk, so that they will know that their merchant is going to marry such a woman."

He agreed and took very good wine which he had on board and gave it to them, and they got very drunk. And he went home to inform his father and friends. And the sailors became drunk and left the ship, and fell down drunk and lay there. And while they were preparing to greet her with the entire family, she went and untied the ship from the shore. And she spread the sails and left with the ship.

And all the merchant's family came to the ship and they found nothing. And the merchant (the son's father) was furious with his son. And the son shouted and said: "Believe that I brought a ship with merchandise, etc. . . ."

But they did not see a thing, so he said to them: "Ask the sailors."

And he went to question them and they were lying drunk. Afterwards, they sobered up, and he questioned them, but they did not know what had happened to them. They only knew that they brought a ship with all the merchandise, but did not know where it was. And the merchant was furious with his son and exiled him from home, so that he would not come into his presence. And he went away from him as "a fugitive and a wanderer."

And the emperor's daughter sailed upon the sea.

3

And it came to pass that there was a king. The king built himself palaces near the sea, because he enjoyed the sea breezes, and ships used to pass by. And the emperor's daughter was sailing upon the sea and she came near the king's palace. The king looked and saw the moving ship without oars and there were no people on board. He thought that he was mistaken and ordered his men to look. And they saw this, too.

The emperor's daughter drew near the palace, and reflected: "Why do I need the palace?" So she started back, but the king sent for her and brought her to his house. And the king had no wife because he could not choose one, since whomever he wanted did not want him, and vice versa. And when the emperor's daughter came to him she told him he must swear he would not touch her until he married her legally. And he swore to her. And she told him it was proper that he neither open her ship nor touch it, but that it stay at sea until the wedding. Then everyone would see how much merchandise she had brought and would not say he took an ordinary woman. And he promised her this, too.

And the king wrote to all the countries that they should come to his wedding. And he built palaces for her. And she ordered that they should bring her eleven ladies to stay with her. And the king ordered and they sent her eleven ladies, daughters of lords, and they built a special palace for each of them. She had a special palace, too. And they used to gather in her palace to play musical instruments and games with her.

Once she told them she wanted to sail with them upon the sea. They went with her, and played there. She told them she would serve them some of the good wine she had on board. She gave them some of the wine which was on board, and they became drunk and fell down and lay there. And she went and untied the ship and spread the sails and escaped with the ship.

The king and his men looked and saw that the ship was not there and they were very alarmed. And the king said: "Be careful not to tell her suddenly, because she will have great grief." (For the king did not know that she herself escaped with the ship. He thought that she was still in her chamber.) She might also think that the king had given the ship to somebody else. They should only send one of the ladies to tell her tactfully.

And they went to one chamber and did not find anyone. And likewise to the second chamber and to all eleven chambers, but they found no one. So they agreed to send an old noble woman at night to tell her. They went to her chamber but found no one there and they were very alarmed. And the fathers of the ladies saw that they had no letters from their daughters. They sent letters, but no one answered. So they set out and went there themselves, but did not find their daughters. They were furious and wanted to banish the king (to a place where they banish those condemned to death) because they were the nobles of the kingdom. But they reconsidered: "Is the king so guilty that he deserves banishment?" It was forced upon him. And they agreed to depose him from his kingdom and to exile him. They dismissed and exiled him and he went away.

And the emperor's daughter who had run away with the eleven ladies sailed with the ship. After a while, the ladies woke up, and began to play again, as they had done before, because they did not know the ship had already left the shore. Later, they said to her: "Let us return home." And she answered them: "Let us stay here a little longer." After a while, a storm wind rose. And they said: "Let us return home." And she informed them that the ship had left the shore long ago. And they asked her why she did this. And she said that she had been afraid that the ship would break because of the storm wind, and that was why she had to do so.

And they sailed upon the sea, the emperor's daughter and the eleven ladies, and they played musical instruments there. They came upon a palace, and the ladies said to her: "Let us draw near it," but she did not want to do so. And she said that she regretted having drawn near the palace of that king who wanted to marry her.

Afterwards they saw something like an island in the sea and they came near it. There were twelve robbers there and they wanted to kill the women. So she asked: "Who is the greatest among you?" And they showed her. She said to him: "What do you do?" He told her they were robbers. She said to him: "We, too, are robbers. Only you are robbers with your might, and we are robbers with our wisdom, because we are proficient in languages and play musical instruments. What good will it do you to kill us? It is better that you marry us so you will have our riches, too."

And she showed them what was in the ship. The robbers were pleased by her speech. And the robbers showed them, too, their riches and led them through all their places. They agreed not to marry all at once, but rather one after the other, each choosing a young lady as befit him, according to his greatness. Later, she told them she would serve them a very good wine which she had on board, but she never used since it was being saved for the day when the Lord would select her intended mate. And she gave them the wine in twelve goblets, and she asked each one to drink to all twelve. And they drank and became drunk and fell over.

And then she cried to the other ladies: "Now go and slaughter your men." And then went and slaughtered them all. And they found there immense riches which are not to be found with any king on earth. And they agreed not to take copper or silver, but only gold and gems. So they cast overboard things that were not important to them, and loaded the entire ship with the valuable things, with the gold and gems they found there. And they decided not to dress as women anymore, so they sewed for themselves men's clothing in the German style, and sailed on with the ship.

4

And it came to pass that there was an old king. He had an only son and married him off and handed his kingdom over to him. Once the prince told his father he wanted to cruise at sea with his wife, so that she would become used to the sea air, in case they should have to escape by sea. And the prince with his wife and his ministers embarked upon a ship and were very merry and played pranks. They decided to take off their clothes. And they did so, and when nothing was left on them except their shirts, several of them tried to climb the mast. And the king's son clambered up the mast.

In the meanwhile, the emperor's daughter arrived in her ship, and saw the ship (of the prince and the ministers). And at first she was afraid to draw near it. Later, they drew a little closer. And when she saw that they were very playful, she understood that they were not robbers and she began to come nearer. The emperor's daughter told her people: "I can knock that bald pate down into the sea." (The prince, who was clambering up the mast, had a bald pate.) They said to her: "How is this possible? We are very far from them." She answered that she had a burning lens and with it she would knock him down. And she decided she would not knock him down until he reached the very top of the mast. Because if he were at the middle of the mast, he would fall into the ship, but if he were at the top when he fell, he would fall into the sea.

She waited till he reached the very top of the mast, and took her burning lens and directed it at his brain until it burned his brain and he fell into the sea. When the people in the prince's ship saw that he fell, there was a great clamor, for how could they return to their homes? The king would die of sorrow! And they decided to draw near the ship (of the emperor's daughter) that they had seen, for perhaps there was a doctor there who could give them advice. And they approached her ship and told its crew to have no fear, since they were not going to harm them. They asked them: "Perhaps there is a doctor among you who would give us advice?" And they told them the whole story, that the prince had fallen into the sea.

The emperor's daughter told them to pull him out of the sea. They went and found him and pulled him out. She felt his pulse with her hand and said that his brain had been burned. They tore open his brain and found it as she said. And they were astonished that the doctor (the emperor's daughter) had been so accurate. So they begged her to come home with them and become the king's doctor, and she would be very important. She did not want to do so and said that she was not a doctor, but that she just knew these things.

And the people of the prince's ship did not want to return home, so the two ships sailed along together. And the noblemen approved of the idea that their queen (the prince's widow) should marry the doctor, because of the great wisdom that they found in him. (The noblemen of the prince who fell and died thought that the emperor's daughter and her noble ladies were men, because they were dressed in men's clothes. Thus, they wanted their queen to marry the doctor—who was really the emperor's daughter—since he knew in his wisdom that the prince's brain had been burned when he fell.) They wanted him to be their king, and they would kill their old king. They were embarrassed to tell the queen to marry a doctor, but she was very pleased to marry this doctor. She was only afraid that the country might not want him to be king.

And they agreed to hold banquets so that during the drinking, in a moment of bliss, they would be able to discuss the problem. And they held banquets, each on his assigned day. When the doctor's banquet day arrived (that is, the emperor's daughter's day) he gave them his wine and they became drunk.

In an hour of bliss, the ministers spoke up: "How nice it would be if the queen were to marry the doctor!"

And the doctor spoke up: "It would be very nice if they spoke about it with a mouth that was not drunk."

The queen, too, spoke up: "It would be very nice if I were to marry the doctor, only the country has to agree to it."

The doctor spoke up again: "It would be very nice if they spoke about it with a mouth that was not drunk."

Afterwards, when they sobered up from their drunkenness, the ministers recalled what they had said and they were embarrassed because of the queen, since they had said such a thing. But they reflected: "The queen herself has said it, too." And she, too, was embarrassed because of them. But she reflected: "They, too, have said so." So they began discussing it and it was agreed between them. And she agreed to marry the doctor (that is, the emperor's daughter, whom they thought a doctor) and they went home to the queen's country.

And when the country caught sight of them they were jubilant, because it had been a long time since the prince had gone with the ship. They did not know where he was and the old king had died before their arrival. Afterwards, the people noticed that the prince who had become their king was not there. And they asked: "Where is our king?" And the travelers told them the whole story, that he had died and they had already accepted a new king who had come with them. And the people were very happy that they already had a new king.

And the king (that is, the emperor's daughter who had now become king), ordered it proclaimed in every country that whoever one was, whether a foreigner or a visitor, an escapee or an exile, he should come to his wedding—no one should be absent—and he would receive great gifts. And the king also ordered fountains built around the whole city, so that when one wanted to drink, one should not have to walk far. Everyone should find a fountain near him. The king also ordered his image drawn at each fountain, and the guards posted there to watch. If someone came and looked at the image very carefully and frowned, they should imprison him. And they did everything so.

All three of them arrived: the first prince (the true bridegroom of the emperor's daughter who had become king) and the merchant's son (exiled by his father since the emperor's daughter had fled with the ship and all its merchandise) and the king who had been deposed from his kingdom (since she had fled from him with the eleven ladies). And everyone of them recognized her image. They looked, recalled, and grieved so the guards imprisoned them.

During the wedding, the king (that is, the emperor's daughter) ordered the prisoners brought before him, and they brought those three, and she recognized them. But they did not recognize her, because she was wearing men's clothing.

The emperor's daughter spoke up and said: "You, King, were deposed from your kingdom because of those eleven ladies who were lost. Here are your ladies. Go home to your country and your kingdom."

"You, Merchant, were exiled by your father because of the ship and the merchandise that was lost. Here is your ship with all the merchandise. And since the money has been delayed for so long, you now have in the ship riches many times more than there originally were." (The ship itself, with all the merchant's son's merchandise with which she had escaped, still remained intact, and in addition there were in that ship all the riches that she had taken from the robbers. And it was immensely richer.)

"And you, Prince (that is, her true bridegroom). Come here! Let us go home!"

And they returned to their home.

III. THE CRIPPLE

One of the most complicated of the Bratslav tales, "The Cripple" is a story of spiritual growth. The hero, a cripple at the beginning of the story, is not only cured —as one might expect —through a miraculous and morally instructive sequence of episodes, but learns the true religious meaning of the enigmatic riddle posed by his dying father in his last testament: "You must always water trees." What seems to be a simple horticultural instruction turns out to be the spiritual secret the son learns in the second part of the story after he has been cured of his physical impediment.

As a description of spiritual growth, the story dwells upon the aspect of power, implying that spiritual growth involves power gained through religious knowledge —here knowledge of the world of demons, portrayed comically. The son regains the power of mobility, then goes on to learn that the watering of trees is the crucial act which nourishes and preserves the source of sanctity without which the world disintegrates into a zoo of demons. The reader learns that the power of the source can be restored either by the act of an individual, like the crippled son, or by an internal cataclysm within the world of the demons. The demons are portrayed with such human features that the reader often feels the author has in mind the chaotic corruption of contemporary society.

ONCE there was a wise man who summoned his children and his family before his death, and ordered them in his will to water trees: "You may earn your livelihood in other ways, but you must always try to water trees." Afterwards the wise man died, and he left many children. He had one son who could not walk. He could stand, but he could not walk. And his brothers supplied him with enough for his livelihood. They supplied him with so much that something was left over. And that son gathered bit by bit from what was left over from his livelihood until he gathered a considerable sum. He thought to himself: "Why should I receive my allotment from them? It is better that I start some trade even though I cannot walk." So he decided to hire a wagon, a faithful servant, and a wagon-driver, and travel with them to Leipzig where he would be able to trade even though he could not walk. When the family heard about this, they were pleased and said: "Why should we give him an allotment? It is better that he has his own livelihood." And they lent him more money so that he could trade.

He hired a wagon and a servant and a driver and set out. And he came to an inn. The servant said that they should spend the night there, but the cripple did not want to. They implored him, but he insisted, and they traveled on. They became lost in a forest, and robbers attacked them. Those robbers had become robbers because once there had been famine. And a person came to the city and proclaimed that whoever wanted food should come to him. Several people gathered around him, and he acted cunningly and rejected whomever he knew he did not need. To one he said: "You can be an artisan." And to another he said: "You can work in a mill." He chose only the clever men and went with them to the forest and he told them that they would become robbers: "From here the roads go to Leipzig, to Breslau, and to other places, and merchants travel here, and we shall rob them and gather money."

And these robbers attacked that son who could not walk and his servant and driver. The driver and the servant, who could flee, fled, but the crippled son remained on the wagon. The robbers came and took the chest with the money, and asked him: "Why are you sitting?" And he answered that he could not walk. They stole the chest and the horses, but he remained on the wagon. The servant and the wagon-driver who had fled reasoned that since they had taken deeds from lords, why should they return home, to be put in chains? It was better that they remain there, in the place they had fled to, and be a servant and a driver there.

As long as the son had food which he had taken from home, dry bread that was in the wagon, he ate it. Afterwards, when he finished and had nothing to eat, he started thinking what to do. And he threw himself from the wagon to eat grass. He spent the night in the field, lonely and frightened. His strength ebbed till he could not even stand, just crawl, and he ate the grass around him. As long as he could reach out and eat, he ate. After he had eaten all the grass around him and could no longer reach it, he moved himself further and ate there. And he ate grass for some time.

2

Once he came across grass he had not yet eaten. And that grass pleased him, for he had been eating grass for a long time and he recognized it, but he had not yet seen such grass. He decided to pluck it up with its root. And under the root there was a diamond and the diamond had four sides, and each side had a different magic quality. On one side it was inscribed that whoever held this side would be carried to a place where day and night come together, that is, where sun and moon come together. When he plucked up the herb with its root, he happened to hold that side, and it carried him, and he came to the place where day and night meet. He looked and saw that he was in the place where the sun and the moon come together.

He heard the sun and the moon talking. The sun was complaining to the moon: "There is a tree that has many branches, and fruit and leaves, and each branch and fruit and leaf has a special quality. One is effective for producing sons, and one is effective for livelihood. One is effective for curing this illness and one, that illness. Each is effective for one thing. And they should have watered this tree, and if they had watered it, it could have had great effectiveness. And not only do I not water it, but by shining on it I dry it up."

The moon answered and said: "You worry about others' worries. Let me tell you my own concern. I have a thousand mountains, and around those thousand mountains there are a thousand more mountains. And *there* is the place of the demons, and the demons have cocks' legs. They have no power in their legs, but they suck from my legs, and therefore I have no power in my legs. I have a dust that is a cure for my legs, but the wind comes and carries it away."

The sun answered: "Is this why you worry? I shall tell you about a cure. There is a road that divides into several roads. One is the road for *zadikim*. For the *zadik*, they spread under his feet the dust on that road at each step. At each step he takes, he treads upon that dust. And there is a road for heretics. For the heretic, they spread that dust under his feet at each step. And there is the road for the madmen. For the madman, they spread under his feet, etc. And thus, there are several roads. There is, furthermore, one road for those *zadikim* who accept suffering, and cruel lords lead them in chains. And since those *zadikim* have no power in their legs, they spread underneath their feet some of the dust from that road, and they gain power in their legs. So, you should go there, where there is much dust, and you will find a cure for your legs." (All this is the sun's words to the moon.)

And the crippled son heard all this.

In the meantime he looked at another side of the diamond and he saw written there that whoever held that side would be carried to the road out of which came those several roads. He held that side, and it carried him there, and he put his legs on that road whose dust was a cure for legs. And he was immediately cured. He went and took dust from all the roads and made packets. He tied the dust of the *zadikim* road by itself, and he tied the dust of the other roads, each by itself, and took them with him. And he decided to go to that forest where they had robbed him. When he came there, he chose a tall tree that was near the road where the robbers set out to rob. He took the dust of the *zadikim* and the dust of the madmen and mixed them and spread them on the road, and climbed the tree and sat there to see what would happen to them.

And the robbers, who were sent by the chief robber, set out to rob. When they came to that road, as soon as they trod on that dust, they became *zadikim*. And they started to cry for their souls, for they had previously robbed and killed many souls. But since it was mixed with madman's dust, they became mad *zadikim* and they started quarreling with each other. One said: "We robbed because of you." And the other said: "We robbed because of you." Till they killed each other. And the chief robber sent another group, and this time, too, it happened as before. They, too, killed each other. And so it happened afterwards, until they were all killed. When the son understood that all the robbers had been killed and no one was left but the chief robber and another man, he descended from the tree. He swept away the dust from the road, and spread only the *zadikim* dust. And he went and sat in the tree.

That robber, the chief among them, wondered why he had sent all the robbers and not one had returned to him. So he went himself with the one that remained with him. As soon as he came to that road, where that son had spread only the *zadikim* dust, he became a *zadik*, and he started to cry to his friend for his soul, crying that he had killed so many souls and had robbed so much. He plucked weeds from graves and repented and had remorse. And when that son, who was sitting in the tree, saw that he had remorse and repented so much, he descended from the tree.

When the robber saw that he found a human being, he started to cry out: "Woe for my soul! I did this and that. Alas, assign me a penance!"

The son answered him: "Give me back the chest you have robbed from me." (They had recorded everything they had robbed with the date it was robbed and from whom it was robbed.)

The robber told him: "I will give it back to you immediately and I will even give you all the stolen treasures that I have. Just assign me a penance!"

The son said to him: "Your penance is to go to the city and cry and confess: 'I am the one who uttered the proclamation then and enlisted several robbers, and killed several souls.' This is your penance!"

The robber gave him all the treasures, and he went with him to the city. The robber did as he had promised, and they decided in that city that since he had killed so many souls, they should hang him so that others would learn.

3

Afterwards, the son who had formerly been crippled decided to go to the two thousand mountains which had been mentioned, to look and see what was going on there. When he arrived there he stood at a distance from the two thousand mountains and saw that there were thousands and tens of thousands of families of demons there. Because they multiply like human beings, they were very many. He saw their royalty sitting on a throne, the like of which no mortal had ever occupied, and he saw that they were making jests. One told how he had harmed a certain baby, and another told how he had harmed somebody's hand, and another told how he had harmed somebody's foot. And similar mockery.

In the meantime the (formerly) crippled son looked and saw two demons, a father and a mother, walking and weeping. And he asked them: "Why are you weeping?" And they answered that they had had a son who used to depart and return at a certain time. And now, a long time had passed, but he had not come. The parents had been brought to the king, and the king ordered messengers sent throughout the world to find him. When the father and mother were returning from the king, they met someone who was their son's friend, and used to travel with their son. But now they met him alone. And he asked them: "Why are you crying?" And they told him. He answered them: "I will tell you. We had an island in the sea which we made our place. Later, the king who owned the island wanted to build buildings there and he laid the foundations. Your son said to me that we should do harm to that king, so we went and took the power away from the king. That king engaged doctors but they could not help him, so he began to engage sorcerers. And there was one sorcerer who knew your son's family, but he did not know my family. Thus, he could do nothing to me. But, since the sorcerer knew his family, he caught him, and tortured him severely."

And the parents brought the demon who had told them all this to their king, and he retold it in the presence of the king. The king said: "They should give that king's power back to him." The son's friend stated: "There was one among us who did not have power, and they gave him that power." The king said: "They should take the power away from him and give it back to the king." They answered the king that he had become a cloud. The king said that they should call the cloud and bring it there. And they sent a messenger for it.

4

That (formerly) crippled son who had come there and seen all that said: "Let me go and see how a cloud is made out of these people." He went after the messenger and came to the city where the cloud was. And he asked the people of the city: "Why does the cloud cover the city so much?" They answered him: "On the contrary, there is usually no cloud here, but it has been some time since the cloud has covered our city." The messenger came and called the cloud, and it went away. That (formerly) crippled son decided to go after them, to hear what they were saying. And he heard the messenger ask it: "How did you become a cloud here?" And he answered him: "I'll tell you a story:

"Once there was a wise man. The emperor of his country was a great heretic, and made all the people of the country heretics. The wise man went and called all his kinsmen. He told them: 'You see that the emperor is a great heretic and he made all the country heretics, and he made some of our kin heretics, too. So, let us retreat to the desert, so that we may remain with our faith in the Lord, blessed be He.'

"And they agreed with him. The wise man said a Name (that is, he mentioned one of The Names), and brought them to the desert, but the desert did not please him. And he said a Name, and he carried them to a different desert, but it, too, did not please him. And he said another Name and he brought them to a different desert, and it pleased him. That desert was close to the two thousand mountains, and the wise man went and made a circle around his kinsman, so that no one could come near them.

"And there is a tree. If that tree had been watered, none

89

of the demons would have remained. Thus some of us demons stand day and night and dig, and do not let water come to the tree."

And the messenger asked him: "Why do they stand there day and night? If they dig once to prevent the water from coming, it is enough."

The cloud answered him:

"There are speakers among us, and those speakers cause controversy between one king and another. This brings about a war, and this, in turn, brings about an earthquake. The earth around the ditch falls and the water can come to the tree. That is why they are always prepared to dig.

"And when one among us becomes a king, the people present all kinds of jest in his presence and are merry. One jests how he has harmed a baby, and how the mother mourns it. And others show different kinds of mockery. And when the king comes to the celebration, he takes a walk with his nobles and tries to uproot the tree. Because, if there had been no tree at all, it would have been very good for us. He takes courage to uproot the whole tree, but when he comes to the tree, the tree shouts loudly. Then, fear seizes him and he retreats.

"Once, a new king was crowned, and they performed great jests in his presence. He came in great celebration, and he took courage, and decided to uproot the whole tree completely. He went on a walk with his ministers, and he took courage, and ran to uproot the tree completely. But when he came to it, it shouted at him loudly, and fear seized him. He retreated and came back in great anger.

"As he was returning he looked and saw that wise man's sect of people sitting, and he sent a few men of his to harm them as was their wont. When they saw the demons, that family of human beings was seized with great fear. That old man told them: 'Don't be afraid.' When the demons came nearer, they could not approach them because of the circle that was around them. The king demon sent other messengers, and they could not approach either.

"The king of the demons came in great anger and went there himself, and he, too, could not come near them. And he asked the old man to let him in.

"The old man said to him: 'Since you ask, I will let you in. But it is not the custom that a king should go by himself. I will let you in with one more person.' And he made an opening for them and they entered. And he went and closed the circle again.

"The king said to the old man: 'How did you come to settle in our place?'

"The wise man said: 'Why is it your place? It is my place!'

"The king said: 'Aren't you afraid of me?'

"He answered him: 'No.'

"The king said: 'Aren't you afraid?' And he spread himself and became very huge till he reached the sky, and threatened to swallow the old man.

"The old man said: 'Nevertheless, I am not afraid at all. But if I want, you will be afraid of me.' And he went and prayed a little and a heavy cloud came, and there were great thunders. The thunder killed all the noblemen who were with him and no one was left but the one who was with the king there, inside the circle. The king asked him to stop the thunder, and it stopped.

"The king stated: 'Since you are such a person, I shall give you a book of all the families of the demons. Because there are Baalé Shem who know only one family, and they do not know even that family completely. I will give you a book where all the families are inscribed. For they are all inscribed in the king's archives, even one who has just been born.' And the demon's king sent the one who was inside the circle with him for the book. (It turns out that the old man did well to let the king in with another person. Otherwise, whom would he have sent?) He fetched the book, and the wise man opened the book and saw inscribed there the names of thousands and tens of thousands of their families. The king promised that they would never harm the old man's family. And he ordered the old man to bring all the portraits of all his family members. Even if a new baby is born, they were immediately to bring his portrait, so that no one of the old man's family might be harmed.

"Later, when the time came for the old man to depart from this world, he called his sons, declared his last will, and told them: 'I leave this book to you. You have seen that I have the power to use this book in sanctity, and nevertheless I have not used it. But I have faith in the Lord, blessed be He. You, too, should not use it. Even if there is someone among you who can use it in sanctity, he should not use it. He should only have faith in the Lord, blessed be He.'

"The wise man died, and the book was inherited by his grandson. He had the power to use it in sanctity, but he had faith in the Lord, blessed be He, and did not use it, as the old man had ordered. The speakers among them tried to seduce the old man's grandson: 'Since you have grown-up daughters and no way to support them and marry them off, use the book.'

"He did not know that they were seducing him, but thought that his heart was advising him. He traveled to his grandfather's grave, and he asked him: 'You left in your will that we should not use that book but that we should only have faith in the Lord, blessed be He. And now, my heart seduces me to use it.' The departed old man answered him: 'Even though you have the power to use it in sanctity, it is better that you have faith in the Lord and do not use it, and the Lord will help you.' And the grandson did so.

"Once, the king of that country where the old man's grandson lived was ill. And he engaged doctors but they could not find a cure. Because of the great heat in that country, the medicines were to no avail. (The king decreed that the Jews should pray for him.) And our king (of the demons) said:

'Since that grandson has the power to use the book in sanctity, and he does not use it, we shall act in his favor.' And the king ordered me to be a cloud so that the king would be cured by the medicines which he had already taken, and by the medicines he would yet take. And that grandson did not know anything about it. And this is why I have become a cloud here."

(All this the cloud told the messenger. And that son, who at first did not have power in his legs, walked behind them and heard it.)

And they brought the cloud to the king. The king ordered them to take the power and return it to that other king, and they returned the power to him. And then, those demons' son returned. He came severely afflicted and without power, because they had tortured him there. He was very angry with the sorcerer who had tortured him so, and he ordered his sons and his family always to lie in wait for that sorcerer. But there were among them speakers. And they went and told the sorcerer to take heed because they were lying in wait for him. The sorcerer devised stratagems and called other sorcerers who knew families, to be on guard against them. That son was very angry with the speakers because they had revealed his secret to the wizard. Once, it happened that members of that son's family and the speakers met in the king's guard. Those family members made a false charge against the speakers, and the king killed the speakers. The speakers who remained were very angry and they incited a rebellion among all the kings. The demons suffered famine and weakness and sword and pestilence. Wars broke out among all the kings, and this brought about an earthquake. The whole earth fell in and the tree was completely watered. And no one remained of them, as if they had never existed. Amen.

IV. THE KING WHO DECREED CONVERSION

One of the ingenious achievements of 16th- and 17th-century Kabbalah was its compelling fusion of two themes as inseparable analogues: the exilic condition of the Jews and the exilic status of the cosmos. "The King Who Decreed Conversion" points to a corollary of this theological fusion. What seems to be the source of real power in our experiential world is merely an illusion, since above and beyond what human beings call "history" or "politics" is a realm of divine purpose which mocks human claims to meaning and truth. The world of double exile which the Kabbalist experienced must have a deeper meaning not readily apparent to our senses.

In this story, the monarchs who seem to be all-powerful are really fragile and beset with insecurities, while the Jews who maintain the pious practices of their religion are secure and control the destiny of nations. Furthermore, the Marrano minister who feigned conversion in order to protect his property lives at the whims of these temporal monarchs while his coreligionists who have remained steadfast in their religion are invulnerable and associated with the realm of real cosmic power. Though the Marrano question was not a live issue as such in the early 19th century, Nahman could have been referring in this story to enlightened Jews who had adopted the practices of the local or Western European nobility.

ONCE there was a king who decreed for his country exile or conversion. Whoever wanted to stay in the country would have to convert, and if not, he would be exiled from the country. There were some who renounced all their property and riches and left in poverty so as to remain with their faith as Jews. Some of them felt sorry for their riches and remained and became Marranos. Secretly they practiced the Jewish religion, but in public they were not allowed to do so. Then the king died and his son became king. And he began to govern the country sternly. He conquered several countries and was very "wise." And since he controlled the ministers of the kingdom harshly, they took counsel and conspired to destroy him and his seed.

Among the ministers there was one of the Marranos, who thought to himself: "Why am I a Marrano? Since I felt sorry for my money and property. Now that the country will be without a king the people will eat each other alive. It is impossible to have a country without a king." That is why he decided to go, himself, to the king, without their knowing it, and tell him. And he went and told the king that they were conspiring against him. The king tried to test whether this was true. And he saw that it was true and stationed guards. On the night they attacked him the guards caught them. And the king judged them each according to his case.

The king spoke out and said to the Marrano minister: "What honor shall I give you for saving me and my seed? If I want to make you a minister—you are already a minister! And if I want to give you money? You have it. Say what honor you want and I shall do it for you."

The Marrano answered and said: "Will you do what I tell you?"

The king answered: "Yes."

Said he: "Swear to me by your crown and your kingdom." And he swore.

The Marrano spoke out and said: "The honor which is most important to me is that I should be allowed to be a Jew in public, to put on *tallith* and *tefilin* in public."

The king was very angry, since in all his country people were not allowed to live as Jews, but he had no choice because of his oath. In the morning, the Marrano went and put on *tallith* and *tefilin* in public.

Afterwards the king died, and his son became king. And he began to govern the country gently, since he had seen that the people had wanted to destroy his father. He conquered many countries, and was very, very wise, and he ordered all the astrologers to assemble, to predict by what his seed would be destroyed, so that he could take heed. They told him that his seed would be destroyed unless he took heed of the ox and the lamb. And they wrote this in the book of records. And he ordered his sons that they, too, should govern the country gently, the way he had done, and he died.

His son became king and he began to govern the country sternly and forcibly, like his grandfather. He conquered many countries and he hit upon the idea of declaring that there should not be found in his country an ox or a lamb, so that his seed would not be destroyed. Thus he had no fear of anything. He governed his country sternly and became very "wise" and fell upon the idea of conquering the entire world without war. That is: There are seven parts to the world, because the world had been divided into seven parts. And there are seven planets. Each planet shines upon one part of the world. And there are seven kinds of metals, for each of the seven planets shines with one kind of metal.

He went and gathered all the seven kinds of metal and ordered his men to fetch all the golden portraits of all the kings which hung in their palaces. From this he made a man: his head of gold, and his body of silver, and the rest of the limbs of the other kinds of metal. There were in that man all seven kinds of metal. And he placed him on a high mountain. All the seven planets shone on that man. When a man needed some advice, whether to make a certain deal or not, he would stand opposite the limb made from the kind of metal that corresponded to the part of the world where he came from, and would think whether or not to do it. If he was supposed to do it, that limb would light up and shine, and if not, the limb would darken. The king did all this, and thus, he conquered the entire world and collected much money.

This image of the man was capable of all this only on condition that the king would humble the proud and exalt the humble. So he sent orders to all the generals and noblemen who had appointments and ranks. They all came and he humbled them and stripped them of their appointments. He stripped even those who had been appointed and worked for his great-great-grandfather. And he exalted the humble and put them in their place. The Marrano minister was among the noblemen whom the king acted to humble. The king asked him: "What are your privileges and appointment?" And he replied: "My privilege is to be allowed to be a Jew in public, because of the favor I did for your grandfather." The king stripped him of it and he became a Marrano again.

One night the king went to sleep and saw in a dream that the sky was clear. And he saw all twelve Constellations of the Zodiac. (The stars in the heavens are divided into twelve sectors corresponding to the twelve months. One sector looks like a lamb [Aries] and this is the constellation of the month of Nissan. The constellation of the month of Iyyar is called an ox

[Taurus]). The king saw that among the Constellations of the Zodiac the ox (Taurus) and the lamb (Aries) were laughing at him. He woke up in great anger and was terrified. He ordered his servant to fetch the book of records and saw written there that his seed would be destroyed by an ox and a lamb. Great fear seized him and his soul was much disturbed. He summoned interpreters of dreams, but each interpreted to himself and their voices did not reach his ears. A very great fear seized him.

Then, a wise man came to him and told him that he had heard from his father that the sun had three hundred and sixty five courses, and that there was a place where all courses were shining. And an iron staff grows there. When whosoever was fearful came to this place, he was saved from his fear. The king felt better, and he, his wife and sons and all his seed went with the wise man to that place. In the middle of the way stood an angel who was in charge of anger. As a result of anger, a destructive angel was formed, and this angel was in charge of all destructive forces. People would ask him for the way, for there was a way that went straight ahead, and a way full of mud, and a way full of holes and pits, and so on. There was also a way where there was fire, and one could burn at a distance of four miles from that fire. So they asked him for the way, and he showed them the way where the fire was. They walked on and the wise man looked forward every now and then to see whether the fire was there, because he had heard from his father that there was such a fire. In time he saw the fire. And he saw that kings and Jews, wrapped in *tallith* and *tefilin*, were walking through the fire. Since Jews were living in the countries of those kings, they were able to walk through the fire. The wise man said to the king: "Since I have a tradition that one can burn four miles away from the fire, I do not want to walk further." The king thought that since he saw the other kings walking through the fire, he, too, would walk. The wise man replied: "I have that tradition from my father, so I do not want to go. If you want to go, go." The king and his seed went and the fire overcame them, and he and his seed burned and all were destroyed. When the wise man came home, the ministers wondered: "He took heed of ox and lamb. Why were he and his seed destroyed?"

The Marrano minister spoke out and said: "He was destroyed through me. The astrologers saw, but did not know what they saw. From the skin of the ox one makes *tefilin*, and from the wool of the lamb one makes fringes for the *tallith*, and through them he and his seed were destroyed. Those kings in whose country Jews lived dressed in *tallith* and *tefilin* walked through the fire, and were not harmed at all. He was destroyed because Jews who wear *tallith* and *tefilin* were not permitted to live in his country. That is why the ox and the lamb in the planets were laughing at him. For the astrologers saw and did not know what they saw, so he and his seed were destroyed."

V. THE KING WHO HAD NO CHILDREN

"The King Who Had No Children" seems, at first, to be an account of intrigue for power in a royal family —a topic quite foreign to Nahman's interests. Actually, it is a description of the character and struggles of the zadik. The zadik, as we know from many accounts and also from the tales of the Baal Shem Tov (Shivhe HaBesht: In Praise of the Baal Shem Tov), attracted Hasidim not only by his religious piety and intense prayer, but by his ability to effect cures by spells and amulets. Among the maladies he was often called upon to remedy was barrenness.

In this story, the two zadikim perform their cures with much difficulty. At first they express great reluctance to accede to the king's request. When they are forced to pray under duress, the results of their prayers are not precisely those which were requested: The first child born was a daughter, not a son; the son, when born, did not seem to be made of gems. Sorcery as such, furthermore, is not discounted as a barbaric practice; the zadik, too, indulges in sorcery, but his sorcery, deriving from prayer to the true Lord, is the more effective.

The birth and revelation of the prince of gems is, to be sure, the ultimate goal of the story, and he must represent some redemptive figure. Nevertheless, the focus of the story is less on the prince than on the struggle of the two zadikim to assist in his birth by means of their prayers and to protect him with their sorcery, particularly in the struggle against his demonic sister.

ONCE there was a king who had no children. He went and engaged doctors so that his kingdom would not be turned over to strangers. But they did not help him. He decreed that the Jews should pray for him to have children. And the Jews searched for a *zadik* to pray and act so that the king might have children. They sought and found a hidden *zadik*, and told him to pray that the king should have children. He replied that he knew nothing. They informed the king of this. The king sent his decree to him, and they brought him to the king.

The king began to talk to him in good spirit: "You know that the Jews are in my hands to do with as I wish. Thus I ask you in good spirit to pray that I may have children."

The *zadik* promised him that in the same year there would be a child, and he returned home.

The queen gave birth to a daughter, and this princess was a remarkable person. When she was four years old she knew all wisdoms and languages and could play all instruments. Kings traveled from all countries to see her. Great happiness overcame the king, but afterwards he longed very much for a son, so that his kingdom would not be transferred to a stranger. And he decreed again that the Jews should pray that he would have a son. They searched for the *zadik*, but did not find him for he had already died. They searched further and found another hidden *zadik*, and told him to give the king a son. He said that he knew nothing. They informed the king of this. The king said to him, too, as he said before: "You know that the Jews are in my hands, etc."

That *zadik* said to him: "Will you be able to do what I command?"

The king said: "Yes."

The wise man said to him: "I must have you bring me all sorts of gems, because each gem has a special quality. For the kings have a book in which all sorts of gems are written."

The king said: "I will spend half my kingdom in order to have a son."

The king went and brought the wise *zadik* all sorts of gems. The wise man took them and ground them into fine dust and took a goblet of wine and put them into it. He offered half the glass to the king to drink, and half to the queen. He told them they would have a son who would be entirely of gems, and there would be in him all the special qualities of all the gems. And the *zadik* went home.

The queen gave birth to a son and great happiness overcame the king. But the son who was born was not made of gems. When the son was four years old, he was a remarkable person and very wise in all wisdom and knew all languages. Kings traveled to see him. The princess saw that she was not important, and became jealous of him. She had only one consolation: the *zadik* had said he would be entirely of gems, but he was not of gems.

Once the prince was cutting wood and he cut his finger. The princess rushed to bandage his finger. She noticed a gem there and grew very jealous of him and feigned sickness. Several doctors came but could not cure her. And they called the sorcerers. There was one sorcerer to whom she revealed the truth, that she was feigning sickness. She asked him if he could charm a man so that he would become scabrous. He said: "Yes." She said to him: "What if he would ask a different sorcerer to cancel the charm and he would be cured?" Said the sorcerer: "If the charm is thrown into the water they will not be able to cancel it." And she threw the charm into the water.

And the prince became very scabrous. There were scabs on his nose and on his face and on the rest of his body. The king engaged doctors and sorcerers to no avail. He decreed that the Jews should pray, so they sought the *zadik* and they brought him to the king. The *zadik* had always prayed to the Lord, blessed be He, particularly since He had promised that the prince would be entirely of gems. Yet it was not so. And he argued before the Lord, blessed be He: "Did I do it for my own honor? I only did it for your honor, and now, what I said has not come true."

The *zadik* came to the king and prayed, but to no avail. They informed him that a charm had been used. Now that *zadik* was high above all the sorcerers, so he came and informed the king that a charm had been used, but they had thrown it into the water, and there was no remedy for the prince, unless they throw the sorcerer who had performed the witchcraft into the water. Said the king: "I give you all the sorcerers to throw into the water so that my son shall be cured."

The princess became frightened and she ran to the water to take the charm out of the water, because she knew where the charm was placed. She fell into the water and there was a great tumult since the king's daughter had fallen into the water. The *zadik* came and told them that the prince would be cured. And he was cured. The scabs dried and fell off, and all the skin peeled off him and he was made entirely of gems. (After the skin peeled off, it was discovered that the prince was entirely of gems, as the *zadik* had said.)

VI. THE KING AND THE WISE MAN

For all his spiritual severity and messianic anxiety, Nahman was not averse to comic moods. We have seen a clear protracted satire about the world of demons in "The Cripple"; "The King Who Decreed Conversion" and "The King Who Had No Children" are not devoid of touches of irony. Though dealing with theodicy, one of the central problems perplexing to men of faith, "The King and the Wise Man" is presented as an ironic burlesque —Swiftian without the scatology.

The first king, obviously temporal, is puzzled by the titles (attributes) applied to the second king because he cannot envisage a king who is either truthful or humble, and, since he has no portrait of the second king in his gallery, he doubts his existence. The wise man selected to solve this riddle and bring back the portrait has several salient characteristics: He can tell truth from sham and deception; he is relentless in his quest; he is fearless even in his questioning of the second king, obviously God himself. And, in a sense of self-parody, Nahman endowed his wise man with the perception that one can judge a country from the nature of its jokes.

When the wise man undergoes his predictably frustrating experiences, which finally bring him to the Supreme Magistrate, God, his report to God of his findings and conclusion regarding the kingdom He apparently rules startles Him. Hearing his praises from such a perceptive and knowledgeable human being, God reduces his substance to nothing so that when the curtain is finally pulled aside, the portrait seen by the wise man —and returned to his own king —is obviously blank. For the perceptive Hasid versed in the intricacies of Bratslav theology, the portrait of God must be blank.

ONCE there was a king who had a wise man. The king said to the wise man:

"There is a certain king who designates himself 'a mighty hero,' 'a man of truth,' and 'a humble person.' As to his might, I know that he is mighty, since the sea surrounds his country, and on the sea stands a fleet of ships with cannon, and they do not let anyone approach. And inland there is a big swamp surrounding the country. Through the swamp there is only one narrow path and on the path only one man can walk at a time, and there, too, there are cannon. When someone comes to fight them, they shoot the cannon, and it is impossible to approach. But why he designates himself 'a man of truth' and 'a humble person,' this I do not know. And I want you to fetch me the portrait of that king."

That king (who spoke to his wise man) had all the portraits of all the kings, but no portrait of the king who had designated himself (with these titles) was available because he is hidden from men, since he sits under a canopy and is far from his subjects.

The wise man went to that country. The wise man made up his mind that he had to know the essence of the country. And how could he know the essence of the country? By the country's jokes. Because when one has to know something, one should know the jokes related to it. There are several kinds of jokes. Sometimes one really intends to harm his friend with his words, and when the friend becomes angry, he says to him: "I am joking as is written: 'As a madman who casts firebrands, arrows, and death.'" (It is like one who shoots arrows into his friend's heart and says, "I am only joking.") And sometimes one does not intend it as a joke, but even so his friend is harmed by his words. Thus there are all kinds of jokes.

Among all countries there is one country which includes all countries (in that it serves as the rule for all countries). In that country there is one city which includes all cities of the whole country which includes all countries. In that city there is a house which includes all the houses of the city which includes all the cities of the country which includes all countries. And there is a man who includes everybody from that house, etc. And there is someone there who performs all the jests and jokes of the country.

The wise man took with him much money and went there. He saw that they were performing all kinds of jests and jokes, and he understood through the jokes that the country was full of lies from beginning to end because he saw how they were making fun, how they deceived and misled people in commerce, and how, when he turned for justice to the magistrate, everyone there lied and accepted bribery. He went to the higher court, and there, too, everything was a lie and in jest they faked all those things.

The wise man understood through that laughter that the whole country was full of lies and deceit, and there was no truth in it. He went and traded in the country and he let himself be cheated in commerce. He went to trial in court, and he saw that they were all full of lies and bribery. On this day he bribed them, and on the next they did not recognize him. He went to the higher court, and there, too, everything was a lie, until he reached the senate and they, too, were full of lies and bribery. Finally he came to the king himself.

When he came to the king he stated: "Over whom are you king? For the country is full of lies, all of it, from beginning to end, and there is no truth in it!"

He started telling all the lies of the country. The king bent his ears toward the curtain to hear his words, because he was amazed that there was a man who knew all the lies of the country. The ministers of the kingdom who heard his words were very angry with him but he continued to tell about all the lies of the country.

That wise man concluded: "And one could say that the king, too, is like them, that he loves deceit like the country. But from this I see how you are 'a man of truth.' You are far from them, since you cannot stand the lies of the country."

He started praising the king very much. The king was very humble, and his greatness lay in his humility. And this is the way of the humble person: The more one praises and exalts him, the smaller and humbler he becomes. Because of the greatness of the praise with which the wise man praised and exalted the king, the king became very humble and small, till he became nothing at all. And the king could not restrain himself, but cast away the curtain, to see the wise man: "Who is it who knows and understands all this?" And his face was revealed. The wise man saw him and painted his portrait and he brought it to the king.

VII. THE KING WHO FOUGHT
MANY WARS

The nature of religious insight has intrigued man since antiquity: Why do some human beings have these insights while others do not? Can one induce them? Why can't a human being possess these insights at all times? In "The King Who Fought Many Wars" Nahman addresses himself to these problems in the literary form germane to them: a composite of vision, nightmare, and trance.

Superficially, the story resembles "The King Who Decreed Conversion," where we found the distinct contrast between the Gentile king and the pious Jews, between Gentile culture and Judaism, the Law of God. What interests the author here is not so much the king's discovery that he has been saved twice by the Law of the Jews (the page or the tablets), but that the king is not satisfied with this information. His desire for authentication —hence the trance —stems from his will to convince his entire people and, more importantly, to discover why he has had this insight and why it is not permanent. What he discovers is that he was indeed destined in heaven to be a zadik, perhaps even the messiah; but Samael, the devil, fearful that this act would annihilate his powers altogether, protested to God who then allowed Samael to create obstacles, including the enigmatic "hunched old man," which prevented this precious soul from descending to the earth as a zadik or the messiah. In its deformed state, the soul was forced to descend as a mere king with only occasional religious insights.

ONCE there was a king who had to fight several difficult wars. He won them, and captured many prisoners. The king used to hold a great ball each year on the day he won the war. All ministers of the kingdom and the lords were at the ball, as is the custom of kings. They used to produce comedies there, and made fun of all nations, of the Turks and of all nations. They distorted, in jest, the manners and customs of each nation, and obviously made fun of the Jews, too. The king ordered his men to fetch him the book where the manners and customs of each nation were written. Wherever he opened the book he saw that the manners and customs of the nation were written exactly as the jesters had performed them. Obviously, the one who produced the comedy had seen that book, too.

When the king was sitting over the book, he saw a spider crawling on the edges of the pages. And on the other side there stood a fly. Naturally, where does a spider go? To the fly. But when the spider was going toward the fly, a wind came and raised the page of the book. The spider could not go toward the fly, and retreated. Cunningly, he pretended that he was retreating and did not want to go to the fly. The page returned to its place. The spider again started toward the fly, but then the page rose and did not let the spider go toward the fly. And it retreated. This happened several times. Later, the spider started toward the fly again. He crawled forward until he caught the page with one leg. Again the page rose, but he was already a little on the page. Then the page set itself down completely and the spider remained underneath, in the space between the pages. He crawled there and remained underneath until nothing remained of him.

The king saw all this, and wondered. He understood that this was no empty matter, but that he was being shown something. All the ministers saw that the king was looking and wondering at it. And he started thinking about it: "What is it and why is it?" And he fell asleep on the book.

2

He dreamt that he had a diamond in his hand. As he was looking at it, grotesque men, came out of it, so he threw the diamond away. It was a custom with kings to hang their portraits above them, and above the portrait, to hang the crown. In his dream the men who came out of the diamond took the portrait and cut off its head, and then took the crown and threw it into the mud. And those men ran to him to kill him but a page rose from the book on which he was lying, and protected him. They could do nothing to him, and they went away. Later the page returned to its place. Again they wanted to kill him and again the page rose. And thus it happened several times. He yearned very much to see what page was protecting him, and what customs of what nation were written on it, but he was afraid to look. He began shouting: "Help! Help!" All the ministers who were sitting there heard him and wanted to wake him. But, since it is not good manners to wake the king, they clapped hands around him to wake him, but he did not hear.

In the meantime, a lofty mountain came to him and asked him: "Why are you shouting like that? For I have been sleeping a long time and nothing ever woke me up, but you woke me."

He said: "Shouldn't I shout? They rise against me to kill me, and only this page protects me!"

The mountain answered him: "If this page protects you, you have nothing to worry about, because many foes rise against me, too, and only this page protects me. Come and I will show you." And he showed him that around the mountain there were thousands and tens of thousands of foes, and they were making banquets and were mirthful, and were playing instruments and dancing. And the reason for the mirth was that a member of one of their sects thought out a plan to climb the mountain. Then they would make a great celebration and a banquet and would play, etc. "And so it is with each of their sects, but this page with these customs which protects you protects me."

On the top of the mountain was a tablet. On it, were written the customs of the page that was protecting him, and to what nation it belonged. But since the mountain was very lofty, they could not read the writing. At the bottom there was another tablet, and on it was inscribed that whosoever had teeth could climb the mountain. And the Lord, blessed be He, made grass grow where they had to climb the mountain, and all the teeth of whosoever came there fell out. Whether he walked on foot, or rode, or came in a wagon drawn by animals—all his teeth fell out. And white heaps of teeth were lying there like mountains.

Later, the men from the diamond took the portrait and restored it as it had previously been, and they took the crown and washed it, and they hung them both back in their places.

3

The king woke up and looked immediately at the page that had protected him to see what customs of what nation were on it, and he saw that the customs of the Jews were inscribed on it. He started looking at the page with the truth and understood the real truth. He thought to himself that he himself would surely become a Jew. But what could one do to correct all of his people, to bring them over to the truth?

He decided that he would go and seek a wise man who would interpret the dream exactly as it had happened. He took with him two men and traveled throughout the world, not as a king, but as a common man. He traveled from city to city and from country to country and asked how he could find a wise man who could interpret his dream as it had happened. They informed him of a place where such a wise man could be found and he went there. He came to the wise man and told him the truth—that he was a king, and had won many wars, and all the events which have been told—and he asked him to interpret his dream.

He answered him: "I myself cannot interpret it, but there is a time on a certain day in a certain month when I collect all ingredients for drugs and I make a mixture out of them. We have the man smoke the drug, and he thinks in his mind what he wants to see and know, and then he will know everything." And the king decided that since he had already spent so much time for that purpose, he would wait for that day in that month.

Then the wise man did this for him and he had him smoke the drug. The king started seeing even what had been done with him before his birth, when the soul had been in the supernal world. He saw that they were leading his soul through all the worlds. They declared and asked: "Whoever has something to plead against this soul should come forward." But there was no one to plead against it. Just then, someone came running and cried: "Lord of the Universe, hear my prayer! If this soul comes into the world, what will I do? Why did you create me?" The one who cried all that was Samael himself. And they answered him: "This soul must surely descend to the world. And you, Samael, take counsel." Thereupon Samael went away. They led the soul further through many worlds until they brought it to the supernal court to adjure it not to descend to the world. Samael had not yet come so they sent a messenger for him and he came. He brought with him a hunched old man whom Samael had known before. And Samael laughed and said: "I have already taken counsel. This soul is permitted to descend into the world." They let the soul descend into the world and it did.

The king saw what had happened to him from beginning to end, and how he had become a king, and the wars he had fought, etc., and the prisoners he had taken. Among them there was a beautiful girl who had all the graces which existed in the world. This grace was not her own, but the diamond's which she hung on herself. The diamond had all kinds of grace, and because of it, it seemed as though she had all kinds of grace. On that mountain only the rich and the wise could climb, etc. (And he did not tell the rest and there is much more in this.)

VIII. THE RABBI'S SON

Patently the most polemical of these tales, "The Rabbi's Son" portrays the spiritual struggle of a brilliant son of a traditional non-Hasidic rabbi of great learning and family lineage. The son is attracted to the charismatic leadership of the zadik because he feels that something is missing in his spiritual life, which has been devoted to intensive study and ordinary ritual piety. Stories of this sort are legion in Shivhe HaBesht (The Praise of the Baal Shem Tov) which often discusses the resistance of the potential Hasid to the new spiritual leader.

In this Bratslav tale, the struggle takes on cosmic dimensions and ends in tragedy with the son's death. Supernal forces seem to attract the son to the zadik, but they are blocked—as in the previous story—by the will of Samael who realizes that the spiritual union of this young man with this specific zadik will bring the messiah and render Samael irrelevant. Samael, who appears in the guise of a reputable merchant, persuades the father to return home with his son by accusing the zadik of frivolous behavior, an unspecified but standard accusation leveled at zadikim.

Only after the son's death, when the deed cannot be remedied, is it revealed to the rabbi in a dream by the zadik himself that the rabbi's obstinacy and incredulity not only caused the son's death, but prevented the initiation of the messianic age. This obstinacy was the work of Samael.

ONCE there was a rabbi who had no children. Finally, he had an only son. He raised him and married him off. The son used to sit in an attic room and study in the manner of rich men and he always studied and prayed. The son had already performed a commandment by which he reached the aspect of "the small light." And yet he felt that there was some imperfection in himself, but he did not know what it was, so he felt no delight in his study and prayer. He told it to two young men and they advised him to go to a certain *zadik*. And the only son went to tell his father that since he did not feel any delight in his worship (his praying, his study, and other commandments) and felt something missing but did not know what, he wanted to go to the *zadik*. And his father answered him: "Why should you want to go to him? You are a greater scholar than he, and of a better family than he. It is not fitting that you should go to him. Turn away from this road!" Thus he prevented him from going.

The son returned to his study and again he felt that imperfection. Again he took counsel with those men, and they advised him as they had before to go to the *zadik*. And again he went to his father. His father dissuaded him and prevented him as before. And so it happened several times. The son felt he was missing something and he longed very much to fulfill this imperfection but did not know what it was. So he came once more to his father and implored him till his father was forced to go with him, because he did not want to let him go by himself since he was an only son. And his father told him: "I shall go with you, and show you there is nothing real in him." They harnessed the carriage and set out.

His father said to him: "This is how I shall test. If the journey proceeds without mishap, it is from heaven. And if not, it is not from heaven and we shall return." They set out. They came to a small bridge and one horse fell down and the carriage turned over and they almost drowned. The father said: "You see that this journey does not proceed without mishap and is not from heaven." And they returned home.

The son went back to his studies and again he saw his imperfection and did not know why. He came again and implored his father as he had done before and the father was forced to go with him again. When they set out his father established the former test: "If it proceeds without mishap . . . ." And it happened that while they were traveling, the two axles broke. And his father told him: "You see that it does not proceed as if we should go, since, is it natural for two axles to break? They have traveled so many times with this carriage and nothing like that has happened!" And they returned home.

The son returned to his way of life, that is, to his studies, etc., and again felt that imperfection. And the men advised him to travel. The son told his father that they should not establish such a test, since it is natural for a horse to fall sometimes or for axles to break, unless there is something very bizarre.

They set out and came to an inn to spend the night. They found a merchant there, and they started talking to him like merchants, but they did not reveal to him where they were going, because the rabbi was ashamed to say that he was going to the *zadik*. They talked about the affairs of the world, until in the course of the conversation, they reached the subject of *zadikim*, and where *zadikim* were to be found. The merchant told them there was a *zadik* there, and there and there so they started talking about the *zadik* they were traveling to. Then the other answered, in amazement, "But he is frivolous! I am coming from him now, and I was there when he committed a sin." The father answered and said to his son: "Did you see, my son, what this merchant has reported while speaking plainly with no intention to malign? And he is coming from there." And they returned home.

And the son died. And he came to his father, the rabbi, in a dream. When he saw his son standing in great anger, he asked him: "Why are you so angry?" He answered him that he should go to the *zadik* whom they had intended to go to, "and he will tell you why I am angry." The father woke up and said it was just a coincidence. Afterwards he dreamt again as before, and he said this, too, was an idle dream. And this happened a third time. Then he understood that there was something in it and he traveled there.

On the way he met the merchant whom he had met before when he had traveled with his son, and recognizing him said to him: "Aren't you the one whom I saw in that inn?"

He answered him: "Of course you saw me."

The merchant opened his mouth and told him: "I can swallow you if I want to."

He said to him: "What are you talking about?"

And he replied: "Do you remember? When you traveled with your son, first the horse fell on the bridge, and you returned. Then the axles broke. Then you met me and I told you that the *zadik* was frivolous. And now that I have done away with your son you are allowed to go on. For your son was in the aspect of 'the small light,' and that *zadik* is in the aspect of 'the great light,' and if they had united the Messiah would have come. But now that I have done away with him, you are allowed to travel."

In the middle of his words he disappeared, and the rabbi had no one to talk to. The rabbi traveled to the *zadik* and he cried: "What a pity, what a pity! A pity on those who are lost and will never be found! May the Lord, blessed be He, return our exiles shortly, Amen."

(That merchant was Samael himself, who disguised himself as a merchant and led them astray. Afterwards, when he met the rabbi again, he teased him for having heeded his advice, because this is Samael's manner, as is known. May the Lord, blessed be He, save us!)

IX. THE *HAKHAM* AND THE *TAM*

(THE CLEVER MAN AND THE ORDINARY MAN)

The contrast between the hakham (the clever man) who really lives foolishly, and the tam (the ordinary man) who lives simply but happily is one of the staples of world folk literature and Nahman was clearly familiar with many prototypes of this story. The specific flavor of Nahman's tale is conveyed by the detailed characterization of the hakham (rather than that of the tam): He is intellectually gifted, skilled in crafts, ambitious, curious, skeptical, arrogant —and utterly miserable since he is so critical that nothing can possibly please him. His critical faculty, in fact, is the matrix of his personality and the cause of his downfall. The hakham resembles not the rabbinical opponents of the Hasidim (called Mitnaggedim), but the Maskilim, the enlightened Jews who had adopted westernized norms of behavior and thought. (Since the story was written in the spring of 1809, Nahman could have referred to the maskilim of Lemberg whom he encountered during his eight-month sojourn in that Austrian city between the fall of 1807 and the summer of 1808.)

After several preparatory chapters (1-3), the hakham denies the existence of God (which no mitnagged would ever do) and ridicules a Baal Shem (a zadik). His modes of empirical reasoning are so deftly caricatured that the reader begins to realize that one who accepts such modes of reasoning must be an arrant fool.

Supernal forces, as usual, parallel the implications of character and as the hakham declines in fortune, the tam rises to the point where he has the power to save his childhood friend, the hakham (to whom he always remains loyal) from the clutches of Azazel, the devil.

ONCE there were two rich men in one town who had great wealth and great houses. And they had two sons, that is, each had a son. The two children studied in the same schoolroom, but of these two sons, one was very clever (*hakham*) and the other was ordinary (*tam*). (He was not a fool, but he had a plain and common mind.) And the two sons loved each other very much. Even though one was a *hakham* and the other was a *tam* and his mind was common, they loved each other very much.

In time, the two rich men began to lose their wealth. And they declined lower and lower till they lost everything and became paupers. Nothing was left to them but their houses. And the sons began to grow up. The fathers said to the sons: "We cannot afford to support you. Do for yourselves whatever you can."

The *tam* went and learned shoemaking. But the *hakham*, who was clever, did not want to engage in a common trade like this, so he decided to travel throughout the world and look for something to do. And he went about the market, and saw a large carriage with four horses in harness coming in a rush.

He asked the merchants: "Where are you from?"
They answered him: "From Warsaw."
"Where do you go?"
"To Warsaw."
He asked them: "Perhaps you need a helper?"

They saw that he was a clever youngster and alert. Since he pleased them, they took him along. And he traveled with them and served them well on the road.

When he came to Warsaw, since he was sharp-witted he reflected: "Since I am already in Warsaw, why should I tie myself to those men? Perhaps there is a better place than theirs. I shall go and look." He went to the market-place and he began to investigate and ask about the people who had brought him, whether there was a better place than theirs. And they told him that those people were honest and it was good to be with them, yet it was very difficult to be with them, since their commerce extended to very great distances. Meanwhile he observed shop-clerks walking in the market in their elegant way with their hats and pointed shoes, their elegant gait and clothes. He was sharp-witted and clever, and it pleased him very much, since it was a nice thing to work at home, in one place.

He went to the people who had brought him and thanked them and told them that it was not good for him to stay with them. And he went and apprenticed himself to a rich man. And this was the order (of advancement) of the servants. First you must be an apprentice servant and do the heavy work for little pay, and later you reach the stage of head servants. And the rich man gave him heavy work to do and sent him to lords to carry merchandise like servants who carry bolts of cloth on their shoulders. And this work was difficult for him. Sometimes he had to climb to upper stories with the merchandise. And this work was difficult for him.

And he reflected, since he was a sharp-witted philosopher: "Why do I need this work? It is important only for the purpose of taking a wife and making a living. I don't have to consider that yet. I shall have time for this later. Meanwhile, I would travel throughout the land and visit various countries."

He went to the market and saw merchants traveling on top of a large carriage. And he asked them: "Where are you going?"

"To Lagorna."

"Will you take me there?"

"Yes."

They took him there, and from there he set out for Italy, and from there, to Spain. Meanwhile, several years passed and he became more clever, since he had been in many countries. And he decided: "Now we have to consider the practical purpose." So he started thinking with the help of his philosophy what he should do. He was eager to learn goldsmithry, since it is a great and fine craft and involves skill. And it is also a lucrative craft. And since he was sharp-witted and a philosopher, he did not have to spend several years to learn the craft. Within only a quarter of a year he mastered the craft and became a very great craftsman, and was more expert in his craft than the craftsman who had taught him. Later, he reflected: "Even though I have such a craft, I am not content with it. Today, this is important. What if, at some other time, something else will be important?" So he apprenticed himself to a gem-cutter and because of his intelligence he mastered this craft, too, in a short time, in a quarter of a year. Afterwards, he reflected with the help of his philosophy: "Even though I have two crafts, who knows, maybe both will not be important? It is best for me to learn a craft that is important for the world."

And he investigated with the help of his intelligence and philosophy the study of medicine since that is always a necessary and important thing. And for the study of medicine one had to learn first Latin and its writing and to study philosophy. And he, because of his intelligence, learned this, too, in a short time, in a quarter of a year, and became a great doctor and philosopher, and learned in all sciences. Afterwards the world began to seem like nothing in his eyes. Because of his wisdom, because he was such a great craftsman and such a wise man and a doctor, every single person in the world seemed to him like nothing. He decided to be practical and to take a wife, and he reflected: "If I take a wife here, who will know what has become of me? I'll return to my home so that they will see what has become of me, that I went away as such a small boy and have now come to such greatness!"

And he traveled home. And he suffered greatly on the road, since he had no one to talk to because of his wisdom. And he did not find lodgings to his liking and suffered greatly.

2

And now we shall set aside the story of the *hakham* and start telling the story of the *tam*.

The *tam* learned shoemaking, and since he was a *tam* he had much to learn before he could master it, and he did not know his craft completely. And he took a wife and earned his living by his craft. And since he was a *tam* and did not know his craft as well as he should have, his livelihood was meagre and scant. And he did not even have time to eat, because he had to ply his craft constantly, since he did not know his craft fully. While he was working, while piercing with the awl and inserting and drawing the coarse thread, he used to bite a piece of bread and eat.

By disposition he was always happy and full of joy, and he had all the foods and all the drinks and all the clothes he needed. And he would say to his wife: "My wife, give me food." And she would give him a piece of bread and he would eat. Then he would say: "Give me the broth with the kasha." And she would cut another slice of bread for him to eat. And he would praise it and say: "How very nice and good is this broth!" And so he ordered her to give him meat and other such good foods. For each food she would give him a piece of bread, and he enjoyed it very much, and praised the food saying how well done and good it was, as if he really ate this food. And, indeed, eating the bread, he used to feel the taste of each food he wanted, because of his great plainness and joy. And so he would order: "My wife, give me beer to drink!" and she would give him water. And he would praise: "How good this beer is. Give me mead!" and she would give him water, and again he offered the same praise. "Give me wine!" and so on, and she would give him water. And he enjoyed and praised the drink as if he really drank it.

And the same with clothes. He and his wife shared one pelt. And he would say: "My wife, give me the pelt," when he had to wear the pelt to go to the market. And she gave it to him. And when he had to wear a sheepskin coat to go among people, he would say: "My wife, give me the sheepskin coat." And she gave him the pelt. And he enjoyed it and praised it: "How beautiful this sheepskin coat is!" And when he needed the kaftan to go to the synagogue, he would order and say: "My wife, give me the kaftan!" and she gave him the pelt and he praised it and said: "How nice and beautiful this kaftan is!" And so it was when he had to wear the jacket, again she gave him the pelt. And he praised and enjoyed it, too: "How nice and beautiful this jacket is!" And so on, and he was always full of joy and gladness.

When he finished a shoe—and it probably had three ends, because he did not know his craft fully—he used to take the shoe in his hand and praise it and enjoy it very much. And he used to say: "My wife! How beautiful and wonderful this shoe is, how sweet this shoe is, what a sugar and honey shoe this shoe is!" And she used to ask him: "If that is so, why do other shoemakers get three *guldens* for a pair of shoes and you get only one half *thaler*?" (that is, one and a half *gulden*.) He answered her: "What does this matter to me? That is his work and this is mine. Furthermore, why should we talk about others? Let's begin to reckon how much clear profit I make on this little shoe. The leather costs this much, the pitch and the threads, etc., cost this much, and other things like these cost this much, tongues cost this much. And so I make a clear profit of ten *groschen*. Why should I be troubled by a clear profit of this amount?"

And he was only full of joy and gladness at all times. Yet

for the world he was a laughingstock, and they enjoyed his company since they found in him someone to joke about to their heart's content, because he seemed like a madman. And people came and intentionally started talking to him, in order to joke about him. And the *tam* used to say: "Only no joking!" And as soon as they answered him, "No joking!" he listened to them and began talking with them. He did not want to think more deeply about witticism since it was a type of joking and he was a simple man. And when he saw that their intention was joking, he used to say: "So what if you are more clever than I? You will still be fools! Because what am I good for? So even if you are more clever than I, you will still be fools."

These were the habits of the simple man. And now, let us return to our first matter.

3

Meanwhile, there arose a tumult, since the *hakham* was about to arrive in grandeur and great wisdom. And the *tam*, too, rushed to welcome him in great joy, and said to his wife: "Give me the jacket quickly, so I can go to welcome my dear friend. Let me see him!" And she gave him the pelt. And the *hakham* was traveling in carriages in grand style. And the *tam* came to welcome him and greeted him with love and joy: "My beloved brother, how are you? Blessed is the Lord who has brought you, so that I am privileged to see you."

And the *hakham* stared at him. The entire world was nothing to him, all the more so such a man who seemed like a madman. Nevertheless, because of the great childhood love that had been between them, he was friendly to him and traveled with him into the city.

And the two rich men, the fathers of the two sons, had died during the time the *hakham* had been traveling through many countries, and left behind their houses. The *tam*, who had been on the spot, entered his father's house and inherited it. But the *hakham* had been in other countries and there was no one to take over the house. The *hakham*'s house was ruined and destroyed and nothing remained of it, so he did not have a house to enter upon his arrival. He went to an inn and suffered there, because the inn was not to his liking. And the *tam* now found a new task. He ran from his home each time and came to the *hakham* with love and joy. He saw that he was suffering in the inn, and said to the *hakham*: "My brother, come to my house and live with me. I shall gather all my belongings in a bag so that my whole house will be yours to do in it as you please."

And it pleased the *hakham*. And he entered the *tam*'s home and stayed there. Yet the *hakham* always suffered because he assumed that he was immensely wise and a craftsman and a doctor. Once a lord came and ordered him to make him a gold ring. So he made him a wonderful ring, and engraved on it drawings with very wonderful paths. And he engraved on it a marvelous tree. When the lord came back, the ring did not please him at all. And the clever man suffered greatly, because he knew that, had the ring with the tree been in Spain, it would have been very important and marvelous. Once, another great lord came and brought a precious gem which came from distant lands and a second gem with a drawing, and he ordered the *hakham* to draw the same drawing on the gem he had brought (from distant lands). And he drew exactly the same drawing, but made one mistake no other man could understand but himself. And the lord came and received the gem and it pleased him. And the *hakham* suffered greatly from that mistake: "See how great my wisdom is—and now, I have made a mistake."

And he also suffered from his medical practice. At times, he came to a patient and gave him medicine which, he knew clearly, was the only thing that would save his life and cure him because it was a wondrous medicine, yet later the patient died. And the people said he died because of him, and he suffered greatly. And once, when he gave medicine to a patient and he was cured, the people said: "It is only an accident." And he was always full of suffering.

And the same thing happened when he needed a garment. He called the tailor and took pains with him till he taught him to make the garment in the style he liked and knew. And the tailor tried to get it right and made the garment as he wished, but made a mistake with just one lapel, and did not get it right. And the *hakham* grieved very much because he knew for himself that it is considered beautiful here, because they do not understand it. "If I had been in Spain with this lapel, they would have laughed at me and I would have been ridiculous."

And so he was always full of suffering. And the ordinary man ran joyfully and came to the clever man all the time. And he found him in sorrow and full of suffering, and he asked him: "A wise and rich man like you, why are you always suffering? Look, I am joyous."

And he was a laughingstock in the eyes of the clever man, and seemed a madman to him. And the ordinary man said to him: "Ordinary people who laugh at me are fools because if they are more clever than I am they are still fools. How much more so a clever man like you. So what if you are more clever than I?" The ordinary man continued and said to the clever man: "May the Lord bring you up to my level." The clever man answered and said: "It is possible that I should reach your level, that my reason, God forbid, will be taken away from me, or I will be ill and become mad. Since what are you? A madman. But that you shall reach mine? It is completely impossible that you shall become as clever as I am."

The ordinary man answered: "With the Lord, blessed be He, everything is possible. And it is possible that in an instant I should attain your cleverness." And the clever man laughed at him very much.

4

And those two sons were called by everyone, one with the epithet *hakham* (clever man), and the other with the epithet *tam* (ordinary man). Even though there were several *hakhamim* and *tamim* in the world, here this contrast was very distinct, since they had both come from the same place and studied in the same schoolroom, and one had become marvelously wise, and the other immensely simple. And in the record hall, where they inscribe every person with his family name, they wrote one with the epithet *hakham*, and the other with the epithet *tam*.

Once the king came to the record hall and found that the two sons were inscribed there, one with the epithet *hakham*, and the other with the epithet *tam*. And he wondered why those two were called *hakham* and *tam*. And the king desired to see them. And the king reflected: "If I suddenly send for them to come to me, they will be very frightened. The *hakham*'s arguments might be silenced, and the *tam* might go mad with fear." And the king decided to send a *hakham* to the *hakham*, and a *tam* to the *tam*. But how do you find a *tam* in a royal city? In the royal city the people are usually "clever." Now the man in charge of the treasury was a *tam*. They did not want to put a *hakham* in charge of the treasury, lest by his wisdom and cleverness he would be able to squander all the treasury. That is precisely why they put a *tam* in charge of the treasury.

The king called a *hakham* and the *tam* (who was in charge of the treasury) and he sent them to the two sons. He gave a letter to each of them, and he also gave them a letter for the governor in whose district the two sons lived. And in the letter he ordered the governor to send the *hakham* and the *tam* letters in his name, so that they should not be afraid, saying it was not obligatory, for the king did not decree that they come, rather it depended on their own will. If they wanted to, they should come. The king, however, wanted to see them. And the messengers, the *hakham* and the *tam*, traveled to the governor and gave him the letter. And the governor asked about the two sons. And they told him that the *hakham* was marvelously clever and very rich, but the *tam* was very common and has all types of clothing from his pelt. And the governor decided that it was certainly not proper to bring him into the presence of the king wearing a pelt. And he made him well-fitting clothes and put them in the carriage of the *tam* and gave the messengers letters as was required. And the messengers traveled there and gave them the letters: the *hakham*'s to the *hakham*, and the *tam*'s to the *tam*. And the *tam*, immediately upon the arrival of the letter, said to the messenger (who was a *tam*) who brought it: "But I do not know what is written in it. Read it for me."

He answered him: "I shall tell you by heart what is written there. The king wants you to come to him."

He asked immediately: "Without joking?"

He answered him: "Surely, it's true, without joking."

And immediately he was filled with joy and ran and told his wife: "My wife! The king has sent for me." And she asked him: "What is this? Why has he sent for you?" And he had no time at all to answer her, but, immediately he hurried with joy, and set out immediately with the messenger. So he sat in the carriage and found the clothes there and became more and more joyful. Now he has clothes, too!

In the meantime, people informed on the governor, saying that he dealt falsely. The king deposed him and reflected that it would be good that the governor be a *tam*, for a *tam* would govern the country with truth and justice, since a *tam* would not know clever tricks and inventions. And the king sent his decree that the *tam* for whom he had sent would be the governor. And since he had to pass through the district capital, they should stand by the city gates, and upon his arrival, they should detain him and present him with his appointment of governor. And they did so. They stood by the gates and as soon as the *tam* passed by they detained him and told him he had been appointed governor. And he asked and said: "Without joking?" They answered him: "Surely, without joking."

And the *tam* immediately became governor with full authority. And now that his luck had risen, and "luck makes one wiser," he acquired a little understanding. Nevertheless, he did not use his wisdom at all, but acted with his original simplicity, and governed the state with simplicity, truth, and honesty, and no injustice was found in him. For in governing a state, one does not need much intelligence and wisdom, but only honesty and simplicity. When two came before him for trial, he would say: "You are innocent and you are guilty." Such was his simplicity and truth, without any cunning or falsehood. And so he governed everything with truth. And the people of the country loved him very much. And he had faithful advisors who loved him truly.

And because of this love, one of them advised him: "You will surely have to appear before the king, for he has already sent for you, and it is the custom that a governor appear before the king. And so, even though you are very honest and no falsehood will be found in the way you govern the country, you must nevertheless follow the custom of the king. When he converses, his speech digresses toward other matters, to sciences and languages. Thus, it is proper and courteous that you should be able to answer him. Therefore, it would be helpful if I teach you sciences and languages." This pleased the *tam* and he thought: "Why should I object to learning sciences and languages?" And he learned sciences and languages. And it suddenly occurred to him that his friend, the *hakham*, had told him that he would never be able to reach his level. And now, he had already equaled him in learning. (Yet, even though he already knew sciences, he did not use this learning at all, but governed all with his original simplicity.)

Later, the king sent for the governor (the *tam*) to come to him. And he traveled to him. At first, the king talked with the *tam* about the governing of the country. And it pleased the king very much, because he saw that he acted with honesty and truth and without any injustice or falsehood. Afterwards, the king started talking about science and languages. And the *tam* answered him properly. This pleased the king more and more. And he said: "I see that he is such a wise man, and nevertheless, he behaves with such simplicity." He pleased the king very much. The king appointed him minister over all the ministers, and ordered that a special city be his seat. And he ordered them to build him beautiful and magnificent walls, as was proper, and gave him a document of appointment to this ministry. And so they built for him magnificent walls where the king had ordered. And he went and assumed his grandeur with authority.

And the *hakham*, when the letter from the king reached him, answered the *hakham* (clever messenger) who had brought it: "Wait and spend the night here, and we shall talk it over and decide." In the evening he prepared a great banquet for him, and while eating the *hakham* tried to show off his wisdom and philosophy. He stated: "Why should such a king send for an insignificant person like me? And who am I that the king should send for me? What is the meaning? He is a king who has such power and grandeur, and I am so insignificant in comparison with such a great king! Is it plausible that such a king should send for me? If I say for my wisdom, who am I in comparison with the king? Doesn't the king have wise men? And the king himself is probably a great wise man, too. And so, why should the king send for me?"

And he wondered about it very much. After being so amazed, he himself said to the clever messenger: "Do you know what I think? It is conclusive that there is no king in the world at all. And the whole world is misled by this nonsense when they think that there is a king. Can you understand how it is plausible that the whole world would give itself up and rely on one man who is the king? Surely, there is no king in the world at all!"

The clever messenger answered: "But I brought you a letter from the king."

The first *hakham* asked him: "Did you yourself receive this letter from the king's own hand?"

He answered him: "No, but another man gave me the letter in the name of the king."

He stated: "You can now see with your own eyes that my words are true, that there is no king at all." And he asked him again: "Tell me—since you are from the capital city and have been raised there all your life—have you ever seen the king?"

He answered him: "No."

The first *hakham* stated: "Now see for yourself that I am right, that surely there is no king at all. Because even you have never seen the king."

The clever messenger asked again: "If so, who rules the country?"

The first *hakham* answered: "This I can tell you clearly because I am an expert in it. You should ask me, because I have traveled in many countries and I was in Italy. And the custom is that there are seventy councillors (called Ratherren) and they ascend and rule the country for a certain period of time, and following them this authority is shared by all the country's people, one after the other." And his words began to penetrate the clever messenger's ears, till they both agreed that there surely was no king in the world at all.

The first *hakham* said again: "Wait till morning, and I will prove to you that there is no king at all in the world." In the morning the first *hakham* arose early, and woke the clever messenger. And he said to him: "Come outside with me and I will prove to you how the whole world is misled and that there surely is no king at all."

Then went to the market, and saw a soldier. And they

took hold of him and asked him: "Whom do you serve?"

He answered: "The king."

They asked him: "Have you ever seen the king?"

"No!"

He (the *hakham*) stated: "Look, is there such nonsense?" Again they went from the soldier to an officer. And they conducted a conversation with him till they asked him: "Whom do you serve?"

"The king."

"Have you seen the king?"

"No."

He stated: "Now you see with your own eyes that it is clear they are all misled and there is no king at all." The *hakham* said: "Let us travel more throughout the world, and I will show you further how the whole world is grossly mistaken." And they went and traveled throughout the world. And wherever they came they found that the world is mistaken. And the king (their proof that there is no king) became an example for them. And wherever they found the world mistaken, they took the king for an example: "This is true just as it is true that there is a king." And they went and traveled until what they had with them was spent. They began selling one horse, and then the second, till they sold them all, and were forced to travel on foot. And they always studied the world and found that it was mistaken, and they became beggars. And they were no longer respected, because no one paid attention to beggars like them.

And they wandered till they came to the city where the minister (the *tam* who was the *hakham*'s friend) lived. And in the city there was a true *Baal Shem*, and he was very respected because he had done wonderful things. And even among the lords he was famous and respected. And those *hakhamim* came to that city and wandered about until they came in front of that *Baal Shem*'s house, and they saw many wagons, forty or fifty, standing there with patients. And the *hakham* thought that a doctor lived there. And since he, too, was a great doctor, he wanted to enter and make his acquaintance. And he asked: "Who lives here?"

They answered: "A *Baal Shem*."

And he laughed most heartily and said to his friend: "This is a lie and nonsense, a greater nonsense than the error about the king. My friend, let me tell you about this falsehood, how the world is misled by such a lie."

In the meantime they were hungry but only had three or four *groschen*. So they went to a soup kitchen for there one could find something to eat for three or four *groschen*. They ordered food and they were served. While eating, they talked and laughed at the lie and the mistake concerning the *Baal Shem*. And the owner of the soup kitchen heard their talk and was irritated because the *Baal Shem* was well respected there. And he told them: "Eat what is in front of you and get out of here!" Later the *Baal Shem*'s son came there and they continued to laugh at the *Baal Shem* in the presence of his son. And the soup kitchen owner screamed at them for laughing at the *Baal Shem* in the presence of his son, till he beat them badly and pushed them out of his house.

They were very irritated, and wanted to sue the one who beat them. And they decided to go to their landlord where they had left their packages, to take counsel with him how to sue the owner of the soup kitchen. They came and told him that the owner of the soup kitchen had beaten them very badly. And he asked them: "Why?" And they told him that they were talking about the *Baal Shem*. He answered them: "Surely, it is not right to beat people, but you were not correct at all in talking about the *Baal Shem*, because the *Baal Shem* is well respected here."

And they saw that he, too, was misled. And they went from him to the magistrate who was a Gentile. And they told him the story, that they had been beaten. He asked: "Why?" They answered that they were talking about the *Baal Shem*.

And the magistrate beat them ruthlessly and pushed them out of his house. So they went to a higher magistrate who was in charge, but they did not get a trial. And they went from one to another, from a governor to a higher governor, till they came in front of the minister (who was the *tam*). And there, in front of the minister's house, stood sentries, and they announced to the minister that a man needed him. And he ordered him to enter and the *hakham* came before the minister. As soon as he entered the minister recognized that he was his friend the *hakham*, but the *hakham* did not recognize him, as he was in such grandeur. And the minister immediately began to talk to him: "See how my simplicity has brought me to such grandeur. And what has your cleverness brought you to?"

The *hakham* answered and said: "Regarding what you say you are, my friend the *tam*, let us talk about that later. In the meanwhile, grant me a trial because they have beaten me."

He asked him: "Why?"

He answered him: "Because I said the *Baal Shem* is a liar and the whole thing is a swindle."

The simple minister answered: "You still cling to your cleverness? You told me that you could reach my level easily, and that I could not reach yours. See, I have already reached yours, but you have not yet reached mine. And I see it is more difficult for you to reach my simplicity."

Nevertheless, since the *tam* knew him long ago when he was great, he ordered that he be given clothes and that he be dressed. And he asked him to eat with him. While eating they started talking. The *hakham* tried to convince him of his opinion that there was no king at all. The *tam* cried out: "What are you talking about? I myself have seen the king!"

The *hakham* answered him laughing: "You yourself know that he was the king! You know him and his father and grandfather who were kings? How do you know that this was the king? People told you that he was the king and deceived you."

And the *tam* was very angry because the *hakham* denied the existence of the king.

In the meantime someone came and said: "The *Azazel* (the devil) has sent for you." And the *tam* was very very shocked. And he ran and told his wife with great fear that the devil sent for him. His wife advised him to send for the *Baal Shem*, and he sent for him. And the *Baal Shem* came and gave him talismans and amulets, and told him that he should no longer be frightened. And he had great faith in this. And they were still sitting, the *hakham* and the *tam*.

And the *hakham* asked him: "Why were you so frightened?"

He told him: "Because of the devil who had sent for us."

He laughed at him: "Do you believe that there is a devil?"

The *tam* asked him: "Who, then, sent for us?"

The *hakham* answered: "Surely, this is my brother who wanted to see me and sent for me in this disguise."

The *tam* asked him: "If so, how did he pass the guards?"

He answered him: "He probably bribed them, and they are lying when they say they did not see him at all."

In the meantime, someone came again and said that the devil had sent for them. And the *tam* was no longer shocked nor did he have any fear because of the amulets of the *Baal Shem*.

He said to the *hakham*: "What do you say now?"

He said: "Let me inform you that I have a brother who is very angry with me, and did this to frighten me." And he stood and asked the one who had come for them: "What kind of face does the one who sent for us have? And what color is his hair?" He answered him so and so. The *hakham* stated: "You see, this is the way my brother looks."

The *tam* said to him: "Will you go with them?"

He answered: "Yes, but you should give me some soldiers for protection so that they will not harm me." And he gave him the protection. And the two *hakhamim* went with the men who had come for them. The soldiers returned and the *tam* minister asked them: "Where are the two *hakhamim*?" They answered they knew nothing about how they disappeared.

And the devil's messenger had kidnapped the two *hakhamim* and brought them to the mire and clay, and the devil was sitting there on a chair in the mire. And they threw the *hakhamim* into the mire, and the mire was thick and sticky like real glue, and they could not move at all in the mire. And the *hakhamim* shouted to the devil and his men who were tormenting them: "Villains! Why do you torment us? Is there any devil in the world? You, villains, torment us for no reason!" (Because the *hakhamim* did not believe that there was a devil, but said that villains were tormenting them for no reason.) And the two *hakhamim* lay in the thick mire and pondered the matter: "The hooligans with whom we once quarreled must be tormenting us now." And they suffered excruciating torments for several years.

Once the *tam* minister passed in front of the *Baal Shem*'s house, and recalled his friend, the *hakham*. So he entered and bowed to the *Baal Shem* as is proper and asked him if he could show him the *hakham*, and get him out of there. And he said to the *Baal Shem*: "Do you remember the *hakham* whom the devil sent for and carried off? I have not seen him since that day." He answered: "Yes. I remember." And the *tam* asked him to show him his place and to get him out of there. And the *Baal Shem* said to him: "Surely, I can show you his place and get him out. But no one should go but me and you."

And they went together. And the *Baal Shem* did what he knew. They came there and saw them lying in the thick mire and clay. And when the *hakham* saw the *tam* minister he cried out to him: "My brother, see how they beat and torment me, those hooligans, for no reason!"

The minister screamed: "Do you still cling to your wisdom and believe in nothing? And you think that these are human beings! Now look, this is the *Baal Shem* whom you denied. He is the one who can get you out (and he will show you the truth)." And the *tam* minister asked the *Baal Shem* to get them out and show them that this is the devil and not men. And the *Baal Shem* did what he did. And they discovered they were on dry ground and there was no mire there at all. And those demons became just dust. Then the *hakham* saw and was forced, against his will, to admit everything: that there was a king, and a true *Baal Shem*, etc.

X. THE BURGHER AND THE PAUPER

"The Burgher and the Pauper" resembles "The King and the Emperor" in that both are essentially romances with happy endings. In both cases, Bratslav commentators have always regarded the stories as allegories of the redemptive process. In "The King and the Emperor," the emperor's daughter represented the Shekhinah in her successful attempt to rediscover her betrothed lover and return home with him. In "The Burgher and the Pauper" the Shekhinah, represented by the daughter of the pauper who has become the rich, cruel emperor is portrayed as a wondrous child who suffers exile in a series of adventurous episodes. Though she is the most forceful figure in the story, our attention is fixed upon her betrothed—apparently the messiah—and the development of his soul. It is interesting to note that he is hesitant while she is aggressive. The document he has lost in the forest when the tempest toppled the trees seems to represent the Torah, which she helps him find. Since he is her true betrothed, only he can read or sing this document correctly. She, on the other hand, must persist in her encouragement of the one destined to redeem her.

Even in early Bratslav commentaries, the parallel is drawn between the exodus from the Egyptian bondage, which was incomplete, and the future exodus from spiritual and political exile which is supposed to be perfect and final. Veiled comparisons between the two are strewn throughout the story. The burgher, for instance, is supposed to represent Moses, and his son, whose development we observe, is the messiah. While all allegorical explanations raise many questions, an ingenious foray into this area by Adin Steinsalz can be found in the commentary.

ONCE there was a burgher who was an immensely rich man. He had much merchandise and his promissory notes and letters were sent all over the world. He had all good things. Beneath him lived a pauper who was extremely poor, the opposite of the wealthy man in every respect. And both were childless. This one had no children, nor had the other.

Once, the burgher dreamt that people came and made bundles. He asked them: "What are you doing?" They answered that they were carrying everything to the pauper. He was very vexed that they wanted to carry all his wealth from his home to the pauper, but it was impossible to vent his anger upon them, because they were many. They made bundles upon bundles of all he had, of all his merchandise and wealth and property, and carried all of it to the pauper's house, and left nothing in his house but the bare walls. And he was very vexed. And he woke up, and saw that it had been a dream. But even though he saw it had been a dream and, thank God, everything remained with him, he was very perturbed. He was very perturbed because of the dream and he could not let it pass out of his mind.

Even before this he used to take care of the pauper and his wife and give them presents. And now, after the dream, he cared for them even more than before, but whenever the pauper or his wife came to his house, his mien changed and he was alarmed by them because of the dream he would recall. The pauper and his wife used to go in and out of his house

quite frequently. Once, the pauper's wife came to the burgher
and he gave her something, but his mien changed and he was
terrified and very astonished. The poor woman asked him: "I
beg your honour's pardon, but would you tell me why your
mien changes so much whenever we come to you?" He told
her what he had dreamt, and that since that day he was perturbed. She answered him: "On that night I, too, had a dream
that I became very rich, and people came to my house and
made bundles upon bundles. And I asked them: 'Where are
you carrying them?' 'To that pauper.' (That is, to the burgher
who was now called a pauper.) So, why do you care about a
dream? I had a dream, too." And he was now terrified and
astonished even more, because he had heard her dream. For it
seemed that they would carry his riches and property to the
pauper and the poverty of the pauper to him. And he was
very terrified.

2

One day, the burgher's wife went on a journey by carriage. She took her friends with her, and she also took along
the pauper's wife. As they drove along a general suddenly
passed with his troops. The women moved aside to clear the
road and the troops passed by. The general saw that the
travelers were women and ordered his men to capture one of
those women who were going on the journey. They went and
took the pauper's wife and kidnapped her in the general's
carriage and rode off. And surely, it was impossible to bring
her back, because he traveled far away. Especially a general
with his troops! And he took her and traveled with her to his
country. But she was a very God-fearing woman and did not
want to obey him at all, and she cried very much. They
begged and enticed her, but she was very God-fearing.

When the women returned home from their journey, the
poor woman was missing. And the pauper cried bitterly and
desperately about his wife. Once, the burgher passed by the

pauper's home and heard him crying bitterly and desperately. He entered and asked: "Why do you cry so mightily?" He answered: "Shouldn't I cry? What is left me? There are those who are left with riches or with sons. I have nothing. My wife, too, has been taken away from me. So what is left me?" The burgher's heart was touched by the pauper and he pitied him very much, because of the great despair he saw in him.

He did a rash thing. Really, it was madness! He inquired in what country the general lived and traveled there. He did a very rash thing and went to the general's house. Guards were standing there, but because of his great confusion, he was distraught, and paid no attention to the guards. The guards, too, were confused and very astonished, since they saw a man running toward them in great confusion. They were perplexed: "How did he get here?" Because of this confusion all the guards let him pass, until he entered the general's house, where she was lying. He came and woke her up and told her: "Come." She saw him and was terrified. But he told her: "Come with me immediately." So she went with him, and they passed all the guards again till they were out.

Then all of a sudden he looked about and realized what he had done. He understood that there surely would be a great tumult at the general's. And there was. He went and concealed himself and her in a cistern which was full of rain water until the tumult should pass. And he stayed with her two days in the cistern. The woman saw the great devotion he had for her, and the troubles he suffered for her. So she swore by God that all the good fortune she would have (since it was possible she should have some good fortune, some greatness and success), all the success that would be hers would not be denied him. And if he wanted to take all her greatness and success for himself, leaving her as she was, it would not be denied him at all. But how does one find a witness there? She took that cistern for a witness. After two days he left with her and went on.

He went with her further and further. And he understood that in that place, too, they were looking for him. He went further and concealed himself with her in a *mikveh*. Again she noted his great devotion and the trouble he suffered for her, and swore as before, and took the *mikveh* for a witness. After they were there, too, approximately two days, they left and journeyed further. And so it happened several times that he concealed himself with her in other such places, that is, in seven places where there was water, and they were: a cistern, and the *mikveh*, and lakes, and a spring, and streams, and rivers, and seas. And in each place where they concealed themselves she recalled his devotion and his trouble for her, and swore to him and took the place for a witness. They went and concealed themselves every time in those hiding places till they came to the sea. When they came to the sea (he was a great merchant and he knew all the sea lanes) he arranged to get to his country. He completed the trip and reached his home with the pauper's wife, and returned her to the pauper. And there was great rejoicing.

3

And the burgher, as a reward for doing such a thing and for having resisted temptation with her, was remembered, and a son was born to him in the same year. And she, the pauper's wife, too, as a reward for having resisted temptation with the general, and with the burgher as well, was also rewarded and gave birth to a daughter. And she was a very beautiful person. She was beyond the beauty of the human species, since among human beings no such beauty exists. And people would say: "Would that she grew up!" (Because it is difficult for such an extraordinary marvel to grow up.) Her beauty was so extraordinarily great that such a thing had never been seen in the world at all. People came to see her and were very astonished at the greatness of her extraordinary beauty, and they gave her presents upon presents out of their love. And they gave her presents until the pauper became rich. And it occurred to the burgher that he should arrange a match with this pauper because of the daughter's great beauty that was such a marvel. And he said to himself: "Perhaps this is the explanation of the dream's vision that they were carrying my possessions to the pauper and from the pauper they were carrying his possessions to me? That is, we should arrange a match and join the families together."

Once the pauper's wife came to him, and he told her he wanted to arrange a match with her since it was possible that in this way the dream would be realized. She answered him: "I, too, have considered this, but I did not have the courage to speak about arranging a match with you. But if you want it, I am surely ready and will not deny you, because I swore that all my property and success would not be denied you."

And the son and daughter studied languages, etc., in one schoolroom, as was their practice. People came to see the daughter because she was a great marvel, and gave presents until the pauper became rich. Lords came to see her and she pleased them very much. Her beauty was a great marvel among them, because it was no human beauty at all. And because of her extraordinary beauty it occurred to the lords that they should arrange a match with that pauper.

A certain lord who had a son wanted to arrange a match with her, but it was not becoming for nobles to arrange a match with such a person as the pauper, so they had to try to elevate him. They arranged to have the pauper serve the emperor, and he became at first an ensign, and later rose higher and higher. Since they tried to elevate him quickly, he climbed quickly from rank to rank until he became a general. And the lords wanted to arrange a match with him. But there were many eager candidates, because several lords were engaged in elevating him for this purpose. And also it was impossible for the pauper to arrange a match because of the burgher, for they had already agreed to arrange a match with him. The pauper who became a general was more and more successful, and the emperor sent him to war and he succeeded very well. When the emperor died, all the citizens of the state took counsel to make the former pauper emperor. All the lords gathered and agreed that he would be the emperor. The pauper became emperor and fought wars and was very successful. He conquered countries and he fought and succeeded and conquered more and more until the other countries took counsel to yield voluntarily to him, because they saw his great success, that all the world's beauty and all the world's fortune were his. Thus, all the kings gathered and agreed that he should be emperor over the whole world. And they presented him a document with golden letters.

4

And the emperor now refused to arrange a match with the burgher, because it was not becoming for an emperor to arrange a match with a burgher. But his wife, the empress, did not forsake the burgher at all. And the emperor saw that he could not enter into another marriage agreement because of the burgher, especially since his wife strongly supported the burgher. Thus he plotted against the burgher and at first considered impoverishing him. He tried stratagems so that it would seem as if he was not the one to cause his loss. The emperor could surely do it and he made him lose all his money till he was destitute and became a complete pauper. But the empress continued to support him. Later, the emperor saw that as long as the burgher's son existed, it was impossible for him to enter into another marriage agreement. So he tried to kill the burgher's son. And he plotted to eliminate him, and had him sentenced to be put into a sack and thrown into the sea. The empress's heart ached very much because of it, but even an empress can do nothing against the emperor.

What did she do? She went to those who were in charge

of throwing him into the sea. She came to them and fell at their feet and implored them very much that they should let him live for her sake. Why should he be condemned to death? And she begged them very much to take another prisoner who had been sentenced to death and throw him into the sea, and let the young man live. And her pleas persuaded them. So they swore to her that they would let him live. And they did so. They took another man and threw him into the sea, and they released the young man, telling him: "Go away! Go away!" And he went away since he was already a sensible person.

Before he fled, the empress called her daughter and told her: "My daughter, know that the burgher's son is your bridegroom!" And she told her all that had happened to her: "The burgher risked his life for me, and he was with me in those seven places, and I swore to him by God that all my property would not be denied him, and I took those seven places for witnesses, and they were the cistern, the *mikveh*, etc. And now, you who are my entire property and good fortune, you are surely his, and his son is your bridegroom. Your father, because of his haughtiness, wants to kill him for no reason. I have already endeavoured to save him and have influenced them to let him live. Thus, you should know that the burgher's son is your bridegroom, and do not accept anyone else at all."

She accepted her mother's words because she, too, was God-fearing. And she answered that she would surely fulfill them. The daughter went and sent a document to the burgher's son in prison, saying that she considered herself his and that he was her bridegroom. She sent him something like a piece of a map. And she drew on it all the places where her mother hid with his father, that were the seven witnesses: a cistern and a *mikveh* which she drew as a cistern and a *mikveh*, etc. She warned him very very much to guard this document very very closely. And she signed her name below.

Afterwards events happened as was told above. The authorities took another man, but let the son go. He walked on and on until he came to the sea, and embarked on a ship and crossed the sea. And a great tempest came and carried the ship to a shore where there was a desert, and from the force of the storm the ship was smashed. But the people in it were saved and disembarked on the land. There was a desert there and each person went by himself to look for food to sustain his soul, because ships were not accustomed to landing at that place, as it was a desert, and thus they did not expect any ship to arrive to take them to their destination. They walked in the desert to look for food and dispersed here and there. The young man walked in the desert on and on until he was far from the shore, and he wanted to return, but could not do so. The more he wanted to return, the further he walked, until he saw that he could not go back. And he walked on in the desert. He had a bow in his hand with which he saved himself from the fierce beasts of the desert. And he found there a few things to eat. He walked and walked till he walked out of the desert. He came to a place which was formerly settled but now unoccupied. There were fruit trees and water all over so he ate from the fruit and drank from the water. He decided to settle there for the rest of his days, because it was difficult for him to return to a settled place. And who knows if he could reach such a place even if he would leave this one? So he intended to settle and live out his life there, for it was good that he had fruit to eat and water to drink. Sometimes he would go and shoot a hare or a deer with his bow and he had meat to eat. He also would catch fish for himself, because there were very good fish in the water. And he thought it good to live out his days there.

5

The emperor thought that he could now marry his daughter to a king since the sentence of the burgher's son had

174

been carried out and he was rid of him. And they began to talk about her marrying this king and that king, etc. And he built her a court as was proper and she resided there. She took the daughters of the lords to be her friends, and she resided there. She played musical instruments, etc., as they used to do. Whenever they talked to her about marriage engagements she would answer that she did not want to discuss the engagement unless the prospective bridegroom himself should come. And she was a great expert in the art of poetry. She skillfully made a place where the prospective groom would come and stand in front of her and recite love poetry, the way a lover speaks words of affection to his beloved. Kings came to win her into marriage and climbed to that place and each recited his own poem. To some of them she sent her reply through her friends in poetry and affection, and to the few whom she preferred she answered herself and raised her voice in song and answered each one with words of affection. To the few whom she preferred even more she showed herself face to face and answered each one with words of poetry and affection. And to all of them she finished by saying:

"The waters have not passed over you!"

But there was no one who understood what she meant, and when she showed her face they used to fall over because of her great beauty. Some remained faint, and some went mad from love sickness, because of her extraordinarily great beauty. Nevertheless, even though they went mad and remained faint, kings came to win her in marriage. And she answered all of them as was told.

The burgher's son resided in that site, and made a place to live in for himself. He, too, could play musical instruments and knew the art of poetry. He chose trees that were fit for the making of musical instruments, and he made himself a musical instrument. From the sinews of animals he made strings, and he played and sang for himself. He would take the document he had, which the emperor's daughter had sent him, and he sang and played, and recalled all the events that had happened to him, how his father had been a burgher, etc., and how he was here. He went and took the document and made a sign on one tree. He made a place in it and concealed the document there. And he lived there for some time. Once there was a great tempest which broke all the trees that stood there, and he could not recognize the tree where he had concealed the document. As long as they stood he had a sign to recognize it, but now that they had fallen, the tree was confused with the other trees which were numerous, and he could not recognize the tree. And it was impossible to split all the trees to look for the document, because they were very numerous. And he cried and grieved over it very much.

The burgher's son saw that if he stayed there he would surely go mad because of his great sorrow, so he decided that he had to go away, no matter what would happen to him. Otherwise he was in great danger because of his great sorrow. So he took meat and fruit and his satchel and went on his way. And he made himself signs at the place which he left. He walked till he came to a settled place, and he asked: "What country is this?" They answered him. And he asked: "Have you heard about the emperor?" They answered him: "Yes." And he asked: "Have you heard here about his beautiful daughter?" They answered him: "Yes, but it is impossible to marry her." And he came to a decision, that since he could not go there, he would go to the king of this country and tell him all he had concealed in his heart, that he was her bridegroom, and for his sake she did not want to marry any other man. Since he could not go there, he would give him all the signs he had, that is, the seven water places. And now the king should go there and marry her, and should give the burgher's son money in return. The king recognized that his words were truthful, because it was impossible to invent them. It pleased him, but he thought: "If I brought her here, and the young man were here—this would not do!" It was hard for him to kill him for why should he kill him for the favor he had done him? So he decided to send him two hundred miles away.

The burgher's son was very angry because the king sent him away for the favor he had done him. He went to another king and told him, too, and gave him all the signs, and to the second he added one more sign, and urged him to make haste and travel immediately. Perhaps he could precede his colleague. And even if he did not precede him, he had one sign more than his colleague. The second king, too, decided as did the first, and sent the son two hundred miles away. And again, he was very angry, and went to a third king. And he gave the third king even more distinct signs.

So the first king immediately went and traveled, and came to the emperor's daughter's place. He composed a poem, and embedded in it according to prosody all those places, that is, all those seven witnesses. But it turned out that he did not put those places in the right order in the poem because of the prosody. And he went to the recitation place and recited the poem. When the emperor's daughter heard those places she thought it a marvel, and it seemed to her that he had to be her childhood friend. But she found it difficult that he did not put them in the right order. Nevertheless she thought: "Perhaps he put them in that order because of the prosody?" She felt firmly that he was the one, and she wrote him that she was engaged to him. And there was great happiness and tumult because her friend was found, and they prepared him for the wedding.

In the meantime the second king came, and he, too, rushed over there. They told him that she was already engaged, but he did not pay any attention to it and said that he nevertheless had something to tell her that would surely be effective. He came and recited his poem and put all the places in the right order, and he gave one more sign. And she asked him: "How did the first king know?" But since it would not help his suit to tell the truth, he said he did not know. She found it an extraordinary marvel and was left confused, because the first one, too, had told about those places, and where would anyone learn about those signs? Nevertheless, it seemed to her that he was her friend, since she saw that he recited in order, etc. And as for the first, it was possible that on account of the prosody it turned out that he mentioned those places. So she remained undecided.

And when the second king sent the young man away, he was again very angry and went to a third king and told him, too, and gave him even more distinct signs. To the third king he told all that was in his heart, and that he had a document where those places were drawn. So he, too, should draw those places on a piece of paper and bring it to her. And the third king, too, thought it would not do to bring her here if that young man were around and he, too, sent the young man over two hundred miles away. So the third king rushed there, too, to take the beautiful maiden. When he came there they told him that those two were already there. And he answered: "Nevertheless," since he had something that would surely be effective. (The people did not know at all why she preferred these three to the others.) The third king came, too, and recited his poem with more distinct signs, and showed a document with the drawing of the places. And she was very alarmed, but could do nothing, since the first king, too, seemed to be the one, and after him the second. Thus she said that she would not believe anyone until they brought her her own handwriting.

Later, the young man thought to himself: "How long will they send me further away each time?" So he decided that he himself would set out to go there, and perhaps he would be successful. So he walked till he came there. He said he had something, etc., and came and recited his poem, and gave more and more distinct signs. He reminded her that he had studied with her in one schoolroom and so on, and he told her he had sent all those kings, and had concealed the document in a tree, and what had happened to it. But she did not pay any attention to this, for surely, those first kings gave some reasons for not having had the document, and it was surely impossible to recognize him, because a long time had elapsed. And she did not want to pay any attention to signs until they brought her the document, because she had thought the first king was the one, and the second, etc. So she did not want to accept any signs. And the young man concluded that it was dangerous to tarry there (since the emperor might kill him), so he decided to return to his place, to the desert where he had been, and there he would live out his days. And he walked and walked to reach that desert and he finally arrived there.

While all this took place many years passed. And the young man remained firm in his intention to reside in the desert and live out his days there. According to his estimation of the life of man in this world, it seemed clear that it was best to live out one's life in the desert. So he stayed there and ate fruit, etc.

6

And on the sea there was a murderer. That murderer heard that there was such a beauty in the world and intended to abduct her, even though he did not need her since he was a eunuch. He desired to abduct her in order to sell her to some king for a great fortune. And he began to make efforts to this end. The murderer was a reckless person and decided to take the risk: "If it works, it works. And if it does not, then it does not. What can I lose?" He was reckless like all murderers. And the murderer proceeded to buy much merchandise of immense variety. He also made golden birds with such art that they seemed to be alive. They seemed to be as natural as live birds. He also made golden cornstalks. And the birds stood upon the cornstalks. It was marvelous that the birds could stand on the cornstalks and the cornstalks would not break since the birds were large. He employed artful devices so that the birds seemed to be playing: One clicked with its tongue, one chirped, and one sang. And everything was done with artful devices since men stood in a room on the ship behind the birds performing everything by pulling strings. It seemed as if the birds themselves were playing because they were made so artfully with strings.

And with all this merchandise the murderer traveled to the country where the emperor's daughter resided. He came to the city where she lived and positioned his ship on the sea and dropped anchor. He disguised himself as a great merchant and people came aboard to buy his precious merchandise. He stayed there for some time, a quarter of a year and more while people carried from him the beautiful merchandise which they had bought from him. The emperor's daughter, too, was eager to buy merchandise from him, so she sent word to him to bring the merchandise to her. But he replied that he didn't have to bring merchandise to the purchaser's house—even though she was the emperor's daughter—and that whoever needed merchandise should come to him.

And since no one could force the merchant to send his merchandise, the emperor's daughter decided she would go to him. Ordinarily, when she walked in the market-place, she put a veil on her face so that people would not look at her, because they could collapse and faint because of her beauty. So the emperor's daughter covered her face and took her friends with her and a guard walked behind her. She came to the murderer who had disguised himself as a merchant and bought merchandise from him and went away. The merchant told her: "If you come again I will show you more beautiful things that are truly wonderful." And she returned home. Once again she came and bought and went away. The murderer stayed there for some time and the emperor's daughter became used to him, and went in and out.

Once she came to him and he opened for her the room where the golden birds stood, and she saw that it was an extraordinary marvel. And the others (that is, the guard, etc.) wanted to enter, too. But the merchant said: "No, no! I will not show it to anyone but you who are the emperor's daughter. I do not want to show it to the others at all." And she entered by herself. He, too, went into the room and locked the door, and acted coarsely, and took a sack and forced her into it. He took off her clothes, and put them on a sailor, and covered his face, and pushed him out and said: "Go!" (And the sailor did not know what was happening to him.) And as soon as he walked out, with his face covered (the guard did not recognize him), they started walking with him. It seemed to them that he was the emperor's daughter. And the sailor went with the guard who escorted him and did not know at all where he was, until he came to the chamber where the emperor's daughter used to sit. And they uncovered his face and saw that he was a sailor. And there was an extraordinary uproar. And they slapped the sailor's face hard and pushed him away, because he was not to blame, as he did not know a thing.

The murderer took the emperor's daughter, and since he knew they would surely pursue him, he left the ship and concealed himself with her in a cistern where there was rain water, till the uproar passed. And he sent orders to the sailors to cut the anchors off at once and escape immediately, since they would surely pursue them. They certainly would not shoot upon the ship because of the emperor's daughter who they thought was in it. "They will only pursue you, and so you should flee immediately. And if they catch up with you, what of it?" He spoke like murderers who are reckless. And so it was. There was an extraordinary uproar and they immediately pursued them, but did not find her there.

The murderer concealed himself with her in a cistern of rain water and they stayed there, and he terrified her so that she wouldn't shout, so that people would not hear. He told her: "I have risked my life to catch you, and if I lose you, my life is not worth anything to me. Since you are now in my hands, if I lose you again, and they claim you from me, my life will be worthless. So if you let out one shout, I shall strangle you at once, no matter what will happen to me. Because I do not consider myself of any worth." And the emperor's daughter was afraid to shout because of her fear of the murderer. Later, he left with her and walked with her in the city and they walked and walked till they came to another place, and he understood that they were searching there too. And he concealed himself with her in all the seven places where the burgher had concealed himself with her mother (these are the seven witnesses, seven kinds of water places that are a cistern, a *mikveh*, a spring, etc.), till they came to the sea.

And he searched there hoping to find even a small fishing boat to cross the sea with her, and he found a ship. He took the emperor's daughter, though he did not need her because he was a eunuch, but he wanted to sell her to some king. And since he was afraid that she would be taken away from him, he made her wear sailor's clothes so she would look like a man. As he crossed the sea with her, a tempest came and carried the ship to the shore and smashed it. And they came to the desert shore where the young man was. When they came there, the brigand, who was an expert in roads, knew that this was a deserted place and that ships did not arrive there. Thus, he was not afraid of anyone here, and released her. The murderer and the emperor's daughter went, one here and one there to seek food, and she went away from the brigand. And the brigand walked his way and presently saw that she was not with him. He started calling for her, but she decided she would not answer him, for she said: "Since he will eventually sell me, why should I answer him? And if he returns, I shall answer him that I had not heard him, especially since he does not want to kill me, because he wants to sell me." So she did not answer him and walked on. The brigand looked for her here and there and did not find her, and walked on and did not find her. And wild animals probably ate him.

She walked on and on and found some food for herself. And she walked till she reached the place where the young man lived. Her hair had already grown and she was dressed like a man in sailor's clothes, as was told. Thus they did not recognize each other. And immediately, upon her arrival, he was overjoyed that another human being had come. And he asked him: "Where did you come from?" She answered: "I was with some merchant on the sea, etc." And she asked him: "Where did you come from?" He answered her: "With some merchant, too, etc." And they both dwelled there.

7

And after the emperor's daughter had been abducted from the emperor, the empress lamented and beat her head against the wall over the loss of her daughter, and chided the emperor saying that by his haughtiness he had first lost the young man and had now lost their daughter. She said: "She was all our fortune and success and we have lost her! And what more do I have today?" Thus she chided him severely. And surely, he was also very bitter that his daughter had been lost. The empress chided and angered him more, so that there were intense quarrels between them. She said harsh things to him until she infuriated him and he decided to exile her. He appointed judges and they decided to exile her. And they exiled her.

Later the emperor sent [troops] to war and did not succeed. He blamed some general for this: "Since you did so, we lost the war." And he exiled him. Later he sent more [troops] to war and did not succeed. He exiled another general, and so he exiled several generals. The people of the country saw that he did strange things: "First he exiled the empress, then—the generals!" And they thought: "Perhaps [we should do] the opposite? We will send for the empress and exile him, and the empress will rule the country!" They did so and exiled the emperor and brought the empress back, and she ruled the country. And the empress sent immediately to bring back the burgher and his wife and took them into her palace.

And when the emperor was exiled, he asked his guards to let him go: "Even though [I am your prisoner], I was once your emperor and probably did you favors, so please, pity me now and let me go. For I will surely not return to this country so you do not have to fear, and I shall at least be free for the days I still have to live." And they let him go. And he walked and walked.

In the meanwhile several years passed, and the emperor walked and walked till he came to the sea. And the wind carried his ship, too, to that desert, until he came to the place where those two lived, the burgher's son and the emperor's beautiful daughter who was dressed in male clothes. They did not recognize each other, since a few years had passed and the emperor's hair had already grown and their hair, too, had already grown. They asked him: "Where did you come from?" He answered them: "With a merchant, etc." And they answered him likewise. And they all stayed there together. They ate and drank and they played musical instruments, as all of them knew how to play, because they had been of noble circles. The young man was the resourceful one among them, since he had been there longer. He brought them meat and they ate. They burnt wood that was more precious there than gold in a settled place.

And the young man would argue with them that it was good to live out their lives there. In comparison with the possessions that people had in the settled world, it was good for them to stay and live out the days of their lives there. They asked him: "What possessions did you have that you say it is better for you here?" He answered and told them all he had gone through, that he was the burgher's son, etc., until he came here. And even though when he was the burgher's son he had all good things, here, too, he had all good things. And he argued with them that it was good to live out their days here.

The emperor asked him: "Have you heard about the emperor?" He answered that he had heard. He asked him if he had heard about the beautiful one. Again he answered him: "Yes." And the young man began to speak angrily: "That murderer!" (referring to the emperor they were talking about, since he did not know that the one he was talking to was the emperor himself. And the young man spoke angrily, as if he was gnashing his teeth over him). And the emperor who was disguised as another man asked the young man: "Why is he a murderer?" He answered him: "Because of his cruelty and haughtiness I have come here." He asked him: "How?" And the young man decided that he had no one to fear here, and told him all the events that had happened to him. At the beginning he apparently had not told him the main thing but only that he was the burgher's son. The emperor asked him: "Were that emperor in your hands, would you take revenge of him now?" He answered him: "No! (For he was compassionate.) On the contrary, I would support him the way I support you."

Again the emperor began to sigh and moan: "How bad and bitter that emperor's old age is!" Since he knew that the beautiful one had been lost and he had been exiled. And the young man added: "Because of his cruelty and haughtiness he has wasted himself and his daughter and I was sent here. All is his fault!" The emperor asked the young man again: "Were he in your hands, would you take revenge?" He answered him: "No, on the contrary, I would support him the way I support you." And the emperor made it known that he himself was the emperor, and what had happened to him, etc. And the young man fell on him, and embraced and kissed him. And she (that is, the beautiful one who was there but was disguised as a male) heard all that they said to each other.

8

And the young man's routine was to go every day, and make signs on three trees and look for the document there. Since there were thousands upon thousands of trees he made signs on the trees he inspected so that on the morrow he would not have to examine those three trees. He labored so much that he might find that document! And when he returned from there he came with tearful eyes, since he cried that he had sought and did not find it. They asked him: "What are you looking for in those trees that you return later with your eyes full of tears?" He answered and told them the whole story, that the emperor's daughter had sent him a document, and he had concealed it in those trees, and a tempest had come, and now he was looking for it. They told him: "Tomorrow, when you look for it, we shall go with you, perhaps we shall find that document." And so it was. They, too, went with him and the emperor's daughter found the document in a tree. She opened it and found her own handwriting. She thought to herself: "If I tell him at once that I am she, when I return and take off these clothes and become as beautiful as before, he might collapse and perish." And she wanted (their marriage) to be proper and legal. (She could not marry him in the desert for she needed a proper wedding.) So she returned the document to him and told him that she had found it. (But she had not yet told him who she was.) And he fainted at once. They revived him and made him well. And there was great rejoicing among them.

Afterwards, the young man said: "What good is this document? Where shall I find her? Since she must now be with some king, what good is this? (He believed she had been sold by the murderer.) I shall spend the rest of my days here." He gave the document back to her and told her: "Take the document and you go marry her." (The emperor's daughter was disguised as a male.) And as she set out to make the journey, she asked him to go with her saying: "I will surely win her and if things go well for me, I will give you half of my property." The young man saw that he (the emperor's daughter) was a wise man and would certainly win her, and so he agreed to go with him. But the emperor remained alone since he was afraid to return to his country. So he (the emperor's daughter) asked him to come along for he would certainly win the beautiful one and the emperor would have nothing to fear since his luck would return.

So the three went together. They hired a ship and came to the country where the empress still lived, and came to the city where she resided. And they anchored the ship. The emperor's daughter thought to herself: "If I inform my mother at once that I have come she might die." So she sent to her [saying] that there was a man who had some information about her daughter. Afterwards she, herself, went and told the empress everything that had happened to her daughter and told her the whole story. At the end she said to her: "And she, too, is here." Afterwards she told her the truth: "I am she!" And she informed her that her bridegroom, the burgher's son, too, was there. She told her that she would not wish it to be otherwise, but that they would return her father, the emperor, to his place. Her mother was not at all pleased with this, since she was very angry because he was to blame for all this. Nevertheless, she had to comply with her daughter's will. They wanted to bring him back, and sought him, but the emperor could not be found at all! And her daughter told the empress that he was here. And the wedding took place and the happiness was complete. And the young couple took over both the kingdom and the empire and they ruled over the entire world. Amen and Amen.

XI. THE KING'S SON AND THE MAIDSERVANT'S SON WHO WERE SWITCHED

In 1809, Nahman composed three stories involving contrasting personalities: "The Hakham *and the* Tam*," "The Burgher and the Pauper," and "The King's Son and the Maidservant's Son Who Were Switched." Each story, however, has its own literary mode and theme. "The* Hakham *and the* Tam*" utilized realistic situations and was an attack on Maskilim; "The Burgher and the Pauper" was a romance which embodied a study of the growth of the messianic personality. "The King's Son and the Maidservant's Son Who Were Switched" commences as a common folktale about two children who were switched in infancy by a malicious nurse, but rapidly develops into a study of psychological types with lengthy, meaningful digressions into the realm of the fantastic.*

The restoration of the king's true son to his status in society comes as no surprise. What interests Nahman is the state of the true son's soul. At first dejected by his unwarranted exile from his rightful home and patrimony, the son sinks into a life of dissolution. Once he realizes how low he has sunk, he takes hold of himself, at times unwittingly, and despite frightening experiences in the forest becomes the master of the maidservant's son who had become the pretender to the throne. In two trials of courage and ingenuity, the true son both exorcises a bewitched garden and repairs a disjointed throne-room, thus regaining his sense of self by proving to himself that he is the rightful heir. The trials of the son and his feats of exorcism and repair have naturally led Bratslav exegetes to explain this story as an allegory of the process of tikkun

ONCE there was a king in whose house there was a maid-servant who served the queen. (Probably no cook was allowed to attend the king, so this maid performed some other minor service.) And the time came for the queen to give birth. And the maidservant, too, had to give birth at the same time. And the midwife switched the infants, to see what would develop from it and what would happen. She switched the infants and placed the king's son next to the maidservant, and the maidservant's son next to the queen. Afterwards, the two sons began to grow up. And "the king's son" (the one who was reared by the king, because they thought he was the king's son) was elevated from rank to rank until he became an important person. And "the maidservant's son" (the king's real son, who was raised by the maidservant) was brought up in the maid's home. And both of them studied together in one schoolroom. And the king's real son, who was called "the maidservant's son," was attracted by nature to the manners of royalty, even though he was brought up in a servant's house. And, conversely, the maidservant's son, who was called "the king's son," was attracted by nature to other manners, not the manners of royalty, even though he was raised in the king's house and had to behave according to the royal manners by which he was brought up.

And the midwife (since "women are frivolous") told someone the secret of how she exchanged the sons. And that person told a friend, and the secret was revealed by one person to the next in the way of the world, until everyone was gossiping about the way the king's son was switched. But they were not allowed to speak out lest it be revealed to the king. Certainly they were not allowed to let the king know about it, since what could the king do? He could not rectify the situation. He could not believe it because it might be a lie. And how could another switch be made? Thus, surely, they were forbidden to reveal it to the king. The people, nonetheless, gossiped about it among themselves.

One day, someone revealed the secret to "the king's son," that people said that he had been switched. "But," (said the informer) "it is impossible for you to investigate it, because it is beneath your dignity. And how does one investigate such a thing? I have informed you about this, because there may be a plot against the throne, and this plot may be strengthened by their saying that they are taking the king's son for their king, that is, the one they speak about as the king's real son. So you have to contrive against this son." (All these are the words of the man who revealed the secret to the maidservant's son who was called "the king's son").

And "the king's son" (the one who was called "the king's son") began to plot mischief against the other son's father, who really was his own father, and always endeavored to cause him evil. And he always inflicted harm upon him, again and again, so that he would be forced to move away with his son. And as long as the king was alive he did not have much influence. Nevertheless "the king's son" plotted mischief against the other son's father. But later, the king grew old and died. And the maidservant's son, who had been switched and was now called "the king's son," took over the throne. And then he plotted more harm against the other son's father. And he did it with cunning, so that the world would not understand that he was inflicting harm, as it was not proper [to behave that way] in public. But he only concealed it and always inflicted harm upon him.

And the other son's father understood that "the king's son" was inflicting harm upon him because of the aforesaid matter, and told his son (the king's true son, who, because of the switch, seemed to be his son) everything. And he told him that he had great concern for him: "Why should you wonder? If you are my son, I surely should have concern for you. And if you are the true king's son, my concern for you is even greater, because he wants to eradicate you completely, God forbid. Thus, you have to move away from here." And it troubled the king's real son greatly. But the king (the one who had become king after his father since, as a result of the switch, he seemed to be the king's son) shot his evil arrows at the king's real son time after time. And the latter decided to move away from there. And his father gave him much money, and he went away. And the son, who was the king's true son, was deeply chagrined for having been exiled from his country for no reason. He pondered: "Why do I deserve to be exiled? If I am the king's son, certainly I do not deserve all this! And if I am not the king's son, I also do not deserve to be a fugitive for no reason. For what is my sin?" And he was deeply chagrined, and because of that he took to drinking. And he went to a brothel. And in this way he wanted to spend his days, getting drunk and behaving wantonly, because he had been exiled for no reason.

And the (false) king took over the throne firmly. And when he heard that people were gossiping and talking about the switch, he would punish them severely and take his revenge. And he ruled mightily and forcefully.

Once day the king traveled with his lords to hunt animals and they reached a beautiful site, and there was a stream full of water in front of it. And they stopped there to rest and to walk about. And the king lay down, and he thought about the deed that he had done, exiling the other son for no reason. For it's either/or! If the exiled son is the king's son, is it not enough that he was switched? Why should he also be exiled? And if he is not the king's son, then, in this case, too, he does not deserve to be exiled, since how has he sinned? And the king thought about it and regretted the sin and the great injustice he had done, and he did not know what to do about it. And it was impossible to talk with any man about the matter and consult with him, and he was anxious and worried. And he told the lords to return home. Since worry had descended upon him, they would not travel any more. And they returned to their homes. And when the king returned to his home he probably had many affairs of state to take care of, and he busied himself with his affairs, and the matter left his mind.

And the exiled son, the king's true son, did what he did and squandered his money. Once he went out alone for a walk, and he lay down. And his mind was occupied with what had happened to him, and he thought: "What has God done to me? If I am the king's son, surely I do not deserve this! And if I am not the king's son, in this case, too, I do not deserve to be a fugitive and an exile." And he reconsidered the matter: "On the contrary, even if the Lord, blessed be He, can do such a thing and switch the king's son and make all this happen to him, is what I have done right? Was it proper for me to behave the way I have?" And he became sorry and regretted all the evil things he had done.

Afterwards he went back to his place and returned to his drunkenness. But since he had started to regret, thoughts of remorse and repentance overcame him from time to time. Once, he lay down and dreamt that at a certain place on a certain day there was a fair, and he should go there, and perform whatever gainful labor he found first, even if it was not according to his dignity. And he woke up. And the dream entered his mind deeply. Some things would pass away immediately from his mind, but this dream was very much on his mind. Nevertheless, it was hard for him to perform this labor, and he took more to drinking. And he dreamt this dream a few times more, and it confused him greatly.

Once they told him in a dream: "If you want to help yourself, do what you dreamt of." And he had to fulfill the dream. And he paid for his lodgings with the remainder of his money. He also left his fine clothes there. And he put on a simple merchant's garment, and traveled to the fair. And he arrived there, and got up early and went to the fair. And a merchant met him and said to him: "Do you want to earn money by some kind of labor?" He answered him: "Yes." He told him: "I have to drive cattle. Will you hire yourself out to me?" And he had no time to think about it because of the dream and he answered at once: "Yes." And the merchant hired him promptly. And right away he began to abuse him and order him the way a master does with his servants. And he began to consider his position. "What have I done? Certainly, such labor does not befit me. I am a delicate man and now I will have to drive cattle and will be forced to walk with the animals." But he could not change his mind. And the merchant would order him like a master. And he asked the merchant: "How can I walk alone with the cattle?" And he answered him: "There are other herdsmen who drive my cattle and you will go with them." And he gave him some animals to drive. And he drove them out of the town. And there, all the rest of the herdsmen who drove the cattle gathered, and they walked together. And he drove the animals.

And the merchant rode them cruelly. And he treated the king's son with the greatest cruelty. And he was much afraid of the merchant because he saw his great cruelty toward him. And he was afraid that he would hit him once with his club and he would die immediately. (Since he was a very delicate man, it seemed to him that this would happen.) And he walked with the cattle and the merchant was with them. And they came to some place and took the bag in which the herdsmen's bread was placed, and the merchant gave them some to eat. And they also gave the king's son some of this bread and he ate.

Later, they walked through a very thick forest and two of

the cattle of the son who had become a herdsman strayed away. And the merchant shouted at him, and he went after them to catch them. And they fled further and he pursued them. And since the forest was thick, as soon as he entered it the herdsmen did not see each other and he disappeared at once from the eyes of his friends. And he continued pursuing the animals and they fled. And he pursued them for a long time until he came into the thickest part of the forest. And he thought: "I will die in any case, for if I come back without the animals, the merchant will kill me. (Because of his fear of the merchant it seemed to him that he would kill him if he came without the animals.) And if I stay here, the beasts of the forest will kill me. So why should I return to the merchant? How can I come to him without the animals?" He had great fear of him. And he went and pursued the animals further, and they fled.

Meanwhile, night came. And a thing like that had never happened to him. He had never before had to spend the night alone in the thickness of such a forest. And he heard the roar of the beasts which were roaring as was their nature. And he decided to climb a tree, and he spent the night there. And he heard the sound of the beasts that were screeching as was their nature. In the morning he looked and saw that the cattle were standing very close to him. And he descended from the tree and went to catch them, but they fled. And the further he went the further they fled. The cattle would find some grass there and would stand to graze. And he went to catch them and they fled. And so he went after them and they fled, he pursued them and they fled, until he came to the very depth of the forest where there were beasts which were not afraid of man at all, because they were far from any human settlement. And again night came. And he heard the roaring of the beasts, and he was terrified. And he saw a very big tree standing there, and he climbed the tree. When he climbed it, he saw a human being lying there. And he was frightened, but nevertheless, it was consoling to find a man there. And they asked each other:

"Who are you?"

"A human being. Who are you?"

"A human being."

"How did you come here?"

And he did not want to tell him what had happened to him, and he answered him: "Because of the cattle which I herded. Two of the animals strayed here, and this is how I came here." And he asked the man whom he had found on the tree: "How did you come here?" He answered him: "I came here because of my horse. I was riding on my horse and I halted to rest, but the horse strayed into the forest. So I ran after it to catch it, and he fled further till I came here."

And they joined company, and they decided that they would stay together even when they came to an inhabited place. And they both spent the night there. And they heard the sound of beasts screeching and roaring loudly. At dawn he heard great laughter over the forest. The laughter was so great that the tree was shaking because of the sound. And he became very terrified and very frightened of it. And the other man, whom he had found lying on the tree, told him: "I am not afraid of it any more, since I have already spent several nights here. And each night, close to daybreak, this laughter is heard until all the trees shake and tremble." And the king's son was very terrified and said to his friend: "It seems that this is the place of the devils, since in an inhabited place such laughter is not heard. Who has heard such laughter in the whole world?" And immediately after this, day came. And they looked and saw the animals standing there, too. And they descended and started pursuing—one, the cattle, and the other, his horse. And the cattle fled further and he pursued them: And the second pursued the horse and the horse fled further, till the distance between them grew and they lost each other.

Meanwhile, the king's son found a bag of bread, and this was very important in the wilderness. And he put the bag on his shoulders and went after the animals. Doing so, he met a man, and at first he was terrified. Nevertheless, it was consoling to find a man there. And the man asked him: "How did you get here?" And he asked the man in return: "How did you get here?" He answered him: "My father and my forefathers grew up here, but how did you get here? No man from an inhabited place comes here at all." And he was terrified, since he understood that this was no man at all. But, nevertheless, the forest-man did not do anything to him and befriended him. And the forest-man said to the king's true son: "What are you doing here?" He answered him that he was pursuing the cattle. The man told him: "Stop pursuing your sins! Because those are not animals at all but your sins that drive you like that. That is enough. You have already suffered your punishment. And now, stop pursuing them further, come with me and you will come to what is fitting for you." And he went with him. And he was afraid to speak with him and ask him, lest the man would open his mouth and swallow him, because he understood that this was no man at all. And he went after him.

Meanwhile, the king's son met his friend who was pursuing his horse. And as soon as he saw him, he gestured: "Know that this is not a man. Don't have anything to do with him, because he is not a man." And he went and whispered all this in his ear. And his friend (the horseman) looked and saw a bag of bread on his shoulder, and he began to implore him: "My brother! It has been several days since I ate. Give me some bread!" The king's son answered him: "Here in the wilderness nothing will help you, for my life comes first, and I need the bread for myself." And he began begging and imploring him greatly: "I shall give you anything." (But surely no gift or payment for bread is of use in the wilderness.) He answered him: "What will you give me? What can you give me for bread in the wilderness?" The horseman replied to the herdsman who was the king's true son: "I shall give myself completely away. I shall sell myself to you for bread!" And the herdsman thought to himself: "To buy a man, it is worth giving him bread." And he bought him as an eternal slave. And the horseman swore to him with many oaths that he would be his eternal slave even when they came to an inhabited place. And the herdsman would give him bread—that is, they would eat from the bag till the bread ran out. And they walked together after the forest-man. And the slave (the horseman) walked after him (the herdsman) and both walked after the forest-man. And in this way the king's son had things a little easier for himself. When he had to raise something or do something else, he would order his slave to raise it or to do his will. And they went together after the forest-man.

And they came to a place where there were snakes and scorpions. And the king's son was very frightened. And because of his fear he asked the forest-man: "How shall we pass through here?" He answered him: "If you think this is difficult, how will you enter my house?" And he showed him his house that was standing in the air. "And how will you enter my house?" And they went with the forest-man, and he led them across safely, and brought them into his house, and gave them food and drink, and went away.

And the king's true son who was the herdsman made use of his slave as much as he had to. And the slave was very vexed that he sold himself into slavery because of one hour when he needed bread to eat. For now they had something to eat, and because of one hour only he would be an eternal slave. And he sighed and groaned: "How did I come to this stage, to be a slave?" The king's true son, who was now his master, asked him: "And what greatness had you, that you sigh so much for having come to this stage?" And he answered and told him that he had been a king and people had gossiped that he had been switched, etc., for this horseman was indeed the king who was really the maidservant's son who had exiled his (childhood) friend. And once he began to realize he had done wrong and he repented it, etc. And feelings of repentance over the evil deed and the great injury he had done his friend came over him continuously. Once he dreamt that the remedy would be to give up his throne and go to the place where his eyes would lead him, and this is how he would atone for his sin. And he did not want to do so. But those dreams used to confuse him all the time until he decided to do so. And he gave up the throne and wandered about until he came there, and now he would be a slave. And the king's true son heard all this and kept silent, but thought: "I shall see and decide how to behave with him."

At night the forest-man came and gave them food and drink. And they spent the night there. At dawn they heard a sound of great laughter (as was told) until all the trees shook and trembled. And the slave enticed his master, the king's true son, to ask the forest-man what it was. And he asked him: "What is this sound of great laughter before morning?" He answered him: "This is the day laughing at the night! Since the night asks the day: 'Why is it that when you come I have no name?' And then the day laughs greatly, and afterwards day comes. And this is the sound of laughter." And it amazed the king's son because it was a wonder that the day should laugh at the night! (He could ask no further when the other answered in such language.)

In the morning, the forest-man went away again. And they ate and drank there. At night he returned, and they ate and drank and slept. Then they heard the beasts screeching and roaring with strange voices, since all the beasts and fowl raised their voices. The lion roared, and the leopard growled with another voice, and the fowl whistled and clattered, and so did the others howl with their voices. And at first they were very much shaken, and did not listen to the sound properly because of their fear. Later, they listened more carefully and heard that it was the sound of wonderfully beautiful melody, an extraordinary marvel. It was an extraordinarily immense pleasure to hear it, that all the pleasures in the world were naught and pointless in comparison with the wonderful pleasure of this music. And they talked and agreed to stay there, because they had food and drink and such wonderful pleasure, that all other pleasures were null in comparison.

And the slave enticed his master, the king's true son, to ask the forest-man what it was. And he asked him. He answered him: "This is the way the sun makes a garment for the moon. And all the forest beasts have called out since the moon does them such great favors. Their main activity is at night, because sometimes they have to enter an inhabited place and cannot do it during the day. And the moon does them the favor of shining for them. Thus they decided to create a new melody in honor of the moon, and this is the music you hear. All the beasts and fowl are playing a new melody for the moon who has received a garment from the sun."

And when the master and the slave heard that this was a melody, they listened more carefully and heard that it was a very pleasant and wonderful melody. And the forest-man called out to them: "Is *this* a marvel in your opinion? Even greater is the instrument I received from my parents who had inherited it from their forefathers, an instrument made of leaves and colors, and when one puts this instrument on an animal or a water-fowl, it starts at once to play this melody." Afterwards the laughter returned and day came.

And the forest-man went away, and the king's true son went to look for the instrument. And he searched all over the room and did not find it. And he was afraid to go further. And both of them (the master who was the king's true son and the slave who was the maidservant's true son and had been a king) were afraid to ask the forest-man to take them to an inhabited place. Later, the forest-man came and told them that he would lead them to an inhabited place. And he led them there. And he took the instrument and gave it to the king's true son, and said to him: "I give you the instrument. And you will know how to behave with this man." (That is, the slave, the maidservant's true son.) And they asked him: "Where shall we go?" He told them to inquire after a country called "The Foolish Country with the Wise Government." They asked him: "Where and in what direction shall we begin to search for this country?" And he pointed with his hand in one direction. And the forest-man said to the king's true son: "Go to that country, and there you will achieve your greatness."

And they went off. While walking they desired very much to find a beast or an animal to try out the instrument, if it could play as before, but they did not see any animal. Later, they came to an inhabited place and found an animal. And they put the instrument on it and it started to play as before. And they walked and walked until they came to that country. And there was a wall around the country, and one could enter it only through one gate, and one had to walk around the wall for many miles till one came to the gate and entered the country. And they walked around till they came to the gate.

When they came to the gate they were not allowed in, since the king of the country had died and the king's son remained, and the king left a will stating that until that day the state had been called "The Foolish Country with the Wise Government," but now it should be called the opposite: "The Wise Country with the Foolish Government." And whoever undertook to restore the original name, "The Foolish Country with the Wise Government," would be king. Thus they did not let anyone in, unless he undertook to bring back the country's original name. That is why they did not let him in, and told him: "Can you undertake to bring back the country's original name?" He could not possibly undertake such a thing, so they could not enter. And the slave tried to persuade him to return to their homes. But he did not want to return because the forest-man had told him that he should go to this country and there he would achieve greatness.

In the meanwhile another man came, riding a horse. And he wanted to enter but they did not let him in for the same reason. Meanwhile the king's son saw that the man's horse was standing there. And he took the instrument and put it on the horse. And it started playing the very wonderful melody. And the man with the horse asked him earnestly to sell him the instrument. But he did not want to sell it, and he answered him: "What can you give me for such a wonderful instrument?" The man on the horse told him: "What can you accomplish with this instrument? All you can make with it is a comedy for which you will get a *gulden*! But I know something that is better than your instrument. I know something that I received from my parents' parents, how to be one who deduces one thing from the other. When someone says something, one can, through what I have received, deduce another thing. And I have not yet revealed it to any man. But if I will teach you this thing, you will give me this instrument!" And the king's true son who had the instrument thought that it was indeed a great marvel to be one who deduces one thing from another, and he gave him the instrument. And the owner of the horse taught him to understand one thing from another.

And since the king's true son was now able to deduce one thing from another, he went near the gate to the country, and deduced that it was possible for him to undertake to bring back the country's original name, because he had already been able to deduce one thing from the other. Thus he deduced that it was possible, though he did not know yet how. Nevertheless, since he was able to deduce one thing from another, he deduced that it was possible. And he decided to order them to let him in, and he would undertake to bring back the country's original name. Since what would he lose by that? And he told the men who had not wanted to let him in to let him in, and he would undertake to restore to the country its original name. And they informed the ministers that there was such a man who wanted to undertake to restore the country's original name. And they brought him to the state's ministers. And the ministers told him: "Know that we, too, are not fools, God forbid. But the late king was such an exceptionally wise man, that in comparison with him we are all considered foolish, and that is why the country was called 'The Foolish Country with the Wise Government.' But later, the king died and only the king's son remained, and he, too, is wise, but in comparison with us he is not wise at all, thus, the country is now called by the opposite name: 'The Wise Country with the Foolish Government.' And the king left a will that when a wise man like this, who can bring back the country's original name, will be found, he will be king. And he ordered his son to give up the throne when such a man is found, and that man will be king, that is, when a wise man is found, who is so exceptionally wise that in comparison with him we shall all be foolish, he will be king, since this is the man who will be able to restore to the country its original name, because they will call it again: 'The Foolish Country with the Wise Government.' Because they will all be fools in comparison with him. So, better know what you are undertaking."

All this the ministers told him, and they continued: "This will be the trial to prove that you are such a wise man. There is a garden that remained from the days of the late king who was a great wise man. And the garden is an extraordinary marvel, since iron, silver, and gold instruments grow in it. And it is an extraordinary marvel. But it is impossible to enter it, because when a man enters it, immediately they start to pursue him. And they pursue him and he shouts, and he does not know and does not see who pursues him, and so they chase him out of the garden. In this way we shall see if you are wise: If you can enter this garden!" And he asked if they beat the man who entered. They told him: "The main thing is that they pursue him and he does not know who is pursuing him and he flees in great panic." Because this was what people who had entered told them.

And the king's true son went to the garden and he saw a wall around it, and the gate was open, and there were no guards there, since surely they did not need guards for that garden. And he went near the garden, and he looked and saw a man standing by the garden, that is, a man was drawn there. And he looked further and saw that above the man there was a tablet, and on it was inscribed that this man had been king several hundred years ago. And in the days of this king there had been peace, since until the time of that king there had been wars. And likewise after him there had been wars, but during the days of that king there had been peace. And he understood, since he was able to deduce one thing from another, that everything depended on this man, that when one entered the garden and was pursued, one did not have to flee at all. One just had to stand by that person, and thus one would be saved. Moreover, if one took that person and placed him in the middle of the garden, everybody would be able to enter this garden in peace. All this the king's true son deduced since he could deduce one thing from another.

And he went and entered the garden. And immediately, when they started pursuing him, he went and stood next to the person who stood next to the garden on the outside. In this way he came out in peace and with no harm. Others, when they had entered the garden and they had begun to pursue them, had run away with great fear and had been beaten and thrashed because of it. And he came out in peace and calm since he stood next to that person. And the ministers saw and were amazed that he had come out safely. Then the king's true son ordered them to take that person and place him inside, in the middle of the garden. And they did so, and then the ministers passed through the garden and went in and came out safely, without any harm.

The ministers told him: "Nevertheless, even though we

have seen you do such a thing, for one reason only it is not proper to give you the throne. We shall try you with one more thing." They told him: "There is a chair of the late king here, and the chair is very tall, and next to the chair stand all kinds of wooden animals and birds, which were carved of wood. A bed stands in front of the throne, and by the bed stands a table, and on the table there is a lamp. And from the chair come out paved roads. These roads are walled, and come out from the chair in each direction. No man understands the meaning of the chair with these roads. And where those roads come out and extend for some distance there stands a lion of gold, and if a man approaches it, then the lion will open its mouth and swallow him. And away from that lion the road extends further. And the same is true for the other roads that come out of the chair. The second road that comes out of the chair in another direction is the same. After it extends and continues for a certain distance, there stands some other kind of animal, like a leopard made of iron and there, too, it is impossible to get close to it, and from there the road extends further. And so it is on the other roads. And those roads extend and go all over the country. And no man knows the meaning of this chair with those things and those roads. Thus, in this you shall be tried: If you are able to know the meaning of this chair and all the above!"

And they showed him the chair. And he saw that it was very tall. And he went close to the chair and saw that it was made out of the wood of the instrument that the forest-man had given him. And he looked and saw that a rose was missing from the tip of the chair, and if the chair had that rose, it would have the power of the box, the instrument that had the power to play a melody when it was put on any kind of beast, animal, or fowl. And he looked more closely and saw that the rose missing from the top of the chair was lying at the bottom of the chair. One had to take it from there and put it on top, and then the chair would have the power of the box. For the late king had done everything with wisdom, so that no man would deduce the meaning, till an exceptionally wise man came who would understand it and would be able to direct and put all things in proper order. And so the king's son understood that the bed should be moved from its place a little, and the table, too, should be moved, so as to change its place a little, and the lamp, too, had to be moved a little from its place. And the fowl and animals had all to change their places, too. They had to take one fowl from this place and put it in that, etc. Because the king had done all with cunning and wisdom so that no man would understand, till the wise man who could understand their proper order came. And the lion that stood at the place from which the road extends, should be placed here, etc. And he ordered them all put in the right order: to take the rose from the bottom and insert it at the top, and to put all the other things in the proper order. And then they all started to play the most wonderful melody. And they all performed their proper function so that they would give him the royal power. Then the king's true son, who had now become the king, told the maidservant's son: "Now I understand that I am truly the king's son, and you are truly the maidservant's son."

XII. THE MASTER OF PRAYER

The longest of the Bratslav tales, "The Master of Prayer" is often cited as Nahman's characterization of the zadik, a man totally engaged in worship of the true Lord and in persuading others to follow his righteous path. The first few pages of the story are, indeed, devoted to this description, but the story soon develops into two seemingly disassociated sagas involving the Master of Prayer.

In the first, a lengthy satire on people who actually think that money is both the measure of personality and the source of divinity, the Master of Prayer is requested to save these people from a terrifying Warrior who is marching upon their country. The Master of Prayer would prefer to deliver them from their spiritual delusion, but he is compelled to accompany these foolish men.

In the second saga, we hear a thinly veiled Kabbalistic cosmogony telling how the Holy Community of the King was scattered by a tempest during the period of creation. These two sagas are linked not only by the figure of the Master of Prayer, who was a member of the original Holy Community, but by the chaos which descended upon the world with the dispersion of the Holy Community. Having no exemplars to guide them, especially no king, mankind searched for a variety of absurd substitutes for worship of the true King. One of these foolish solutions was the worship of money. Impelled by the ever-solicitous Master of Prayer, the Holy Community reassembles and can thus save the people of the Country of Riches from their mad lust after money. The tale which begins as a description of the zadik thus embraces a Kabbalistic cosmogony and a hilarious satire on bourgeois society.

ONCE there was a *Baal Tefilla* (prayer leader) who was always engaged in prayers and songs and praises to the Holy One, blessed be He. And he dwelled outside inhabited places. And he used to come into town to visit someone. Naturally, he would visit lowly people, like the poor. And he would talk to them of the purpose of the entire world, saying that there is truly no purpose except for the worship of the Lord all the days of one's life, spending one's days in prayer and songs and praises to the Holy One. And he would speak such inspiring words so often to the man he visited that they entered his heart and the man was willing to join him. As soon as he was willing, the *Baal Tefilla* led him to his place outside the town which he had selected. And in that place was a river, trees, and fruit. And they would eat of the fruit. But they paid no attention to clothes—anything was all right. And he would always come into town to persuade people to worship the Holy One, to go in His way and to be engaged in prayer, etc. And he would take whomever he persuaded and lead him to his place outside the town. And there they would engage in prayers, songs, and praises to the Holy One, and in confessions, fasts, mortifications, repentance, and the like. And he would give them books which he had of prayers, songs, praises, and confessions.

And they were always engaged in this until there were among the men whom he had brought to that place certain individuals who were also worthy of attracting men to the worship of the Holy One. Sometimes he permitted one of them to enter the town to awaken people to the service of the Almighty. And thus the *Baal Tefilla* would attract people each time and take them out of the town until this made an impression in the world and the matter became publicized that certain people among them would suddenly disappear from the country and their whereabouts would remain unknown. And so it might happen that a man suddenly lost his son or a son-in-law, and it was not known where they were until it became known that there existed a *Baal Tefilla* who used to persuade people to worship the Holy One. But it was impossible to capture him because the *Baal Tefilla* would behave cleverly and would disguise himself differently with each person. With one, he would disguise himself as a pauper and with another as a merchant. And furthermore, when he came to speak to people, if he saw that he could not accomplish his purpose with them, he would confuse them with words until they could not understand that his purpose was to attract people to the Holy One. And the *Baal Tefilla* was engaged in this matter until he made an impression and a reputation among people. And they wanted to capture him, but it was impossible.

The *Baal Tefilla* and his men would dwell outside inhabited places and engage in these matters only, in prayer, songs, and praises to the Holy One, and confessions, fasts, mortifications, and repentances. And the *Baal Tefilla* had the talent to provide each one with what he needed. If he understood that one of his men needed, by temperament, to wear golden brocade in order to worship the Lord, he would provide him with it. And vice versa: Once a certain rich man became an intimate of his and he took him out of the town. And he understood that this rich man had to go about dressed in torn clothes, so he led him accordingly. He would provide each one with what he knew he needed. And among those whom he drew near to the Holy One, a fast or a severe mortification was more precious than all the pleasures in the world, because they derived more pleasure from severe mortification or from the fast than from all the pleasures in the world.

2

And it came to pass that there was a country where there were great riches and everyone was rich there. But their behavior was very strange because everything among them was conducted according to riches. Everyone's rank and status was determined by riches. He who had so many thousands and tens of thousands would have one rank and status, and he who had a certain sum of money would have another rank and status. And he who had so many thousands and tens of thousands, according to the sum established among them, would be king. And they also had banners. He who had a certain sum of money would be under this banner and would have the rank of this banner. And he who had a certain sum of money would be under that banner, according to the amount of his money. And so it was established among them that when one had a certain sum, he was an Ordinary Man, but if he had less, he was no longer a Man, but a Beast with a human face or a Bird or the like. For the most important thing among them was money, and the rank and status of each person was determined according to money.

And it became widely known that such a country exists and the *Baal Tefilla* sighed over it, saying: "Who knows how far they can go astray this way?" And there were among the *Baal Tefilla*'s men those who did not ask his opinion at all, but went to that country to return its people to the right way, since they had great pity on those who had strayed so far in their lust for money, especially since the *Baal Tefilla* told them that they might return them to the right way. So they went there and came to that country and visited one of them, probably a man who was called a Beast among them. And they began to speak to him, as was their custom, saying that money was not the purpose of life, but that the chief purpose was worship of the Lord. And he did not listen to them at all because it was already rooted in him that the chief purpose was only money. They spoke to another person, but he, too, did not listen to them. They wanted to speak to him at length, but he answered: "I have no more time to speak to you." They asked why. He answered: "Because we are all preparing now to migrate from this country to another country. Since we have seen that the chief purpose of life is only money, it has been agreed to go to another country where people make money. There is ore there from which one makes gold and silver. So we must all go now to that country."

And it was agreed among those people that there should be among them Stars and Constellations, too. Whoever had a certain previously established sum would be a Star. Since he had so much money, he had the power of that star by which gold grew. The very existence of the ore which could be made into gold was due to the star. Consequently, he who had so much gold had the power of that star, and he himself would be a Star. And they also declared that there should be among them Constellations, that is, whoever had the previously established sum, should be a Constellation. And thus they made themselves Angels, in accordance with the additional sum of money. Finally, they agreed that they should also have Gods. Whosoever's money increased so many thousands and tens of thousands, as previously established, would be a God, since God had given him so much money, he himself should be a God.

And they also said that it did not become them to dwell in the atmosphere of this world or to mingle with other people lest they defile themselves, since the rest of mankind were unclean in comparison with them. They therefore decided to seek the highest mountains in the world and dwell there, so that they would be loftier than the atmosphere of the world. They sent people to search and seek such lofty mountains. And all the citizens of the country went to dwell on the lofty mountains, that is, on each mountain dwelled a certain group from that country. And they built around the first mountain a great fortification, with huge trenches and the like, until it was absolutely impossible for any man to reach them since there was only one hidden path to the mountain. Similarly, on the second mountain and on all the mountains they made fortifications. And they placed guards at a distance from the mountains so that no stranger could approach them. And they dwelled there on the mountains and behaved in this way. And they had many Gods, each according to his money.

And since the chief purpose among them was money, and through money they became Gods, they were afraid of murder and robbery, because everyone would become a murderer and a robber in order to become a God with the money he would steal. So they said that since the rich man with much money was a God, he would protect them from robbers and murderers. And they ordained rituals and sacrifices to offer and pray to the Gods. And they also sacrificed human beings. And they would sacrifice themselves to the Gods, so that they would be incorporated in the Gods and would afterwards be transformed into rich men because the principle of faith among them was money. And they had rituals, sacrifices, and incense which they would offer to the Gods, that is, to the possessors of much money. Nonetheless, the country was full of murder and robbery because whoever did not believe in these rituals would become a murderer and a robber to get money. The chief principle among them was money, because (they observed that) with money they could buy all food and clothing, and that the chief support of human life was by means of money. (This was their foolish and misled opinion.) Therefore they endeavored not to lack money because money was the principle of their faith and their God.

So they endeavored to bring money from other places. And merchants set forth to trade in other countries in order to earn money and to bring more money into the country. And charity was surely severely forbidden, according to their opinion, because it lessened the abundance of money which God had given a man. Since the chief purpose was to have money and charity diminished and lessened one's money, it was surely severely forbidden among them to give charity.

And they also had officials to supervise each person to see if he had as much money as he claimed since everyone had to exhibit his wealth at all times so that he could remain in the rank and status he had in accordance with his money. (And they used to inspect all the wealthy people who were Gods and Stars and Angels in accordance with their wealth, to see if they had enough money so that they were not Gods, etc., for nothing. And people were appointed to oversee this.) And sometimes a Beast became a Man, and a Man became a Beast. That is, when one lost his money, he lost his human status since he had no money. And, vice versa, when one earned money, a Beast became a Man. And likewise in the other ranks, according to money. (And it once happened that one lost his divine status because he no longer had enough money.) And some of them had portraits of the God *Baal Mammon*, and they would embrace them and kiss them because this was their devotion and their faith.

And the pious men of the *Baal Tefilla* returned to their place and told the *Baal Tefilla* of the enormity of the error and folly of that country, that the people were misled by the lust for money and wished to migrate to another country to make themselves Stars and Constellations. The *Baal Tefilla* answered that he feared lest they stray more and more. Afterwards, it was heard that they made themselves Gods. The *Baal Tefilla* answered that he had been fearful and concerned about this from the very beginning, and he had much pity for them. He decided to go there himself; perhaps he could lead them back from their error.

3

And the *Baal Tefilla* went there and came to the guards who stood around the mountain. And the guards were, of course, men of low rank for they were permitted to stand in the atmosphere of this world. The men who had rank because of their money cannot mingle at all with the people of this world or stand in its atmosphere lest they be defiled. And the guards could not speak at all with people of the world lest the latter defile them with their breath. And though the guards were of low rank, even they had these portraits and would embrace and kiss them because among them, too, the principal belief was money.

And the *Baal Tefilla* came to a guard and began to speak to him concerning the purpose of life, saying that the chief purpose is only the worship of the Lord, Torah, prayer, and good deeds, and that money is folly and not the true purpose at all. The guard did not listen to him at all because it had long been established among them that the main principle was only money. And so the *Baal Tefilla* went to a second guard and spoke to him also. And the second guard did not listen to him either. And thus he went to all the guards and they did not listen to him at all. So the *Baal Tefilla* decided to enter the city on the mountain. How he got there was a marvel to them, and they asked him, "How did you get here?" Because no man had been able to reach them before. He answered them, "Why do you ask me about this? I have already entered." And the *Baal Tefilla* began to speak to one man about the purpose of the world but he did not listen to him at all. The same was true for the second and for all of them, since they all had been deluded in their folly. And it was astonishing to the people of the city that a man had come among them and had spoken to them of these matters which were the opposite of their belief. And they guessed that this man must be the *Baal Tefilla* because they had previously heard that there was a *Baal Tefilla* like this in the world. For the reputation of the *Baal Tefilla* was already widely known in the world and people called him "the Pious *Baal Tefilla*." But it was impossible for them to recognize him or capture him since he disguised himself with each person. With one he appeared as a merchant and with another as a pauper. And suddenly, he escaped from there.

4

It came to pass that there appeared a Warrior around whom many warriors had gathered. And this Warrior with his warriors used to go and conquer countries. He wanted nothing but submission. If the people of a certain country would submit to him, he would leave them alone; if not, he would destroy them. He would conquer, but did not want money, only submission to him. And this Warrior used to send his warriors to a country while he was still a great distance from it—fifty miles—saying that the country should submit to him. And thus he conquered countries.

And the merchants of the country of riches who used to trade in foreign countries would come and tell of the Warrior. And great fear befell them. At first they were disposed to submit to him, but they heard that he despised money and did not want money at all. And this was contrary to their belief. Therefore it was impossible for them to submit to him because it was for them like conversion since he did not believe at all in their belief, that is, in money. And they feared him very much, and began to perform rituals, and to offer sacrifices to their Gods (to those who had much money). And they took a Beast (one who had little money) and offered him as a sacrifice to their Gods and performed similar rituals.

And the Warrior drew closer and closer to them and began to send them his warriors to ask what they wished, as was his custom. And they were terrified and did not know what to do. And their merchants advised them that they had been in another country where everyone was a God and traveled "with Angels." All the people of that country, from the lowly to the mighty, were so enormously wealthy that even the most lowly among them possessed the established amount of money to be a God among them. And they traveled "with Angels," since their horses were covered with such great wealth, with gold and the like, that the covering of one horse costs as much as the amount that one of their Angels possessed. Consequently, they traveled "with Angels," that is, they harnessed three pair of "Angels" to a chariot and traveled with them. "Therefore you should send to that country and they will certainly help you since all the people in that country are Gods." And the advice seemed right to them because they believed that they would surely get help from that country since they were all Gods there.

5

And the *Baal Tefilla* decided to go again to that country; perhaps he would bring them back from their folly. And he came to the guards and began to speak with one guard as was his custom and the guard told him about the Warrior, that they were terrified of him. And the *Baal Tefilla* asked him: "And what do you intend to do?" And the guard told him that they intended to send to the country where they were all Gods. And the *Baal Tefilla* laughed at him heartily and said to him: "All this is great folly. Those people are all human beings like us, and you and your 'Gods' are human beings like us, and not God. There exists only one God in the world who is the Creator, blessed be He, and to Him alone is it fitting to worship and to pray and this is the main purpose of life." And the *Baal Tefilla* spoke words like these to the guard. And the guard did not listen to him because their folly had long been embedded in them. Nevertheless, the *Baal Tefilla* argued at great length with him until the guard finally answered him: "What more can I do than this? I am only one person." And this answer was encouraging for the *Baal Tefilla* because he understood that his words were beginning to penetrate the ears of the guard. The words the *Baal Tefilla* spoke previously with the guard and the words he spoke now joined together and made an impression on him so that he began to doubt and to incline a bit toward the *Baal Tefilla*. And thus the *Baal Tefilla* went to the second guard and spoke with him, too, but he did not listen to him until finally he, too, answered him: "I am only one person, etc." And so all the guards finally made this reply.

Then the *Baal Tefilla* entered the city and began again to speak with the people as was his custom, saying that they were all living in great error and this was not the purpose of life at all, that the chief purpose of life was to be engaged in Torah and prayer. And they did not listen to him because they had all been deeply rooted in money for a long time. And they told him about the Warrior, and said that they intended to send to the country where they were all Gods, etc. And he laughed at them, too. And he said to them, "This is folly. They are all human beings and cannot help you at all, because you are human and they are human and not Gods at all. But there is One, blessed be He." And regarding the Warrior he cried out: "Isn't this the Warrior?" And they did not understand what he meant, and so he went from one to the other and spoke with them, and concerning the Warrior he said to each one as before: "Isn't this the Warrior?" And they did not understand what he meant. And there was a tumult in the city since there appeared a person who spoke this way making fun of their belief, saying that there exists only one God, the Holy One, etc. And regarding the Warrior he said: "Isn't this the Warrior?" They understood he surely must be the *Baal Tefilla* for he had already become famous among them.

And they ordered him hunted and captured. Even though he changed his disguise each time they knew that he did so and ordered an investigation so they would capture him. And they searched for him and captured him, and brought him to their elders and began to speak to him. And he said to them, too, that they were all living in great error and folly and that money was not the purpose of life at all. "But there is One who is the Creator, blessed be He, etc. And the citizens of the country who you say are all Gods will not be able to help you at all, because they are only human beings." And they considered him mad, because all the people of that country were so immersed in money, and had become so foolish because of it that whoever spoke against their folly was considered a madman. And they asked him: "What do you mean when you say about the Warrior: 'Isn't this the Warrior?' " And he answered them, "I used to be with a King and he lost a Warrior and if this is the same Warrior, I am acquainted with him. Furthermore, it is foolish for you to trust in the country where you say everyone is a God, because they can't help you. On the contrary, if you trust in them, it will be your downfall." They said to him, "How do you know this?"

He answered them:

"At the palace of the King with whom I stayed was a hand, that is, there was a picture of a hand with five fingers and with all the lines which are on a hand. And this hand was a map of all the worlds. And everything which has been from the Creation of the heavens and the earth until the end of time, and what will be afterwards was drawn on that hand. A drawing of the position of each and every world with all its details was drawn in the lines of the hand, as it is drawn on a map. And there were letters on the lines just as there are letters written on a map next to each item so that one may know what that item is, that is, to know that here is a certain city and here is a certain river and the like. The details of every country, town, river, bridge, and mountain are inscribed there. Precisely the same way were letters inscribed on the lines of the hand. And all the people who moved about the country and all their activities were inscribed there, as were all the paths which led from one country to another and one place to another. And because of this I knew how to enter this city which is impossible for any man to enter. And so, if you want to send me to another city, I know that path, too. I know everything by means of that hand.

"And similarly, the path from world to world was inscribed on it, for there is a path by which one can ascend from the earth to the heavens. (It is impossible to ascend to the heavens if one does not know the path, but the path to ascend to heaven was inscribed there.) And all the paths which go from one world to the next were inscribed there. Elija ascended to the heavens on a certain path, and the name of that path was written there. And Moses, our teacher, ascended to the heavens on another path and that path, too, was written there. And Enoch, too, ascended to the heavens on another path and that, too, was written there. And so it was from one world to the next (even higher) world, everything was inscribed on the lines of that hand.

"And everything was inscribed on the hand just as it was at the time of the Creation of the world, and as it is in its present form, and as it shall be afterwards. For example: Sodom was inscribed there as it existed before it was destroyed, and the destruction of Sodom was also drawn there just as the city was being destroyed, and there is also a drawing of Sodom after the destruction. Because on the one hand was inscribed what was, what is, and what shall be. And on that hand I have seen that the country whose people you call Gods will be destroyed and annihilated together with all the people who come to it to receive help from it."

All this the *Baal Tefilla* replied to them. And the matter was an extraordinary marvel to them because people recognized that this was a true speech, for it was known that all these things are drawn on a map. And they also understood his speech is true because they saw it was possible to compose two lines of the hand so that they form a letter. Therefore, they understood that he did not invent these things from his mind, and it was for them an extraordinary marvel.

And they asked him, "Where is that King? Perhaps He will reveal to us the way to find money." He replied to them, "You still want money? Don't speak of money at all." They asked him, "Even so—where is the King?"

He replied to them, "Even I don't know where the King is. And this is the story of what happened.

"There was a King and a Queen, and they had an only daughter. And she reached the age of marriage. And they summoned counselors to advise who was worthy of marrying her. And I, the Master of Prayer, too, was among the advisors, for the King loved me. And my advice was that they should give her to the Warrior, since the Warrior did us several favors in that he conquered several countries. Therefore, he was worthy to be given the Princess as a wife. And my advice was considered very good and they all agreed to it. And there was great joy because they found a groom for the Princess. And they married her to the Warrior and the Princess bore a child. And the child was a marvelous person, and his beauty was unlike anything human. And his hair was made of gold and had all kinds of hues. And his face was like the sun, and his eyes were the other luminaries. This child was born endowed with great wisdom, and they saw as soon as he was born that he was already a great wise man. When people spoke, he laughed where one should laugh and the like. They recognized that he was a great wise man, though he did not yet have the motions of an adult such as speech and the like.

"The King had an Orator, that is, an eloquent and polished speaker who could make beautiful speeches, songs and praises to the King. And though this Orator was a fine orator on his own account, the King showed him the path where he could acquire the skill of oratory, and thus he became a marvelous orator.

"The King also had a wise man. Though he was wise on

his own account, the King showed him the path where he could acquire wisdom and thus he became a marvelously wise man. And though the Warrior was valiant on his own account, the King showed him a path where he could acquire more valor and thus he became marvelously valiant.

"There is a sword that hangs in the air, and this sword has three powers. When the sword is raised all the army officers flee and the enemy is naturally defeated, because when the officers flee, no one is left to conduct the war, and so the enemy certainly suffers a defeat. The remaining soldiers, nevertheless, could still wage war. The sword, however, has two edges which have two powers. Through one edge all enemies fall and through the other they are afflicted with consumption. They become thin and their bodies waste away just like in the plague, Heaven help us! And with a sweep of the sword, the enemies are afflicted by the two edges and their powers, defeat and consumption. The King showed the Warrior the path to the sword and from there he acquired his valor.

"The King also showed me the path to the thing that I needed. I took from there what I needed. (The *Baal Tefilla* who is telling this said that the King had also shown him the path where he should acquire his thing, that is, prayer.)

"The King had a very faithful friend who loved the King very much. The love between them was so wonderful that they could not be apart for an hour. Still there are times when people must part for an hour. So they had portraits where their images were drawn, and when they were separated, they took pleasure in looking at the images. The images were painted to depict the love between the King and his friend, how they kissed and embraced each other lovingly. The portraits had a magic power so that anyone who looked at the images acquired great love. The loyal friend of the King had also acquired this love from the place designated by the King.

"There came a time when all these people went, each to

his own place, to derive his strength from there. The Orator and the Warrior and all the other King's men went, each to his own place, to renew his strength. On that day there arose a great tempest in the world. And the tempest upset and confused the entire world. It made dry land ocean and turned ocean into dry land. It turned desert into settlement and settlement into desert. The tempest turned the whole world upside down. It entered the house of the King and did no damage there, but it entered and snatched the child of the Princess. In the tumult, when the tempest snatched the precious child, the Princess immediately chased after it. And so did the Queen and the King until they dispersed and no one knew where they were. None of us were there, for we had gone, each to his own place, to renew his strength. When we returned, we did not find them. At the same time, the Hand was also lost. Since then we have all dispersed and we cannot return each to his place, to renew our strength. Since the world was turned upside down we now need new paths. Because of this we can no longer return, each to his own place, to renew our strength.

"Yet the impression (the little bit of power) that was left with each one was nonetheless very great. And if the Warrior is the King's Warrior, he is certainly extremely valiant."

So spoke the *Baal Tefilla* to the people who listened carefully to his words and were astonished. They kept the *Baal Tefilla* with them and were not willing to let him go away in case the Warrior who wanted to attack them was the Warrior with whom the *Baal Tefilla* is acquainted.

The Warrior was coming closer and closer to the kingdom and he kept sending his messengers to them until he arrived. And he remained outside the city and sent his messengers inside to them (to tell him whether they are willing to surrender). They were terrified of him, so they asked the *Baal Tefilla* for advice. The *Baal Tefilla* told them they should examine the behavior of the Warrior in order to recognize whether this was the King's Warrior. The *Baal Tefilla* left to confront the Warrior and came to his army. He began a conversation with one of the warriors of the Warrior to recognize if this was the Warrior. The *Baal Tefilla* asked him: "What are your (heroic) deeds? How did you join the Warrior?"

The guard answered, "This is the story that is written in their chronicles:

"Once there was a great tempest on earth and the tempest turned the whole world upside down turning ocean into dry land and dry land into ocean, turning settlements into deserts and deserts into settlements. And after the tumult and the confusion, the people of the world decided to make a King. They began to consider who is worthy to be crowned their King. They reasoned that the most important matter was the final purpose. Therefore, he who is busy with and strives toward the purpose of all life is worthy to be King. They began to reason what the chief purpose should be. There were many factions among them.

"One faction said that the chief purpose was honor since we see that honor is important in the world, for if a man is not accorded his honor, it leads to bloodshed. The whole world recognizes the significance of honor. One even insists upon the honor of the dead, to bury the corpse with honor, etc. (And people tell the dead person what is being done for him is simply to honor him.) Even though after death one no longer wants money and the dead person certainly does not desire anything, nevertheless, one insists upon the honor of the dead. Consequently, honor is the chief purpose. (And they had other conjectures and deductions as confused and foolish as these.) Because of this they had to find an honored man who also continues to seek honor. If he should be an honored man who both possesses honor and pursues honor, thus abetting the disposition that wished honor, he would consequently strive toward that purpose and achieve it. For the chief purpose was honor. For this reason such a man deserved to be king.

"They walked along and saw people carrying an old gypsy beggar. He was followed by some five hundred people, all gypsies. The beggar was blind and crippled and mute. The people who followed him were his kin, brothers and sisters and progeny, forming the group which followed him and carried him. And the old beggar insisted upon his honor. He was an irate man and always vented his anger upon them. He ordered different people to carry him each time and he was always scolding them. Consequently, this old beggar is indeed a greatly honored man for he possessed such honor and pursued honor and insisted upon his honor. Therefore, this old beggar pleased this faction and they accepted him as their king.

"At times the land is also a factor, for there are countries that generate honor and are congenial to it. Similarly, there is a country that generates a different virtue. Because of this, the faction which reasoned that the chief purpose was honor sought a country that generates honor. They found a country that was congenial to this quality and settled there.

"A different faction said that honor was not the chief purpose. They reasoned that the chief purpose was murder. Inasmuch as we see that all things on this earth cease to exist and perish, and everything on earth such as grass and fruit and people must cease to exist and perish, the chief purpose of all things is ceasing to exist and perishing. Thus a murderer who kills and destroys people does much to bring the world to its chief purpose. This was why they concluded that murder was the chief purpose. They looked for a person who would be a murderer, an irate and extremely envious person, for such a person was closer to the chief purpose (according to their mistaken opinion) and deserves to be a king.

"They set out to find such a person. They heard a great outcry and asked the reason for this outcry. They were answered that someone had just slaughtered his father and mother. They asked themselves, 'Could a greater murderer than this be found so impudent and so impetuous as to kill both his father and his mother? This man has achieved the chief purpose.' He pleased them and they accepted him as king. And they searched for a land that generates murder. They chose a place of mountains and hills where murderers were found, and they went there. They settled there with their king.

"Another faction said that the person who was fit to be king should be one who had an abundance of food and did not eat the same food as everyone else, only more noble food (so that his intellect should not become coarse). Such a man would make a proper king. Only they could not find immediately such a man who did not eat the same food as everyone else. For the meanwhile they selected a rich man who had an abundance of food that was a bit more noble until they could find the person they desired who would not eat, etc. At that time the rich man would abdicate the throne and the other would become king. They chose a land that would be fit for this virtue and they went there and settled.

"Another faction said that a beautiful woman was fit to rule, since the chief purpose was for the world to be populated and for this the world was created. And because a beautiful woman stirs the passion through which the world population increases, she achieves the chief purpose. Because of this a beautiful woman was worthy of ruling. They chose a beautiful woman and she ruled over them. They searched for a land that would be fit for this virtue and went and settled there.

"Another faction said that the chief purpose was speech, because the advantage man has over an animal is speech. And since this is the only advantage man has, it is the chief purpose. Thus they sought an orator who was eloquent and knew several languages and always talked a great deal, for such a person has achieved the chief purpose. They went and found a mad Frenchman who went around talking to himself. They asked him if he knew any languages. He knew several. And such an individual had obviously achieved the chief purpose

(according to their confused opinion) since he was eloquent
and spoke several languages and he talked a great deal, because he even talked to himself. Because of this, he pleased
them and they accepted him as king. And they chose a country that would be fit for this virtue and they went and settled
there with their king. He obviously led them along the right
path.

"Another faction said that the chief purpose lay in rejoicing. For one is joyous when a child is born, and joyous at a
wedding. One is joyous when a land is captured. And so,
everyone's chief purpose lies in rejoicing. So they searched for
an individual who was always joyous, for he was already at
the chief purpose and would be fit to be a king over them.
They went to search and saw a Gentile walking along in a foul
shirt and carrying a flask of whiskey. Many Gentiles followed
him. The Gentile was very joyous since he was very drunk.
They noticed that the Gentile was very joyous without a care
in the world and he pleased them greatly for he had reached
his final purpose which was joy. They accepted the Gentile as
king over them and he surely led them along the right path.
They chose a land that would be fit for this virtue, where
there are vineyards so they could make wine and from the pits
of the grapes they would make brandy. Nothing should go to
waste from the grapes for the chief purpose was drinking and
drunkenness and continuous joy. Even though there was no
reason for their joy, their chief purpose was still to be happy
and they chose a land that would be fit for this virtue and
settled there.

"Another faction said that the chief purpose was wisdom.
They searched for a wise man, and they made him king over
them. They searched for a land that would be fit for wisdom
and settled there.

"Another faction said that the chief purpose was that one
should pamper oneself by eating and drinking thus enlarging
the limbs. They looked for a full-limbed individual, one with

large limbs who also pampered himself to enlarge them. Since he had such large limbs he had a greater share in the world because he took up more space. This person was closer to the chief person because of this enlargement of limbs. That is why such a person would be fit to be king. They went out and found a long, eel-like man and he pleased them. He was full-limbed and, therefore, at the chief purpose, so they chose him for their king. They searched for a land that would be fit for this virtue and they went and settled there.

"Another faction said that none of these things had the chief purpose, but that the only true purpose was to be engaged in prayer to the Almighty, to be humble and modest. They searched for a *Baal Tefilla* and they made him king over them. (It is self-evident that all the previously mentioned factions were mistaken and in great confusion. Only the last faction found the real truth. It is they who are blessed!)"

(All this was told by one of the warriors to the *Baal Tefilla* and he added that the warriors who later joined the Warrior stemmed from the faction of full-limbs who selected as king a man of full limbs.)

"And the day came when an army of them marched forth with many wagons behind them to carry their food and water and the like. The whole world surely feared these full-limbed men greatly for they were huge and valiant. Everyone whom they met stepped aside before them. As the army was marching they met a great warrior. (And he was the Warrior who now marches with them.) This Warrior did not step aside before them. He plunged into the army and scattered them (with his hands) far and wide. The men of the army were afraid of him. He also went among the wagons which followed the army and ate everything there. His mighty valor was an extraordinary marvel to the army for he had no fear of them and plunged into their ranks and ate up everything that was on the wagons. They immediately capitulated and said, 'Long live the King!' For they knew that a Warrior like this surely deserved to be king, according to their opinion that the chief purpose was one who has full limbs. And the reigning king was prepared to abdicate his kingdom, since such a full-limbed warrior had been found who especially deserved the kingdom. And so it was. The Warrior who came out to confront them was accepted to rule over this faction. And this is the Warrior whom we march with today to conquer the world. And the Warrior says that he really means something else by marching out to conquer the world. For he does not mean to become a conqueror, with the world under his rule, but he means something else."

All this was told by one of the warriors to the *Baal Tefilla* who had asked him how he joined the Warrior. So he told him all this.

The *Baal Tefilla* asked him, "What are the heroic deeds of the Warrior who is your king today?" He answered: "When a certain country refused to capitulate to him, the Warrior took out his sword. And this sword has three powers. When the sword is raised, all the army officers flee, etc." (Here he retold the story of the three powers.) When the *Baal Tefilla* heard this, he understood this must surely be the Warrior of the King. The *Baal Tefilla* asked if it would be possible to meet the Warrior who was their king. They replied that they would inform the Warrior and ask him if he would grant permission. They asked him and he granted permission to enter. When he entered the Warrior's presence, they recognized each other, and they were greatly elated that at last they were privileged to meet. They laughed and cried, for they recalled the King and his court, and they cried out. Because of this there were rejoicing and weeping. The *Baal Tefilla* and the Warrior began to chat, and talked about how they got to this place.

The Warrior told the *Baal Tefilla* that during the tempest they were all dispersed far and wide and when he returned from where he had gone to renew his strength, he found no King and no court. He then went everywhere, and passed by all of them. He understood that he was at the place where they all were, that the King must surely be there, only he did not know how to search for him or find him. Likewise, he passed by another place and understood that the Queen must be there, only he did not know how to search for or find her. And so he passed by all the King's court. "Only you have I not passed by," said the Warrior to the *Baal Tefilla*.

The *Baal Tefilla* answered: "I have passed by all the places where they were and also by your place. At one place I saw the King's crown, so I understood that the King must surely be there, but I could not seek and find him. And so I traveled on, and I passed a sea of blood. I understood that the sea surely came from the Queen's tears, because she was crying over everything, so I understood that the Queen must surely be here. Only I could not seek or find her. Similarly, I passed by a sea of milk, and I understood that the sea came from the Princess who lost her child and squeezed the surplus of milk from her breast and created a sea of milk. Surely the Princess must be there, only I could not search and find her. So I walked further and saw the golden hairs of the child lying there. I did not take any of them. I knew that this must be the child, only it was impossible for me to search and find him.

"So I walked further until I came to the sea of wine. I knew that the sea came from the words of the Orator who stands and consoles the King and the Queen. Afterwards he turns to the Princess and consoles her. From those words came the sea of wine, as it is written: 'And your palate is like good wine.' Only I could not find him. So I walked along further. I saw a stone inscribed with a picture of the Hand with its lines. I understood that the Wise Man of the King must be there and he carved the picture of the Hand on the stone. But it was impossible to find him, so I walked further. I saw displayed on the mountain the Golden Tables and the Credenza with other treasures belonging to the King. I understood that this must be the Keeper of the treasures of the King only it was impossible for me to find him."

All this the *Baal Tefilla* told the Warrior. The Warrior answered: "I also passed by all these places and I gathered some of the child's golden hairs and I took seven hairs of different shades and they are very dear to me. I sat somewhere and sustained myself with whatever was possible, with grass and other things until there was nothing to sustain me. So I walked wherever my feet would carry me. When I left that place, I forgot to take my bow with me."

The *Baal Tefilla* answered: "I saw the bow and I knew it was surely yours, only I couldn't find you." The Warrior continued to tell the *Baal Tefilla*: "After I left this place I walked along and met the army. I went among them for I was very hungry and I wanted to eat. As soon as I arrived, they accepted me as their king. Today I am going to conquer the world. And my intention is: I hope to be able to find the King and his court."

The *Baal Tefilla* asked the Warrior: "What should be done with those people who had fallen so deeply into the lust for money that they reached the enormous folly: Those with much money are Gods, etc.?" The Warrior answered the *Baal Tefilla* that he had heard from the King that people could be extricated from all the lusts they fall into, but he who fell into the lust of money could in no way be extricated from it. He said, "You will have no effect on them, for it is impossible to extricate them from this at all." Nevertheless, he also heard from the King that through the power of the sword from which he derived his strength one could extricate them from the lust for money into which they have fallen.

The Warrior and the *Baal Tefilla* sat together for a long time. And on the matter for which the people of that country asked the *Baal Tefilla* to meet with the Warrior on their behalf, they extended the time. The *Baal Tefilla* persuaded the Warrior to give them a deadline (until which he would not harm them), and he granted them this extension. And the *Baal Tefilla* and the Warrior established signals so that they could communicate with each other. Afterwards the *Baal Tefilla* departed on his way.

As the *Baal Tefilla* went along, he saw people walking along praying to God, blessed be He, and carrying prayerbooks. He was afraid of them and they were afraid of him. He stopped in order to pray and so did they. Then he asked them, "Who are you?" They answered him, "During the tempest, when the world was divided into many factions, some chose one and some another. At that time we chose that the chief purpose is to be engaged with prayer all the time to the Holy One. We searched and found a *Baal Tefilla*, and we made him king." When the *Baal Tefilla* heard this, he was extremely pleased because this was his desire. He began to speak with them and showed them his order of prayers and his books and other practices of prayer. When they heard him they were astonished and became aware of the stature of the *Baal Tefilla*. They immediately made him ruler over them. Their own king surrendered the kingdom to him for they realized he was indeed a man of exceptional stature. The *Baal Tefilla* studied with them and opened their eyes and showed them how to pray and transformed them into absolute *zadikim*. Previously, they had also been *zadikim* because they engaged only in prayer, but now the *Baal Tefilla* opened their eyes until they became venerable *zadikim*. The *Baal Tefilla* sent a letter to the Warrior informing him that he was fortunate in finding such people, and that he had become king over them.

6

And the people of the Country of Money were engaged in their own affairs and in their worship. The time assigned by the Warrior was rapidly approaching and they were frightened. They performed their worship and sacrificed victims and incense and were engaged in their prayers to their Gods. They seized a little Beast (a person who had little money) and sacrificed him to their Gods. They agreed that they must follow the first suggestion, to send emissaries to the country of exceptional wealth (where, according to their belief, everybody must be Gods). Those people would certainly help them, because they were Gods.

They sent emissaries to that country. As the emissaries were traveling along, they lost their way, and found someone walking along with a cane which was worth more than all their Gods. The cane was studded with precious diamonds and this was more valuable than all the wealth of their Gods. If all the wealth of their Gods were combined, including even the wealth of the country to which they were traveling, this cane would be more valuable than all their wealth. And this person was also wearing a hat inset with diamonds and it was also worth a huge sum. The emissaries immediately kneeled down before him and prostrated themselves. According to their foolish opinion this man was the God of their Gods for he had such tremendous wealth. (The man they met was the Keeper of the King's treasures.)

The man told them: "Do you consider this a marvel? Come with me and I will show you wealth." He led them to the hill where the King's treasure was arrayed and he showed them that treasure. As soon as they saw the treasure, they fell on their knees and prostrated themselves, for this man must surely be the God of all Gods.

However they made no sacrifices (according to their opinion, this man was a God and they would surely have sacrificed themselves to him) because the emissaries were ordered not to make sacrifices along the way, for they feared that if they wanted to make sacrifices along the way, not one of them would remain. For if one might find a treasure along the way, or if one of them went to the toilet and found a treasure there, he would begin to sacrifice himself and no one would remain among them.

The emissaries came to the conclusion: "Why should we go to the country of those Gods, that is, to the country where everyone who is very wealthy is considered a God? This person would be better able to help them, for he is a God over them all (according to their mad opinion) since he has an exceptionally great amount of riches, many times more than all of them." Because of this, they asked this man to accompany them to their country. He was agreeable and followed them, and came to their country. The people held a great celebration because they had received such a God for they were assured that through him they would certainly be saved for he was a God with such great wealth.

The man who was Keeper of the King's treasures and had been accepted as a God decreed that before there could be proper order in the land, all sacrifices should be abolished. (For the Keeper was truly a great *zadik*, since he was one of the King's people who were all great *zadikim* and he surely detested the evil customs and the folly of this land. Only he could not bring them back from their evil ways. For the time being, he decreed that at least no sacrifices be made.)

The people began to question him regarding the Warrior who threatened them. The Keeper told them perhaps it was the Warrior he knew. The Keeper arose and went to meet the Warrior. He requested the guards around the Warrior whether it would be possible to have an audience with him. They answered they would announce him. They announced him and he granted permission. The Keeper went in to meet the Warrior. They recognized each other and there was great joy and weeping.

The Warrior spoke with the Keeper: "Know that the pious *Baal Tefilla* is also here and I have already seen him. He has already become a king." The Keeper told the Warrior how he had passed by the place of the King and the court. Only by

those two he did not pass, that is, by the *Baal Tefilla* and the
Warrior. The Keeper chatted with the Warrior about the
country where everyone was so misled and confused that they
fell into great folly. The Warrior gave the Keeper the same
answer he gave the *Baal Tefilla*, that he had heard from the
King that whoever succumbs to the lust for money can in no
way return and escape it, except through the way of the
sword from which the Warrior derived his power. They extended the time some more, that is the Keeper pleaded with
the Warrior to extend the time for the people. The Warrior
agreed to grant them a longer span of time. Then they established signals (the Keeper and the Warrior).

The Keeper left the Warrior and returned to the Country
of Money. (The Keeper surely rebuked them severely for
their evil way through which they had strayed because of
their lust for money. Only it was impossible for him to save
them for they were already deeply rooted in it. And yet, since
the *Baal Tefilla* and the Keeper rebuked them mightily, they
were a bit confused. They would say, "By all means, lead us
out of our folly," even though they still clung strongly to their
opinion and did not wish to return from their folly. Still they
said to those who rebuked them, "By all means, if it is truly so
that we are misled, lead us out of our folly.")

The Keeper advised the people that he knew the power
of the Warrior, from which he derived his courage. He told
them the story of the sword, from which the Warrior derived
his courage. "Let's go, I and you, to the place of the sword,
and thus you will obtain courage," The Keeper's intention
was that when they got to the place of the sword, they could
be delivered from their folly (for through the path to the
sword they could eradicate the lust for money). They accepted his suggestion, and sent off with the Keeper their
chiefs whom they considered Gods. (And they were, of
course, adorned with gold and silver ornaments because that
was of prime importance to them.)

They set out together. The Keeper informed the Warrior

that he was going to seek the place of the sword so he might be worthy to find the King and all his court. The Warrior announced: "I, too, will go with you." The Warrior disguised himself so that the people accompanying the Keeper would not recognize that he was the Warrior, and thus he went along with the Keeper. The two of them decided to inform the *Baal Tefilla* of their plans. Thus they informed him and he said he wished to go along with them. So the *Baal Tefilla* joined them. However, before leaving, the *Baal Tefilla* ordered his people to pray for them that God should prosper their way, and make them worthy of finding the King and his court. This was the *Baal Tefilla*'s constant prayer. He had constantly ordered his people they should pray and had composed prayers for them. And now, because he wanted to accompany the Keeper and the Warrior so that together they could seek the King and his court, he urged them even more to pray toward this end constantly, so that they should be worthy to find them.

When the *Baal Tefilla* joined the Keeper and the Warrior, there was obviously great rejoicing, both gladness and crying. The three of them went along together, that is, the Keeper, the Warrior, and the *Baal Tefilla*. The Gods, i.e., the officials of the country, accompanied them. They went off and came to a country surrounded by guards. They asked the guards about the affairs of the state and "Who is your king?"

The guards answered: "During the tempest, when the world was dispersed into many factions, the people of this land chose the main principle of wisdom, and chose a wise man to be king. It didn't take long before they found a marvelously wise man who was the wisest of all wise men. The king relinquished the kingdom to him and the wise man was accepted as their king for their ideal was wisdom. The three (the Keeper, the Warrior, and the *Baal Tefilla*) said: "Evidently this must be our Wise Man, the Wise Man of the King's court."

They asked if it would be possible to have an audience

with him. They (the guards) answered that they must announce them. They announced and he ordered them in. When they entered the presence of the Wise Man who had become king over this land, they recognized each other, for this Wise Man was really the King's Wise Man. There truly was great rejoicing, gladness, and sadness, for they cried because they still could not find the King and the others.

They asked the Wise Man whether he knew the whereabouts of the King's Hand. He replied that he had the Hand; however, since they were all dispersed by the evil tempest and the King disappeared, he had refused to look upon the Hand, for it belonged only to the King. But he carved a facsimile of the Hand on a rock so it could be of some help to him in his affairs. He never looked at the Hand itself. They chatted with the Wise Man about how he had come there. He told them that after the tempest he had wandered wherever his feet took him. (Wherever he went he passed by everyone except those three, i.e., the places of the *Baal Tefilla*, the Warrior, and the Keeper.) Finally, he was discovered by the people of the country and accepted as king. For the while, he had to lead them according to their custom, their ideas of wisdom, until he would be able, at a later date, to return them to the truth.

They told the Wise Man about the country where everyone was so misled and confused in the worship of money. And they said: "If only we were not separated and dispersed anymore! If only for the sake of this land, to set it right and return it to the truth, it would have been enough for us! For they have become so stupid and misled. Indeed all the factions are misled and confused, and all need to be returned from their folly and restored to the true chief purpose. For even the faction that chose wisdom as its highest purpose has not reached the true chief purpose. They also needed to be extricated from it for they clung to worldly wisdom and heresies. However, it is easier to turn one from his follies to the truth than to return those who are so misled in the idolatrous worship of money. They are so deeply sunk in this that it is almost impossible to extricate them from it, etc."

And so the Wise Man also agreed to accompany them. All four of them went along and those foolish Gods went, too. They came to a country. Here, too, they asked the guards what type of country this was and who their king was. They were answered that during the tempest the people of the land chose as their chief purpose oratory. They accepted an orator as their king. Later on, they discovered a very fine orator and an exceptional speaker. They accepted him as their king since the existing king surrendered the throne to him because of his very fine language. Since he was a master of language, they surmised that he must be the King's Orator. They inquired if it were possible for them to have an audience with him. The guards told them that they must announce them. They announced them and the king ordered them to enter. So they entered the presence of the king and he was the King's Orator. They recognized each other with great joy and great crying. The Orator accompanied them and they searched further — perhaps they might find the others, especially the King. And they attributed all this to the merit of their worthy *Baal Tefilla* who was always praying for this and through his prayers they always were privileged to find their friends: for they realized that God was prospering their way each time to find friends. They went further — perhaps they would be fortunate to find the others.

They walked along and came to a country and there, too, they asked about the affairs of state and who their king was. They answered that they were of the faction that chose as the chief purpose drunkenness and mirth. They accepted to be king over them a drunk who was always mirthful. Later on they found a man sitting in a sea of wine. And he pleased them more because he was surely an exceptional drunk since he sits in a sea of wine and they took him for their king. And they sought to have an audience with him, too, and they were announced. They entered the presence of the king and it was the Loyal Friend of the King and he was sitting in the sea of wine which had been formed from the consoling words of the Orator. (The people of the land thought that he is a great drunk because he sat in a sea of wine and thus made him king.) As soon as they entered, they recognized each other and there was great happiness and crying among them, too. And the Loyal Friend went along with them, too.

They went along further and came to a land. They asked the guards: "Who is your king?" They answered that their king was the great beauty since she brings people to the chief purpose, for the chief purpose was the populating of the world. Previously, a certain beautiful woman was their queen and after a while they found a woman who was marvelously beautiful and accepted her as queen. They understood that this must surely be the Princess and they sought to have an audience with her, and were announced. They entered the queen's presence and they recognized that she was the Princess. And the joy was unimaginable. They asked her how she came there and she told them when the tempest came and snatched her dear child from his crib, she ran after the child in the moment of panic but did not find it. And the milk spurted out and became a sea of milk. Later on, the people of this country found her and made her king. And there was great joy and they cried bitterly over the dear child who was lost and over her father and mother about whom she knew nothing. Now the country had a king, too, because the husband of this queen was now here. The Warrior was her husband. So the country had a king.

The Princess asked the *Baal Tefilla* to go among her people and cleanse them somewhat of their obscene vice. Since in their opinion the final goal was beauty, they had certainly become extremely obscene in their lust. Therefore, she asked the *Baal Tefilla* to go for a while and cleanse them a bit so that they should not be so debased through this obscenity. For not only was this a lust, but it had also become for them like a faith that this was the chief purpose. (For all the factions, the evil quality which they had chosen as the chief purpose became like a complete faith.) She therefore asked the *Baal Tefilla* to go for a while and cleanse them a bit.

Afterwards they all went to seek the others, especially the King, and they came to a country. They asked there, too, "Who is your king?" They answered that their king was a one-year-old child, because they were of the faction which chose him who had an abundance of food and did not feed on food of other people. He was worthy of being king. For a while they accepted a rich man as king. Afterward they found someone sitting in a sea of milk and he pleased them greatly because this man fed on milk all his life and did not feed on the foods other people eat. Therefore, they accepted him as king. And so he was called a one-year-old child because he fed upon milk like a one-year-old.

And they reasoned that this must be *the* Child and they sought to have an audience. They were announced and entered his presence. They recognized each other, for he also recognized them even though he had been a small child when he was snatched away from them. But since he was fully wise at birth (because he had been born with great wisdom) he therefore recognized them and they surely recognized him. And so there was great rejoicing, but they still cried since they did not know the whereabouts of the King and the Queen.

And they asked him (the Child), "How did you get here?" And he told them that when the tempest snatched him it carried him somewhere, and he stayed there and sustained himself with what he found there, until he came to the sea of milk. He understood that the sea must surely have come from his mother's milk because the milk surely pressed her, and the sea came from it. And he dwelled by the sea of milk and was fed by it until the people came and took him for their king.

Then they went along further and came to a country and asked, "Who is your king?" They answered that they had chosen murder for their chief purpose. And they accepted a murderer as their king. Afterwards they found a certain woman sitting in a sea of blood, and took her for their king since she is surely a great murderer because she sits in a sea of blood. And they also asked to have an audience with her. They were announced and entered her presence and this was the Queen who always cried and the sea of blood was from her tears. And they recognized each other and there was surely great rejoicing, but they still cried because they still did not know the whereabouts of the King.

They went along further and they came to a country and they asked, "Who is your king?" They answered that they chose as king an honored man because among them the chief purpose is honor. After that they found sitting in a field an old man with a crown on his head. And he pleased them greatly, because he was a man of great honor since he sat in a field wearing a crown. So they accepted him as king. And the others guessed that he is surely *the* King (that is, he is their King). They asked if it were possible to have an audience with him. They were announced and entered his presence and they recognized that this was the King himself. And the celebration that took place there is unimaginable.

And the foolish Gods (that is, the great rich men of the Land of Money who were Gods in their land) went with them and did not know at all why they were so joyous.

7

Now the entire holy community had gathered together and they sent the *Baal Tefilla* to those countries (that is, the countries of those factions which chose evil for their purpose) to set them right and to cleanse them from their folly—each land from its specific folly and error, for they were all misled.

And now the *Baal Tefilla* surely had the power to go to them and bring them back to the right way because he took his power and authorization from the kings of all the countries for all the kings were here. (Because this holy community of the King which returned and gathered were the kings of all the lands of those factions.) And the *Baal Tefilla* went with their power to cleanse them and return them in repentance.

And the Warrior spoke with the King about the people who fell into the idolatry of money. He said to the King, "I have heard from you that by means of the path I have to the sword, one can extricate those who have sunk into the lust for money." And the King answered, "Yes, that is so." And the King informed the Warrior that from this path which goes up to the sword is a side path on which one reaches a fiery mountain. On top of the mountain crouches a lion and when the lion has to eat, he falls upon the flocks and takes sheep and cattle and eats them. The shepherds are aware of this and guard their flocks against him, but the lion pays no attention to this. When he wants to eat, he attacks the flocks. The shepherds beat him and storm against him, but the lion does not hear this at all. He takes sheep and cattle for himself. And he roars, and eats them. And the fiery mountain cannot be seen at all.

And from the main path there is another side path on which one reaches a place called: the Kitchen. In this Kitchen are found all types of food, but no fire. The foods are cooked by means of the fiery mountain which is very far away. And troughs and runnels go from the mountain of fire to the Kitchen. And that is how all the foods are cooked. And this Kitchen is not visible, either. However there is a sign: Birds are perched on top of the Kitchen and that is how one knows that the Kitchen is there. The birds fan their wings, thus kindling and extinguishing the fire. That is, by means of the fanning, the birds can either kindle and blow on the fire, or extinguish the fire so that it will not flame too strongly. They blow upon the fire only as much as is necessary for each type of food, since each type requires a different heat.

All this the King told the Warrior. "Therefore, lead them (that is, those people of the Land of Money where they are Gods) first against the wind so that the smell of the foods should reach them. Afterwards, when you give them some of these foods to eat, they will cast away the lust for money."

And this was what the Warrior did. He took the emissaries who came there with the Keeper of the treasures and who, upon leaving their country, were given authority to do whatever had to be done. Their countrymen had to agree to whatever they did and they could not change it.

The Warrior took them and led them along that path and brought them to the Kitchen where all the foods are found. First he led them against the wind and the odor of the foods reached them and they began to implore him that he give them some of these good foods. Afterwards he led them before the wind and they started to scream that there was a great stench. The Warrior did this again. He brought them upwind and they implored him to give them some of the food. Then he led them downwind again and they began screaming there was a great stench. The Warrior said to them, "Can't you see that there is nothing here that should stink? It must be you yourselves who stink, for there is nothing here that should stink."

Afterwards he gave them food to eat. No sooner had they eaten from the foods than they threw away their money. Each one dug a pit and buried himself in it out of great shame, because they felt that their money stank exactly like excrement, for they had tasted of the food. They tore at their faces and buried themselves and could not lift up their heads at all. Each was ashamed of the other. (Such was the virtue of these foods: He who ate of these foods detested money.) For in this place money was the greatest of all disgraces and he who wished to insult another would say to him, "You have money." For money was a very great disgrace and the more money one had, the more he was ashamed of it. And that is why they buried themselves, out of great disgrace. And no one could lift up his head even to look at another, especially before the Warrior. And he who found in his possession a *gulden* or a *groschen* would get rid of it immediately and throw it far away from him.

Afterwards, the Warrior came to them and took them out from the pits they had dug and said to them, "Come with me. You no longer have need to fear the Warrior. I am the Warrior." They asked the Warrior to give them some of the food so that they could bring it back to their country. They themselves would surely detest money, but they wished that the entire country would abandon this lust for money. He gave them some of the food and they carried it to their land. And as soon as they gave their countrymen some of the food, they began to throw away their money and buried themselves in the earth out of shame. And the great rich men and Gods were even more ashamed. The ordinary people whom they used to call Beasts and Birds were ashamed at having been so insignificant in their own eyes because they had no money. For now they knew that it is just the opposite: Money was the real disgrace. Because the foods had in them a special quality that whoever ate of them detested money, because he felt that the stench of money was exactly like the stench of excrement. And so they threw away their money, gold and silver. And afterwards they sent the *Baal Tefilla* there and he gave them prayers of repentance and he cleansed them. And the King became ruler of the whole world, and the whole world returned to God and all engaged only Torah, prayer, repentance, and good deeds. Amen. May it be His will.

XIII. THE SEVEN BEGGARS

"The Seven Beggars," Nahman's last and most-renowned tale, commences with a narrative representative of the cosmic catalysm attending creation according to Lurianic myth. In this tale, most of our attention is focused upon the celebration attending the process of tikkun, here the marriage of a young couple who had been lost during the mass flight following the cosmic cataclysm.

During the wedding banquet, six of the seven beggars whom the young children had met in the forest arrive to present them with wedding gifts and regale them with bizarre, circuitous tales, each of which purports to explain that the beggar's apparent deformity, for example, blindness, is actually a virtue somehow connected with the gift presented. In general, the six beggars who appear to present gifts are similar in one respect: They demonstrate, as delightful raconteurs, that the world of reality we live in is really an illusion.

The seventh beggar, the legless one, never appears, leading us to speculate that Nahman intended an abrupt, abbreviated cloture as in "The Loss of the Princess." Following the principle of inversion embedded in the story, the legless beggar was really a consummate dancer and since dance was so central to Bratslav religious praxis, his appearance would have been associated with the joy of prayerful ecstasy, the completion of the wedding feast, or the concept of the Sabbath —all symbols of the messianic era which we have not yet earned.

I will tell you how our people were once joyous.

1

Once there was a king who had an only son. The king wanted to transfer the royal power to his son during his own lifetime. So he gave a grand ball. Now whenever the king gave a ball, it was surely a very joyous affair. But when he transferred the royal power to his son during his own lifetime, there was surely a great celebration. And at the ball were all the ministers, all the dukes, and all the nobles. And they were all very joyous at the ball. And the people, too, were greatly pleased that the king handed his royal power over to his son during his lifetime, because this was a great honor for the king, and indeed there was a great celebration. There were all sorts of things for the celebration—musical bands and comedians and the like—all things used for a celebration were present at the ball.

And when everybody had become very joyous, the king arose and said to his son: "Since I am a star-gazer, and I foresee that you, too, will at some time abdicate the royal power, see to it that you have no sadness when you abdicate. Only be joyous, for when you are joyous, I shall be joyous, too. Even if you are sad, I shall be joyous that you are no longer king, because you do not deserve to be king if you are the kind of person who cannot always maintain his joy even

255

when he abdicates the royal power. Only when you are joyous, shall I be exceedingly joyous."

And the prince assumed the royal power vigorously. He created ministers, and dukes, and officials, and an army. The prince was a wise man, he loved wisdom dearly, and gathered around him many wise men. Whosoever came to him with some sort of wisdom was highly esteemed by him. He gave them great respect and wealth for their wisdom. He gave each one whatever he desired. If one desired money, he gave him money. If one desired honor, he gave him honor. Everything for wisdom. Since wisdom was so esteemed, everyone adopted wisdom and the whole kingdom engaged in the practice of wisdom. One practiced wisdom because he desired money, and another, because he desired honor and esteem. And because they all engaged in wisdom only, people in that country forgot military tactics. They were all engaged only in wisdom until the least wise man in this country would be considered the wisest man in another country, and the truly wise in this country were marvelously wise.

Because of this wisdom, the wise men of the land fell into heresy and they drew the prince into their heresy. But the common people did not fall into heresy since there was a great depth in the wise men's wisdom which escaped the common people and they were not harmed. Only the wise men and the prince became heretics. And since the prince had goodness in him because he had been born with goodness and had good qualities, he always remembered: "Where am I in the world and what am I doing?" And he would groan deeply and remember: "What is this? I should be carried away by such things? What's happening to me? Where am I in the world?" Yet, no sooner had he begun to use his reason than the heretical ideas were strengthened within him. And so it happened several times. He would remember where he was in the world and what he was doing and would groan and sigh, but suddenly he would again use his reason and his heretical tendencies would be strengthened as before.

2

And it came to pass that there was a mass flight from a certain country and everyone fled. And as they fled, they passed through a forest, and lost two children there, a male and a female. One family lost a male, and another lost a female. And they were still little children, four or five years old. The children had nothing to eat. They screamed and they cried because they had nothing to eat.

Meanwhile, there came a beggar who was going along with sacks in which he carried bread. The children began to badger him and cling to him. He gave them bread and they ate. He asked them: "Where do you come from?" They answered: "We don't know," because they were little children. He started to leave them, but they asked him to take them along with him. He said to them: "I do not want you to go along with me." Meanwhile they looked and noticed that the beggar was blind. And this was to them a marvel: "If he is blind, how does he know where to go?" (It was also a marvel that the children raised this question, because they were little children. But since they were clever children, this was a marvel to them.) And this blind beggar blessed them: "May you be as I am. May you be as old as I am." He left them more bread and went away.

The children understood that The Blessed One was watching over them and sent them a blind beggar to give them food. After a while the bread ran out and again they began to scream for food. Then night came, and they slept there. In the morning, they still had nothing to eat. They screamed and cried. In the meanwhile another beggar appeared who was deaf. They began to speak to him. He pointed with his hands and said to them: "I don't hear a thing." And this beggar also gave them bread and began to leave them. Again they wanted him to take them with him. He didn't want to, but he, too, blessed them: "You should be like I am." And he also left bread and went off. Then this bread also ran out, and again they began to scream.

Again a beggar appeared who stuttered. They started speaking with him, but he stuttered his words, so they couldn't understand what he said. He knew what they were saying but they didn't know what he was saying because he stuttered. The beggar also gave them bread and left them as before. He also blessed them, that they should be as he was, and he left.

After a while another beggar came, who had a twisted neck. The same thing happened as before. Then came a beggar who was a hunchback. Then a beggar without hands came. Then came a beggar without feet. Each one of them gave bread and blessed them, that they should be as he was, exactly as the previous beggars.

Then the bread ran out again. They started walking toward an inhabited place until they reached a path. And they walked along the path until they came to a village. The children went into a house. People pitied them and gave them bread. They went into another house and there they were also given bread. And so they went from door to door. They saw that it was good that people gave them bread. The children agreed that they would always be together. They made themselves large sacks and went from door to door and they used to go to all celebrations, to circumcisions and to weddings. They roamed through all kinds of towns and went from door to door. They also went to fairs and sat among the beggars on the benches with the beggar's plates, until the children became widely known among all the beggars, since everyone recognized them and knew them as the children who had been lost in the forest.

Once there was a large fair someplace in a large city. All the beggars went there and the children went there too. The beggars hit upon the idea to arrange a wedding match between the children. Immediately, as soon as a few of the beggars began to discuss the issue, it pleased them all and they arranged the match. Only how does one make a wedding for them? They decided that on a certain day, when there would be a feast for the king's birthday, all the beggars would gather there, and from the meat and bread which they begged there, they would make a wedding.

And so it was. All the beggars went to the birthday party and begged for bread and meat, and they also gleaned all the leftovers, meat and egg bread. And they went and dug a huge pit which could hold one hundred people, and they covered it with beams and earth and rubbish and they all went in, and there they made the wedding for the children. They raised the wedding canopy and were very, very joyous. The bride and groom were also very joyous. The bride and groom recalled the favors that The Blessed One had bestowed upon them when they were in the forest and they cried and longed: "How do we find the first beggar, the blind beggar, who brought us bread in the forest?"

3

Just as they were longing for the blind beggar, he called out: "I am here, I have come to be with you on your wedding day. I present you with a wedding gift: You should be as old as I. Previously, I offered you my blessing but today I bestow this upon you outright as a wedding gift: You should be as old as I am. Do you think that I am blind? Not at all. It is just that the entire world does not amount to an eye's wink (moment) for me." (He looked like a blind man because he did not look at the world at all, since the entire world did not amount to an eye's wink for him. Therefore seeing and looking at this world did not pertain to him.) "For I am very old and yet I am still young. I haven't even begun to live, yet I am very old. Not only do I say so, but I have an affidavit to that effect from the large eagle and I will tell you a tale:

"Once, people set sail upon the seas in many ships. A tempest arose and smashed the ships, but the people were saved. The people came to a tower. They climbed the tower and found all manner of food and drink and clothes and all the essentials. All the good things and pleasures of the world were there. They called upon each one to recite an old tale, one he remembered from his earliest recollection, that is, what he remembered from the inception of his memory.

"The old and the young were there. They honored the oldest among them by allowing him to be the first to recount. The oldest declared: 'What can I tell you? I can still remember when they cut the apple from the branch.' No one understood what he said, but there were wise men there who said: 'Surely that is a very old tale.'

"They invited the next to tell a tale. The second, who was not as old as the first, declared while asking: 'Is that such an old tale? I remember that tale, too, but I even remember when the lamp burned.' They declared: 'This tale is even older than the first tale.' They wondered how the younger could recall a tale that was older.

"They invited the third old man to tell a tale. He was younger still and declared: 'I even recall the forming of the fruit, that is, when the first fruit began to form.' They declared: 'This is an older tale still.'

"The fourth old man, younger yet, declared, 'I even remember when they brought the seed for the planting of the fruit.'

"The fifth, younger yet, declared: 'I can even remember the wise men who invented the seed.'

"The sixth one, younger yet, declared: 'I remember the

taste of the fruit before the taste entered the fruit.'

"The seventh one declared: 'I even remember the smell of the fruit before it entered the fruit.'

"The eighth one declared: 'I even remember the appearance of the fruit before it was on the fruit.'

"And I (the blind beggar) was at that time only a child. I was also there and declared: 'I remember all of these tales and I remember nothingness.' They all declared: 'That is a very much older tale, older than all the others.' It was a great marvel for them that the child remembered more than all of them.

"In the meanwhile a large eagle arrived and he knocked on the tower and said to them: 'Stop being paupers. Return to your treasures. Use your treasures.' And he told them to leave the tower in the order of their age, the oldest leaving first. He took them all out of the tower. He first took out the child, since truthfully he was the oldest of all. And so he took out the youngest ones first, and the oldest he took out last. For the younger one was older, and the oldest among them was the youngest of them all.

"And the great eagle declared to them as follows:

" 'I will interpret all the tales that were told. He who told that he remembered how the apple was cut from the branch implied that he still remembers when they cut his umbilical cord, that is what occurred as soon as he was born, when they cut his umbilical cord. This, too, he still remembers.

" 'And the second who said that he still remembers when the lamp burned implies that he still remembers when he was an embryo because that is the time when a candle burns over the head. (Thus it is written in the Gemara, that when a child is in the mother's womb a lamp burns over his head.)

" 'And he who said he still remembers when the fruit began to form, still remembers when his body began to form, that is, when the child was created.

" 'And he who still remembers when they brought the seed to plant the fruit denotes that he remembers how the semen was drawn out during copulation.

" 'And he who still remembers the wise man who invented the seed implies that he still remembers when the semen was still in the brain.

" 'And he who remembers the taste, that is the lower spirit; and the smells, that is the soul; and the appearance, that is the higher spirit. And the child who said he remembers nothingness, he is greater than all since he still remembers what existed before the lower spirit, the soul, and the higher spirit and so he said that he still remembers when there was nothing, and what happened there. He is higher than all.'

"And the great eagle said to them: 'Return to your ships. Those are your bodies which were broken. They will be rebuilt. Now, return to them.' And he blessed them.

"And to me (the blind beggar who was a child at that time and who is telling these stories) the great eagle said: 'You come with me, because you are just like me in that you are extremely old and yet very young. And you have not yet even begun to live, though you are very old. And I am the same since I am extremely old and still young.'

"Accordingly, I have an affidavit from the great eagle that I have lived a long life. And now I give you my long life as a wedding gift."

And there was a great happiness and delight.

4

On the second day of the seven feast days, the bride and groom recalled the second beggar, the deaf one, who nourished them and gave them bread. And they cried and longed for him: "How do we bring the deaf beggar here, the one who nourished us?"

Meanwhile, as they were longing for him, he arrived and

said: "I am here." And he embraced and kissed them saying: "Today, I present you with a gift that you shall be like me, that you should live as good a life as I. Previously I offered you this blessing, today I bestow my good life upon you outright as your wedding gift. And you think I am deaf? I am not deaf at all. It is only that the whole world is not worth my hearing its deficiencies. All sounds in the world are due to its deficiencies since people cry out about what they are lacking, about what they haven't got. Even all the world's celebrations are about deficiencies since one rejoices over the deficiencies which have been filled. As for me, the whole world is not worth my listening to its deficiencies, because I live a good life that has no deficiencies. And I have an affidavit from the Country of Riches that I live the good life." His good life was that he ate bread and drank water.

And he told them:

"There is a country where there are great riches and they have many treasures. One day these wealthy men gathered to boast how they live the good life, and each one told of his style of good living. And I declared to them: 'I live a good life which is better than your good life, and here's the proof. If you are living such a good life, let me see if you can save a certain country. For there is a land where they had a garden, and in this garden there were fruits that had all the flavors in the world. And all the odors in the world were also there, all the forms, all the colors, and all the blossoms in the world were all there in that garden. Over the garden there was a gardener and the people of that land lived a good life because of this garden. But then the gardener disappeared, and, of course, everything in the garden withered and died since the gardener was no longer there. However, they were still able to live off the aftergrowth of the garden.

" 'But a cruel king arose in the country, and since he was unable to do anything to them personally, he spoiled the good life of the country which they had derived from the garden.

He did not spoil the garden itself, but left three groups of servants in the land and ordered them to do his bidding. And through their actions they spoiled the people's sense of taste. Consequently, anyone who wished to taste anything sensed only the taste of the carrion. And likewise they spoiled their sense of smell, so that all the odors smelt of galbanum. Likewise they spoiled their sense of vision, so that they dimmed their eyes as if there were heavy clouds. What they did there was as the cruel king had ordered.

" 'Now, if you live the good life, help that country. And I say to you,' so said the deaf beggar, 'that if you do not help them, their deficiencies will harm you.'

"These rich men started out for that country, and I also went along with them. Even along the way each one lived his good life because they had great treasures. As they approached that country their sense of taste and their other senses, too, began to spoil. And they themselves felt that their senses were spoiled. Then I said to them: 'If you haven't even entered the land and your senses of taste and smell and sight have already spoiled, how will it be when you enter? Furthermore, how will you be able to save them?' And I took out my bread and my water and gave it to them. In my bread and water, they felt all the tastes and smells, and that which had been spoiled was repaired.

"And the inhabitants of that country where the garden was began to seek to repair the country where the sense of taste had been spoiled. They came to a decision: Since there existed a country of great riches (the very same country which the beggar had mentioned) it seemed that their lost gardener through whom they had lived the good life was of the same stock as those people of the Country of Riches who also lived the good life. Thus they counseled that they should send to the Country of Riches, for surely they would help them. And that is what they did. They sent out emissaries to the Country of Riches. As the emissaries left, they met with the rich men from the Country of Riches, and the rich men asked the emissaries: 'Where are you going?' They answered: 'We are going to the Country of Riches so that they might help us.' They replied: 'We ourselves are inhabitants of the Country of Riches and we are on our way to you.' I (the beggar who is telling this story) declared: 'You really need me because you cannot go there to help them, therefore remain here and I will go with the emissaries to help them.'

"So I went with the emissaries until I came to the country. I entered a city, and I saw some people telling jokes and then more people gathered around them until there was a whole crowd telling jokes and they all laughed. I listened and heard that they were speaking obscenities. One tells an obscene joke; another one is slightly more subtle. This one laughs; that one enjoys the fun, etc. Then I went further to another city. There I saw two people quarreling over business. They went to court to bring suit. The court decreed: 'This one is innocent and that one is guilty.' They left the court. Later, they quarreled again. This time, they said they would not go back to that court, but they wished another court. They selected another court and brought their case before it. Later, one of this pair quarreled with someone else. They chose a different court this time. And this way they continued to quarrel and to choose different courts each time until the whole city was full of courts. I observed that the reason was that the truth did not exist there. Today this man distorts the judgment and favors his friend; afterwards, his friend favors him, since they take bribes and there is no truth in them. Then I noticed that they were full of lechery and there was so much lechery there that it became permissible.

"I told them that was why their senses of smell and taste and sight were spoiled. The cruel king left them with those three groups of servants who spoiled the country, for they wandered about spreading obscenity and introduced it into the country. And through the obscenity, the sense of taste was spoiled, all the tastes had for them the taste of carrion. And they also introduced bribery into the land. Through this their sight was dimmed and their sense of sight was spoiled as it is written: 'Graft blinds the eyes of the wise.' And thus they also introduced lechery into the land and through that the sense of smell was spoiled since the sense of smell is spoiled through lechery. 'Therefore,' I said, 'see to it that you cure the country of those three sins, seek out those people and banish them. And when you cleanse the country of these three sins, not only will your sense of taste and sight and smell be cured, but even the gardener who mysteriously disappeared will be found.'

"And that is what they did. They began to cleanse the country of these three sins and to seek out those people. They would seize an individual and question him: 'Where do you come from?' until all the people of the cruel king were discovered and banished and the country was cleansed of these sins. In the meanwhile there arose a tumult: 'Perhaps that madman is really the gardener. For there is a madman who wanders about crying he is the gardener and whom everyone considers mad and stones him and chases him away. Perhaps he is really the gardener.' They went and brought him in and I said: 'Of course he is the true gardener.'

"Consequently, I have an affidavit from the Country of Riches that I live the good life because I cured the Country of the Garden. And today, I grant you my good life outright as a wedding gift."

There was great rejoicing and a fine celebration and everyone was very happy. The first gave them long life as a gift and the second gave them a good life.

5

On the third day, the couple again remembered and cried and longed: "Where can one find the third beggar, the one who stuttered?" Meanwhile, he entered and said: "I am here."

He embraced them and kissed them and also said to them: "Previously, I blessed you that you might be as I am. But today I present you as a wedding gift that you should be as I am. And you think that I am a stutterer? I am not a stutterer at all. It is only that worldly words which are not praises of the Holy One have no perfection." That is why he looked like a stutterer, for he stuttered those worldly words which have no perfection. "In fact, I am really not a stutterer at all. On the contrary, I am an extraordinary orator. I can recite riddles and poems and songs so marvelous that there is no creature in the universe who would not wish to hear them. And in these songs lies all wisdom. I have an affidavit to that effect from the great man who is called the True Man of Kindness. There is in this an entire story.

"Once all the wise men were sitting and boasting of their science. One said that with his science he had invented the production of iron from ore; another, that he had invented the production of another metal; and still another boasted that he had invented the production of silver, which is even more important. And yet another boasted that he had invented the production of gold. One boasted that he had invented weapons. Another boasted that he could make all these metals from material other than those used for making these metals. And another man boasted of other sciences, for there are numerous things that were invented through science, like saltpeter, and powder and the like. Each boasted of his science.

"One came forth and said: 'I am wiser than all of you, for I am as wise as the day.' They could not comprehend what he was saying, that he was as wise as the day. And he declared to them that if all their sciences were gathered together, they would only amount to one hour. Even though each science derived from a specific day, according to the creation which took place on that day (all these sciences are only combinations of materials which God had created on specific days), nevertheless, through science one can gather all these inventions into one hour. But I am as wise as an entire day.

"That is how the last wise man boasted. So I (the stutterer) asked him: 'Like which day are you wise?' The wise man declared: 'This man (the stutterer) is wiser than I, because he asks, "Like which day?" But I am as wise as whichever day you wish.' And now the question arises: Why is he who asks 'Like which day?' wiser than the wise man who is as wise as any day he wishes?

"There is an entire tale about this. The True Man of Kindness is indeed a very great man. And I (the stutterer) travel around and collect all true deeds of kindness and bring them to the True Man of Kindness. For the very becoming of time—time itself is created—is through deeds of true kindness. So I travel and gather together all those true deeds of kindness and bring them to the True Man of Kindness. And from this time becomes.

"Now there is a mountain. On the mountain stands a rock. From the rock flows a spring. And everything has a heart. The world taken as a whole has a heart. And the world's heart is of full stature, with a face, hands, and feet. Now the toenail of that heart is more heart-like than anyone else's heart. The mountain with the rock and spring are at one end of the world, and the world's heart stands at the other end. The world's heart stands opposite the spring and yearns and always longs to reach the spring. The yearning and longing of the heart for the spring is extraordinary. It cries out to reach the spring. The spring also yearns and longs for the heart.

"The heart suffers from two types of languor: one because the sun pursues it and burns it (because it so longs to reach the spring); and the other because of its yearning and longing, for it always yearns and longs fervently for the spring. It always stands facing the spring and cries out: 'Help!' and longs mightily for the spring. But when the heart needs to find some rest, to catch its breath, a large bird flies over, and spreads its wings over it, and shields it from the sun. Then the heart can rest a while. And even then, during the rest, it still looks toward the spring and longs for it.

"Why doesn't the heart go toward the spring if it so longs for it? Because, as soon as it wants to approach the hill, it can no longer see the peak and cannot look at the spring. (When one stands opposite a mountain, one sees the top of the slope of the mountain where the spring is situated, but as soon as one approaches the mountain, the top of the slope disappears—at least visually—and one cannot see the spring.) And if the heart will no longer look upon the spring, its soul will perish, for it draws all its vitality from the spring. And if the heart would expire, God forbid, the whole world would be annihilated, because the heart has within it the life of everything. And how could the world exist without its heart? And that is why the heart cannot go to the spring but remains facing it and yearns and cries out.

"And the spring has no time; it does not exist in time. (The spring has no worldly time, no day or moment, for it is entirely above time.) The only time the spring has is that one day which the heart grants it as a gift. The moment the day is finished, the spring, too, will be without time and it will disappear. And without the spring, the heart, too, will perish, God forbid. Thus, close to the end of the day, they start to take leave one from the other and begin singing riddles and poems and songs, one to the other, with much love and longing. This True Man of Kindness is in charge of this. As the day is about to come to its end, before it finishes and ceases, the True Man of Kindness comes and gives a gift of a day to the heart. And the heart gives the day to the spring. And again the spring has time.

"And when day returns from wherever it comes, it arrives with riddles and fine poetry in which all wisdom lies. There is a distinction between the days. There is Sunday and Monday; there are also days of New Moon and Holidays. The poems which the day brings depend upon what kind of day it is. And the time that the True Man of Kindness has, all derives from me (the stutterer) because I travel around, collecting all the true deeds of kindness from which time derives.

" Consequently, the stutterer is wiser even than the wise one who boasted that he is as clever as whichever day you wish. Because all of time, even the days, come about only through him (the stutterer) for he collects the true deeds of kindness from which time derives and brings them to the True Man of Kindness. He in turn gives a day to the heart. The heart gives it to the spring, through which the whole world can exist. Consequently the actual becoming of time, with the riddles and poems and all the wisdom found in them, is all made possible through the stutterer.

"I have an affidavit from the True Man of Kindness that I can recite riddles and poems, in which all wisdom can be found, because time and riddles come into being only through him. And now, I give you my wedding gift outright that you should be like me."

Upon hearing this, they had a joyous celebration.

6

In the morning, when they finished the celebration of that day and had slept through the night, the couple yearned for the beggar with the twisted neck. Meanwhile, he entered and said: "I am here. Previously, I blessed you that you may be as I am. Today I present you a wedding gift that you should be as I am. Do you think my neck is twisted? My neck is not twisted at all. In fact, I have a straight neck, a very handsome neck. Only that there are worldly vanities (empty breaths) which are so numerous that I do not want to exhale the least breath." (It seemed like his neck was twisted, since he twisted it because of the vanities of the world and did not want to exhale any breath into the vanities of the world.) "But

I really have a handsome neck, a wonderful neck because I have such a wonderful voice. I can imitate with my voice every speechless sound made on earth because I have such a wonderful neck and voice. And I have an affidavit to that effect from a certain country.

"For there is a country where everyone is skilled in the art of music. Everyone practices these arts, even little children. There isn't a child there who is unable to play some kind of instrument. The youngest in that country would be the wisest in another country in the art of music. And the wise men, and the king of that country and the musicians are experts in the art of music.

"Once, the country's wise men sat and boasted of their expertise in the art of music. One boasted that he could play on one instrument; another, on another; and still another, on all instruments. This one boasted that he could imitate with his voice the sound of one instrument, and another boasted that he could imitate with his voice yet another instrument. And still another boasted that with his voice he could imitate several instruments. Another one boasted that he could imitate the sound of a drum, just as it is being beaten. Another one boasted that with his voice he could make the sound of cannon firing.

"I, too, was there, so I declared saying, 'My voice is better than all of yours. And here is the proof. If you are such wise men in music, see if you can save these two countries. There are two countries one thousand miles apart from each other where no one can sleep when night falls. As soon as night falls, everyone begins to wail with such anguish —men, women, and children—because they hear a certain wailing sound of mourning. Stones would melt because of this wail. And thus they behave in the two countries: In one, they hear the wail and all wail; and likewise in the other country. And the two countries are a thousand miles apart. So if you are all so very wise in music, let us see if you can save these two countries, or at least imitate the sounds of the laments heard there.' And they said to him: 'Will you lead us there?' He answered: 'Yes, I will lead you there.'

"And they all arose to go there. They left and reached one of those two countries. When they arrived, and night fell, as usual, everyone began to wail and the wise men also wailed. And so they saw that they were of no help at all to the two countries. And I (the one with the twisted neck) said to the wise men: 'Can you, at least, tell me where the sound of the wailing comes from?' They asked: 'Do you know?' And I (the beggar with the twisted neck) answered: 'Of course I know. There are two birds, a male and a female. There was only one pair of this species on earth. The female was lost and the male roamed about seeking her. She was also seeking him. They searched for each other for such a long time that they lost their ways and realized they could no longer find one another. They remained where they were and made nests. The male built a nest close to one of those two countries — not too close by, but considering the bird's voice, close enough. From where he built his nest, his voice could be heard in the country. In the same way, she also built her nest near the second country, also not too close by, but close enough for her voice to be heard. And when night fell, each one of this pair of birds began to lament with a very great wail. Each wailed for its mate. This is the wailing that is heard in these two countries, and because of the sound, everyone must wail and no one can sleep.'

"But they didn't want to believe me, and said to me, 'Will you lead us there?' 'Yes,' he answered. 'I can lead you, but how can you get there? You cannot get there by night because you will not be able to bear the wailing when you approach. Even here you cannot bear it and you must also wail. When you get there, you will not be able to bear it at all. And you cannot get there by day, for by the day, the joy is unbearable. During the day, birds gather around each one, around him and her, and console them and gladden each one of the pair with great rejoicing. They speak words of comfort: "It is yet possible that you will find each other." That is why it is not possible to withstand the great rejoicing that is found there by day. The voices of the birds that gladden them are not heard from far off, but only when you get there. But the sounds of moaning arising from the pair is heard from far off. That is why you cannot get there.'

"The wise man said to me: 'Can you set it right?' I answered: 'Yes, I can set it right, since I can imitate all the sounds of the world. I can also throw my voice, so that in the place from where I throw my voice, nobody hears, but it is heard far, far away. Thus I can throw the voices of the birds, from her to him. I will imitate her voice and throw it close to him. I will also throw his voice close to her, and this way I will bring them together and so everything will be put right.'

"But who could believe me? So I led them into a forest. They heard somebody open a door, and shut it, and lock it with a bolt. Then I shot a gun and sent my dog to retrieve what I had shot. And the dog struggled in the snow. These wise men heard it all and looked around, but they saw absolutely nothing. They heard no sound from me (whose neck was twisted though it was I who had thrown those sounds and thus they had heard them), so they understood that I could imitate all the sounds and could throw my voice and thus could set everything right." (Here he skipped in his narrative.)

"And therefore I have an affidavit from that country that I have a very fine voice and can imitate all the sounds in the world, and today I grant you this outright as a gift in honor of your wedding, that you should be like me."

And there was great celebration and joy there.

7

On the fifth day they also celebrated. The married pair remembered the beggar who was a hunchback. And they yearned greatly, "How do we bring the hunchback beggar

here? If he were here, our happiness would be great indeed."
Meanwhile, he arrived and said: "Here I am. I came to be
with you at your wedding." He embraced and kissed them
and said: "Previously I blessed you that you might be like me.
Today, I present you a wedding gift that you should be like
me. I am not a hunchback at all. On the contrary, I have
shoulders that are characterized *the-little-that-holds-much*. And
I have an affidavit to that effect.

"Once there was a discussion where people prided themselves on having this characteristic. Each one boasted that he
possessed the characteristic of *the-little-that-holds-much* (that is,
a small space that should contain much). One of them was
ridiculed and laughed at. The words of the others who
boasted about having *the-little-that-holds-much* were acceptable.
But *the-little-that-holds-much* that I have was greater than all the
others.

"One of them boasted that his mind was like *the-little-
that-holds-much*. He carried in his mind multitudes of people
with all their needs and all their behavior, with all their ges-
tures and traits. Since he kept all these things in his mind, he
was *the-little-that-holds-much*, for his little bit of a mind carried
so many people. And they made fun of him and declared:
'Your people are nothing and you are nothing.'

"Another one declared and said: 'I saw *the-little-that-
holds-much*. For once I saw a mountain that was covered with
rubbish and filth. This was a marvel to me: Where did this
rubbish and filth come from? There was a man close by the
mountain. He told me, "All this comes from me." Since he
dwelt so close to the mountain he threw everything onto the
mountain, rubbish and filth from his eating and drinking.
From him the rubbish and filth increased on the mountain.
Therefore, this man was obviously *the-little-that-holds-much*.
Because one man could create so much rubbish.'

"Another boasted that he had *the-little-that-holds-much*,
since he had a piece of land which produced much fruit. The

fruit produced by that land was later counted and it turned out that the land was not as large as the amount of fruit it produced. Therefore this was *the-little-that-holds-much*. His words were pleasing, and accepted as truly being *the-little-that-holds-much*.

"And one said, 'I own a wonderful orchard wherein fruits grow. Many people and lords visit it since it is such a beautiful orchard. And when summer comes, many people and lords journey there to stroll in the orchard. Truly, the orchard is not so large that it can accommodate many people. Therefore, it is *the-little-that-holds-much*.' And his words were also pleasing.

"And one said that his speech possessed the characteristic of *the-little-that-holds-much*, since he was the secretary for a great king: 'Many people come to the king. One comes with praise and another comes with petitions. The king cannot listen to all of them so I gather together all their speeches and shorten them and present to the king this digest of all their praises and petitions. Thus my brief words are *the-little-that-holds-much*.'

"Another one said that his silence possessed the characteristic of *the-little-that-holds-much*. There were accusers and slanderers who informed against him severely. They quarrel with him and talk about him a great deal. And he refutes all slanders and accusations against him with silence, only with silence. Therefore, his silence was *the-little-that-holds-much*.

"Another one said that he was *the-little-that-holds-much*. There was a very poor man who was both blind and very big. He (the boaster) was very small and led about the poor blind man who was very big. Therefore, he was *the-little-that-holds-much*. Because the blind man could slip and fall, and he maintains him upright by leading him. Because of this he was *the-little-that-holds-much* because he was small and held up the big blind man.

"And I (the hunchback) was also there. I retorted, 'The

truth is that you all have the characteristic of *the-little-that-holds-much*, and I understand everything that you meant. The last one who boasted that he led the big blind man is greater than all of you. But I am by far superior to all of you, since he who boasted that he leads the big blind man means that he leads the lunar sphere. For the moon has the characteristic of a blind man for she has no light of her own. And he who boasted of this, leads the moon even though he is small and the sphere of the moon is extremely large. Through him the world survives because the world must have a moon. Thus, he is surely *the-little-that-holds-much*. But I am superior to all of you and *the-little-that-holds-much* which I have is superior to all. This is the proof.

"There was once a sect which reasoned that every beast had its own shade where it wished to rest, and so, too, each bird had its branch where it rested and not on any other branch. Because of this, the sect reasoned that there might exist such a tree in whose shade all the beasts could choose to rest, and on whose branches all the birds could rest. They declared that such a tree did exist. They wanted to travel to the tree, because the pleasure found around the tree should be limitless since all the birds and the beasts were there. No beast harmed any other beast, but all the beasts were intermixed and they gamboled there. Surely it would be a great pleasure to be at the tree. They reasoned in which direction to go to reach the tree. A controversy arose among them and one said, 'We must go west.' This one said, 'Go here,' and that one said, 'Go there.' They couldn't possibly decide which way to go to reach the tree.

"A wise man came by and said to them, 'Why are you reasoning which way to go to reach the tree? Reason first which are those people who can reach the tree. For not everyone can reach the tree. Only he who possesses the virtues of the tree can reach it. For this tree has three roots. One root is faith in God; the next root is reverence; and the third root is humility. Truth is the body of the tree from which the branches emerge. Therefore no one can reach the tree unless he has those virtues.'

"Now, not everyone in the sect possessed these virtues; only a few had them. And since the sect was well united, they did not want to separate so that one group should go to the tree and the rest remain behind. So they agreed to wait while each one of them labored and struggled to attain the high degree of all the virtues so that all of them would reach the tree together. This is exactly what they did: They labored and struggled until they all achieved those virtues. And no sooner had they achieved these virtues, than they all agreed upon the one way to go in order to reach that tree. They all set out and after they had traveled a while, they were able to see the tree from afar. When they looked, they noticed that the tree was not rooted in any space. The tree stood on no specific space. And if it had no space, how could it be reached?

"And I (the hunchback) was also there with them. So I declared to them: 'I can lead you to the tree. For this particular tree has no specific space; it is entirely above (superior to) the earth's space. And yet, the characteristic of *the-little-that-holds-much* still involves some space. Although it is a *little-that-holds-much*, it still has a little space in it. And my *little-that-holds-much* is at the very end of space, and beyond it there is no space at all.' (For the hunchback was like the middle stage between space and what is entirely above (superior to) space because he had the highest degree of *the-little-that-holds-much* which is at the very end of space and after it the term space does not exist at all. Therefore, he could lead them from that space to the aspect of *above-all-space*.) 'That is why I can lead all of you to this tree which is totally above (superior to) the space it stands on.'

"And I took them and led them there to that tree. Thus I have an affidavit from it that I have the highest degree of *the-little-that-holds-much*." (And that is why he appeared to be hunchbacked; he carries a heavy load since he himself carries within himself *the-little-that-holds-much*.) "And now I grant you this trait that you be as I am."

And great joy was expressed and there was very great bliss.

8

On the sixth day they were all very joyous and yet they yearned: "How do we bring here the beggar without hands?" Suddenly he arrived and said, "Here I am. I come to you on your wedding." And he spoke to them as the others did. And he embraced them and kissed them and said to them: "You think that I am crippled in my hands. I am not at all crippled in my hands. I do have power in my hands, but I do not use the power in my hands in this world. I need this power for something else and I have an affidavit to that effect from the Water Castle.

"Once a few of us were sitting, each one boasting of the power which lay in his hands. This one boasted that he had a certain prowess in his hands, and that one boasted that he had another type of prowess in his hands. For instance, one man boasted that he had such power and prowess in his hands that when he shot an arrow from his bow, he could pull it back to him. For the power of his hands was such that even though he had shot the arrow, he could still turn it around and make it return.

"And so I asked him: 'What type of arrow can you pull back?' There are ten different sorts of arrows because there are ten different types of poison. When an arrow is smeared with one poison, it does a certain type of harm, and if an arrow is smeared with another type of poison it does more harm. There are ten different types of poison each more deadly than the first and this is why there are ten different types of arrows. (The arrows themselves are all alike, but because they are smeared with ten different types of poison they are called ten different arrows.) That is why I asked him: 'What sort of arrow can you pull back?' I also asked him whether he could pull back an arrow before it hit its mark or could he also recover it after it had hit. To this he answered that even after the arrow had hit its mark he could pull it back, and to the question, what type of arrow can you pull back, he declared: 'Such and such an arrow.' So I replied: 'If this is the case, you cannot cure the Princess. Since you can only pull back one type of arrow, you cannot cure the Princess.'

"One boasted that he had such power in his hands, that no matter from whom he took, he gave. By the very fact that he took something from someone, he was giving because his taking was giving. This automatically made him a giver of charity. Then I asked him, 'What kind of charity do you give?' (Because there exist ten sorts of charity.) He answered that he tithed. I replied: 'If that is so then you cannot heal the Princess. You cannot even reach her place. You can enter only one wall where she dwells and so you cannot come to her place.'

"One boasted that he had a special power in his hands. For there were in the world officials who needed the wisdom which he could impart by laying his hands on them. I asked him, 'What kind of wisdom can you impart through your hands? For there are ten measures of wisdom.' He answered: 'Such and such a kind of wisdom.' I declared: 'You can't heal the Princess at all; you can't even take her pulse. You are aware of only one pulse and there are ten types of pulse, but you know only one, because you know of only one type of wisdom.'

"One boasted that he had such power in his hands that when a tempest arose, he could contain the tempest with his hands. He could catch the wind within his hands and contain it. He could give the wind the proper counter-force that was needed. So I asked him: 'What kind of wind can you catch

with your hands? There are ten types of wind.' He answered:
'Such and such a wind.' I replied: 'You cannot heal the
Princess because you cannot even play her tune. The cure for
the Princess is through music, and there are ten types of tunes
and you can only play one tune for her from these ten.'

" 'And what can you do?' they all questioned. I answered: 'I know what all of you don't know, that is all of the
nine parts of all that you don't know, I know. I know all.'

"There is a tale. Once upon a time a King fell in love with
a Princess. He tried to capture her through stratagems until
he succeeded and then he kept her by his side. One night he
dreamt that the Princess rose up against him and killed him.
When he awoke, this dream remained in his heart. He called
together all the interpreters of dreams and they interpreted as
follows: 'The dream will literally become reality; she will kill
him.' The King was unable to find any counsel: What could
he do with her? Should he kill her? That would sadden him.
Should he banish her? That would irk him, for someone else
would have her. He had worked so hard to get her and now
she would be someone else's. And especially if he banished
her and she asked another's help, the dream could surely come
true; she would kill him, since she would then be with somebody else. On the other hand if he kept her with him, he
feared the outcome of the dream.

"And so the King didn't know what to do about the
Princess. Meanwhile his love for her was spoiled somewhat
because of the dream; he didn't love her as much as before,
each day his love for her was spoiled. And so, too, her love for
him was spoiled, each day more and more, until there existed
within her a hatred toward him, and she ran away from him.
The King sent word to search for her. People came and said to
him that she was circling about the Water Castle. For there
was a Water Castle, with ten walls, one inside the other. All
the ten walls were made of water, and the ground that was
trod upon was also of water. There were trees and fruits, all of

water. The beauty and the marvel of the Castle was inde-
scribable. For surely it was an extraordinary wonder for the
entire Castle to be made of water. To enter the Castle was
obviously impossible. He who would enter would drown,
because the Castle was formed of water. So when the Princess
fled, she went to the Castle. The King was told that she was
circling about the Water Castle.

"The King and his soldiers set out to capture her. No
sooner did the Princess see this than she decided to run into
the Castle. She would rather have drowned than be captured
by the King and remain with him. And perhaps, she would be
saved and would slip into the Water Castle. As soon as the
King saw her running into the water, he said, 'If that is so
. . . . ' He ordered her shot: 'If she dies, let her die.' She was
shot at and hit with all the ten kinds of arrows that had been
smeared with the ten poisons. The Princess fled into the Castle and came inside. She passed through the gates and walls
made of water, for there were gates and walls of water. She
passed through all the gates of all the ten walls of the Water
Castle until she was inside the Castle where she fell in a dead
faint.

"And I (the handless one) am curing her. For he who
does not possess within his hands all the ten types of charity
cannot enter the ten walls of the Water Castle. For he will
drown in the water. The King and his soldiers pursued the
Princess and they all drowned. But I am able to enter past all
the ten walls of the Water Castle. These walls of water are the
billows of the sea that stand like walls. The winds raise up the
billows of the sea and lift them up high, and the billows that
are the ten walls always stand there. The winds hold up the
waves and lift them, yet I can enter through the ten walls.
And I can remove the ten different arrows from the Princess.
And I know all the ten kinds of pulse through my ten fingers.
For through each one of the ten fingers one can feel a specific
pulse out of the ten different pulses. I can cure the Princess

through the ten types of music. And that is how I am curing her. Therefore I have this power in my hands.

"And this is my gift to you this day."

And there was great rejoicing and everyone was very happy.

COMMENTARIES

I. THE LOSS OF THE PRINCESS

"The Loss of the Princess" is frequently presented as the paradigm of the Bratslav tale, a pedagogic practice both useful and deceptive. While it is true that many of these tales are ingenious variations on the basic structure of this story (cf. II, X, XI, XII, XIII), others are not. The attempt to force a complicated tale into a recurring structure which often requires the excessive allegorical identification of the protagonists tends to impoverish and distort the imaginative achievement of the individual stories.

Having offered these caveats, we will present both the standard structure and allegorical interpretations—loosely and flexibly construed—to render this specific story intelligible and demonstrate the great variety of the thirteen tales of the sacred cycle.

The story begins with the disappearance or exile of the princess from her father's home after the latter's fit of unexplained rage. The main action of the story is the viceroy's repeated attempts to find the princess, to redeem her from her exile, a quest not fulfilled even by the end of the tale. Kabbalistic allusions transmute this simple folktale into a model of the cosmic drama which filled Lurianic Kabbalah and obsessed Nahman and other Hasidic masters

The king's anger and the princess's exile are narrative correlatives of the process of *tzimtzum* and *shevirat hakelim* by which God created the world. As explained in the General Introduction, Lurianic kabbalah argued that God, in his will to create a world, contracted his being in order to make room for the world to be created. This contraction (*tzimtzum*) involved a violent cataclysm, an internal struggle within the Godhead (*shevirat hakelim* = the breaking of the vessels) in which at least one part of the sefirotic structure, the lowest of the ten spheres (called the "Shekhinah") is, in effect, exiled. The act of redemption (called *tikkun*) is thus the attempt to restore the primordial harmony. This myth explains

285

both the coexistence of a perfect God with the imperfect world and the phenomenon of exile, and suggests the method for restoring the primordial harmony, the act of redemption.

In our story the king is obviously God in his purest form and his beloved daughter is the Shekhinah, variously envisaged as the manifestation of the Godhead in the world or, on a national basis, Knesset Israel, the eternal corporate soul of the people of Israel which has a meta-historical existence, but is in exile. The viceroy, who is the hero of the story, should not be limited to one allegorical equivalent. He might represent any individual pious person or the figure of the zadik or Nahman himself, the *zadik hador*, or the messiah or the historical people of Israel. The selection of any one allegorical equivalent constricts the polysemous fecundity of Nahman's imagination.

The search for the princess naturally leads the viceroy into a desert, the traditional locus of demonic forces or, at least, a world devoid of the divine presence. The fortress he discovers is easily entered since it is the always-inviting stronghold of the demon where the princess is held captive. It is not at all surprising that the viceroy and the princess recognize each other; not only do they come from the same court, but, if the viceroy does represent the messiah or Knesset Israel, they are destined to marry when the primordial harmony is restored—hence the romantic unions presented in stories II, X, and XIII.

The qualifying trial which the princess sets for the viceroy involves some abstinence (fasting), but mainly yearning for her presence. The viceroy fails this trial twice, first reliving part of Adam's fall (the apple), then Noah's drunkenness. In both cases, the penalty for lack of perseverance is spiritual slumber, hence the loss of a relatively easy opportunity to save the princess. (According to some Kabbalistic sources, Adam could have effected the redemption of the cosmos had he been more vigilant in the Edenic period.) The period of seventy years' sleep after the second failure invokes memories of the Babylonian exile and comprises a turning point in the story. Upon waking, the viceroy discovers the princess's message written in her tears on her kerchief (the Torah?); she has been exiled to a much greater distance, far into the desert to the Golden Mountain and the Pearly Castle, and recovering her is all the more difficult, if not impossible.

The focus of the story, we realize, is not on the princess herself, but upon the viceroy and his struggle to find and retrieve her. In his despair at not finding her in the inhabited world, he enters the desert where he meets the three forbidding giants who repeatedly tell him that his quest is futile, that the object of his search does not exist, and that people have deluded him. Despite these discouraging messages, the viceroy persists and the giants reluctantly respond to his persistence by offering some help. The third giant actually has him transported to the Golden Mountain and the Pearly Castle where he must expend great efforts—and much money—to release the princess from her captivity. How the viceroy does this we are never told since, as most Bratslav exegetes argue, Nahman declined to describe the actual act of redemption.

The missing or declined cloture is a narrative device found in both this story and "The Seven Beggars," Nahman's last story. In both cases the actual redemption is not described to the reader, who is left to ponder and yearn.

II. THE KING AND THE EMPEROR

In "The Loss of the Princess" folk motifs were either shaped by or open to the allegorical impulse which was both eschatological and axiological. The correspondence between the Bratslav theory of literature as presented by Rabbi Nathan in the first Introduction to the tales and the structure of "The Loss of the Princess" is close enough to allow the story to serve as a paradigm of the theory. In "The King and the Emperor" the allegorical substructure is much slighter. If we were to identify the Emperor's daughter with the Shekhinah (like the Princess in "The Loss of the Princess" or the pauper's daughter in "The Burgher and the Pauper") we would be hard pressed to explain some of the other elements in the narrative. In general, there seems to be a tension between the narrative line and the putative allegorical system.

The basic plot of the story is familiar to anyone who has read romances from the Hellenistic period onward. A young couple, destined to marry, is prevented from doing so by one of their parents. To fulfill the pledge they had made to each other, they flee to the sea or the desert. Having been separated, they spend the remainder of the story struggling through many ingenious adventures toward a reunion and a happy ending. Actually, the emperor's daughter is the protagonist here while the king's son remains in exile and servitude until she redeems him at the end of the story. Martin Mantel has observed that while Rabbi Nahman's romance conforms to many of the features of the traditional literary romance, it avoids the exploitation of prurient elements, though opportunities to titillate abound in the story; the pretense of historical realism so common in the romance is absent here, and the story seems to take place in the limbo of fairyland space.

One might add that the tension between the demands of the genre and the allegorical impulse is evident throughout the story. The four episodes in which the emperor's daughter is the protagonist are designed to elevate her to a position of royal power and wealth from which she can declare that all exiles must be returned to the capital for the festivities accompanying her marriage. In the first episode (with the merchant's son) and in the third episode (with the pirates) she amasses great wealth. In the second (with the eleven daughters of the noblemen), the third, and the fourth (in which she kills the prince and, dressed as a male doctor, marries his wife), the bizarre theme of transvestism is dominant; it would otherwise be implausible for a woman to rise to prominence in a world of men without resorting to sexual seduction, a theme Rabbi Nahman clearly would want to avoid. While these episodes lead to a definite goal, the attention and inventiveness invested in them suggest a discernible delight in fabulation. The duplicity and ruthlessness of the emperor's daughter are difficult to reconcile with her figure as a representative of the Shekhinah: She deceives the merchant's son (in the first episode) and the king (in the second episode); she leads the eleven young ladies in the slaughter of the pirates and kills the frolicking prince (in the fourth episode), though he had not threatened her at all.

While broken pledges of marriage are common to the romance as a genre, they are also a standard topos in Jewish literature (cf. the book of Hosea or rabbinic homilies based on the Song of Solomon). Divine forces seem to be manipulating the story throughout. The king and the emperor are childless, but after they have met and pledged their hoped-for children to each other in marriage, they go home and beget children—of the proper genders for a match. Though this pledge is forgotten, it is renewed by the children themselves who "happen" to study together in the same school. The pledge is sealed, as in the Jewish wedding ritual, by a ring given by the prince to the emperor's daughter. When the emperor tries to prevent the match and establishes a difficult trial for the king's son, the young couple take matters into their own hands and, upon the advice of the emperor's daughter, flee the country. But just as the pledge has devolved from the parents to the children, the responsibility for breaking the pledge has become theirs: After a fateful act of negligence, they lose the ring and then lose both each other and the ship in their attempt to find the ring.

The narrative that follows is a description of an attempt not to recover the ring, but rather to reunite the couple. Having been married by the very act of his giving her the ring, they do not need to have the marriage consecrated again. The princess simply says to her newly rediscovered husband: "Let us go home." The original ring does not have to be discovered since the fact it symbolizes, the union of the couple, has been reestablished.

COMMENTARIES

If the emperor's daughter is the Shekhinah, the story is a tale of the breaking of the covenant and its restoration, thus recapitulating the dynamics of *shevirah* and *tikkun* which suffuse so much of Bratslav thinking. The king's son would most likely be Knesset Israel, which is both the historical community of Israel and, in Kabbalistic terms, another aspect of the Shekhinah, both being aspects of the tenth or lowest sefirah of the sefirotic structure.

Were this story a simple romance, the emperor's daughter would have stayed on as king in her new kingdom or, at least, the reader would expect some development to explain how the emperor's daughter revealed that she was really a woman masquerading as a man and how she was received when she returned home. Since, however, the central theme is obviously exile and redemption—whether we accept the Kabbalistic allegory or not—the reader is expected to be satisfied with the simple statement of the emperor's daughter: "Let us go home." Reunion with her husband implies return to their home from their self-imposed exile.

III. THE CRIPPLE

Of dazzling intricacy, "The Cripple" demands careful attention to the development of its central theme. The reader attempting to follow the plot line only will discover not only a bizarre series of episodes, but a baffling bifurcation: The first part of the story deals with the cure and enrichment of the crippled son of a wise man, while the second part presents a sequence of partly comic episodes concerning the world of demons. The seemingly disparate episodes are controlled by the central theme so carefully presented in the opening scene: The development of the hero from dependence to independence and from innocence to profound knowledge. What we are asked to focus upon is the acquisition and understanding of power, particularly an understanding of the power that really controls the world, the power involved in the enigmatic "watering of trees." The father's will contains two statements: His sons may earn their living from any kind of work, but they must water trees. The first statement is clear and immediately developed in the story, but the second, relating to the watering of trees, seems to be a riddle. The selection of the crippled son as hero is significant since he is the least likely to be able to earn his own living and, following the inversion common in Hasidic tales, the most likely to discover the meaning of the riddle.

Although the son acts in the first part and is an observer in the second, his role as observer is not passive. He obviously learns much about the world of the demons—which is remarkably like the world of human beings—and of the cosmic power of "the tree" situated next to the region of the demons. Without reference to any specific literary antecedent, the tree can be perceived as some aspect of human behavior which requires cultivation. It obviously corresponds to the world-tree found in many religious traditions. Reference to a tree in the Jewish tradition immediately evokes memories of the Tree of Life in the Garden of Eden, a favorite topic of rabbinic exegesis. Adam, for example, was commanded to water the Tree of Life, but he in fact ravaged it. The tree, in Kabbalistic literature, is one of the metaphoric representations of the sefirotic structure. In this story, the watering of the tree implies the annihilation of the demons—and the demons are painfully aware of this threat. The watering of trees must be the pursuit of the religious life with all its cosmic implications, leading to the messianic age and the concurrent annihilation of the demons. The complete annihilation of demonic power is countered by the plenitude of power in the messianic sphere.

The conversation of the sun and the moon (which the crippled son overhears by holding one side of the diamond he has found) deals with the limitation of the powers of even the celestial bodies. The sun realizes that it desiccates a certain magnificent tree which actually requires watering. The mighty sun cannot do what the cripple had been commanded to do by his father. The moon complains that the demons had robbed it of the natural power of its legs (perhaps an allusion to the eclipse) and used that power for themselves since they naturally have weak, chicken-like legs. The correspondence with the cripple is obvious and he, in fact, learns from the sun's advice to the moon about the various types of powders and their respective magical powers. We surmise that the crippled son is considered an afflicted zadik since he can properly utilize the powder from the fourth path on which the afflicted zadikim trod. By means of the powders, he cures his legs, manipulates the robbers, and captures their stolen treasures.

No longer crippled, and inspired by his newly gained power, the hero is curious to visit the land of the demons mentioned by the moon in its conversation with the sun. And although he never openly seeks the solution to the riddle, his curiosity draws him to the one place, the land of the demons, where he will discover why his father ordered him to water trees. At first portrayed in all its grotesque sadism, the world of the demons is racked by turmoil and terror. Torture, assassination, political intrigue, and the stealing of demonic power are rampant. The entire demonic kingdom is disrupted by a dissident group of "talkers" who have the power to generate earthquakes. Above all, the demons fear that water might reach the magic tree planted nearby since they know that the watering of the tree implies their annihilation. They realize that their factionalism generates the earthquakes which would let the waters reach the tree, and although the demons specialize in harming human beings, they cannot damage the tree.

The settlement of the wise man who had fled with his family from the land of freethinkers is located strategically near the magic tree which so terrifies the demons. Protected by their enchanted circle, even the demons cannot harm them. The enchanted circle is only the outer manifestation of the religious faith and wisdom of the wise man, who can destroy demons and resist the temptations of the king demon. Relying only on their faith in God, neither the wise man nor his descendents avail themselves of the magic catalog of demons. We learn that they are saintly Jews when a king seeks their prayers to heal his illness (the central theme of the seventh story). In contradistinction to the community of saintly Jews, the neighboring demons live in such social turmoil that the earth quakes and the water reaches the tree, thus annihilating the demons.

What the (formerly) crippled son observes seems to be the opposite of what he had been told. He was told to water trees, but learns that the tree is watered by a cataclysm in the world of the demons. Actually, the two acts are different aspects of the same cosmic phenomenon: the era of redemption. The perfect faith of the believer or the disruption of demonic existence is tantamount to the age of redemption. Since we can assume that the hero has assimilated this message by the end of the story, he can, in effect, disappear from the vision of the reader: The hero has become the experience he was to have learned, the profound mystery about the watering of trees. Rabbi Nahman's narrative progression functions to convey this spiritual message. At first the hero is the main dramatic figure; then he becomes the curious observer; then he simply disappears—or is replaced by the reader.

IV. THE KING WHO DECREED CONVERSION

The choice between forced conversion and martyrdom or exile has been both a recurring fact of Jewish history and an oft-repeated tale type. The figure of the Marrano presents a third, intermediary possibility: The historic or legendary character is outwardly a fully participant member of the dominant community, including its religion, but practices his Jewish rites and worships clandestinely. The wide dissemination of 16th- and 17th-century Hebrew histories of the expulsion of the Jews from Spain and the concomitant Marrano experience gave currency to the Marrano figure in Eastern Europe and afforded a variety of writers with a bifurcated figure living in two realms at the same time.

Rabbi Nahman utilizes this theme to reject, however indirectly, the possibility of living in two realms at the same time, particularly when one is contingent upon the whims of temporal rulers. The Marrano minister preferred wealth and position to poverty and exile and chose to remain in the country after the first king's decree of conversion or exile. Though rewarded by the second king with the privilege of practicing his religion in public, he loses it in the reign of the fourth king. In pointed contrast to the Marrano minister loom the Jews in the fire near the end of the story. They are presented in their most dramatic moment—in Bratslav ideology—donned in *tallith* (prayer shawl) and *tefilin* (phylacteries), prepared to pray. The fire consumes the fourth king and his family precisely because in his country Jews were not permitted to wear *tallith* and *tefilin* in public; the kings who can endure the fire do so because they have allowed Jews to practice their religion openly in their realms. The kings, therefore, are dependent upon the praying Jews and not the opposite.

Many of the passages describing the instability and stupidity of the monarchy are clearly satirical and contrast implicitly with the stability and wisdom of the true King of the Universe who deserves human adoration and prayer. The second earthly king of this story could have been overthrown by his rivals had the Marrano minister not informed him of the plot. This situation, echoing the Esther story among others, is couched in irony: The minister who has to hide his loyalty to the King of the Universe is the one who comes forth to save his earthly king, who then rewards him with the privilege of worshiping the King of the Universe publicly. The fourth king, in his desire to conquer the world without the risk of war, creates a massive statue—described in abundant comic detail—which could function only by inverting all social structures, implying, of course, the eventual overthrow of the king who had commissioned it. Ironically, again, it is precisely this imperious king who is terrified by his dreams and led to his destruction in the fire.

The contrast between the world of ostensible political power and the true strength of faith is born out in the varying interpretations of messages conveyed in dreams. The third king is told by his astrologers that he should beware of an ox and a lamb, which they interpret to mean Taurus and Aries, signs of the zodiac. The fourth king also misinterprets this message by reading it literally and has all oxen and sheep in his kingdom slaughtered. Only at the end of the story are we informed that this warning referred to the *tefilin* and *tallith*, made of ox hides and sheeps' wool respectively. The third king was actually warned that the dynasty would be unharmed as long as Jews would be allowed to practice their religion publicly. The fourth king was also told by one of his wise men that he could assuage the terror of his nightmare if he came to the spot where all the rays of the sun converge and where an iron "staff" grows. Here the misunderstanding derives from the ambiguity of the Hebrew word *shevet* which can mean either a "staff" or, by extension, a "tribe." (In one famous Rabbinic exegesis, this *shevet* even refers to the messiah.) The wise man's message really meant that at the crucial convergence of cosmic energy (there are 365 days in the solar year) one finds a tribe, the tribe of Israel, which, if allowed to worship in peace, could save the king from his terror. In the intense fire near which the king and his family were consumed, there stood Jews dressed in *tallith* and *tefilin*. The correct interpretation of these messages reveals that the true power to affect history is vested not in a monarchy but in those Jews who keep their faith under all conditions.

V. THE KING WHO HAD NO CHILDREN

In Hasidic tales, the zadik is often endowed with miraculous powers to heal illnesses and remedy physical deficiencies, among them barrenness. These powers, derived from the zadik's special closeness to God and particularly manifested in his intensity of prayer, are contrasted with the skills of professional physicians and sorcerers. The success of the zadik is, in effect, a demonstration of the power of the Lord to work his will in this world through the mediation of the zadik in whom the believer should have full faith.

Though this motif has been found in the literature of many religions for centuries, it was given added emotional impact because of the Hasidic preoccupation with the role of the charismatic leader (which varied from sect to sect). In this story, some of the salient features of Bratslav Hasidism shape the narrative line. We find here two hidden zadikim, one after the other, suggesting a continuity of charismatic powers, an obsession of Rabbi Nahman who regarded himself as the true successor of his great-grandfather, the Baal Shem Tov. The zadikim, furthermore, though ultimately successful, must struggle relentlessly to achieve their goal — the king, we notice, is not granted a male heir at first even though the zadik prays for him. In fact, the fulfillment of the prayer comes after three partial failures. At first the king is granted a daughter, not a son; when the king is granted a son, he does not seem to be made of gems as predicted by the zadik; and, finally, the zadik's prayer that the son be cured of his scabs is ineffectual since a charm has been placed on him. The narrative is thus marked by successive points of dramatic tension. Both zadikim are forced to pray for the king against their will; their prayers are not completely answered; the king's daughter has her brother afflicted with scabs. These struggles seem to be necessary for the final successful conclusion, the revelation of the prince as the true prince of gems. Were it not for his sister's jealousy, he would not have been afflicted with scabs; his skin would not have peeled off revealing the true gem constitution of his body.

The dialectical movement of the plot conforms to Bratslav theology, which is characterized by paradoxes and the constant struggle for spiritual ascent. Physical deficiencies—barrenness, in this case—parallel spiritual failings. The king who has no male heir to whom to leave his kingdom seems to reflect Rabbi Nahman's preoccupation with the transmission of his special religious doctrines, particularly after the death of his son in 1806. The author's identification with the central figures, the king and the zadikim, would explain the peculiar balance maintained throughout: Both the king and the zadik are treated sympathetically and comprise the dual foci of the narrative.

Here, as in other stories, magic is not discounted as nonsensical superstition. The second zadik was "high above all the sorcerers" because of his special closeness to the Lord of Israel. While the first zadik effected a miracle by prayer alone, the second zadik resorts to a type of gemological sorcery. His prayers that the prince be made entirely of gems seem, at first, to go unanswered and he berates God for failing him. And when his prayers for the healing of the prince's scabs are also ineffectual, he realizes that a spell has been cast upon the prince and action must be taken to eliminate the sorcerers. The second zadik clearly believes in the power of magic and sorcery and knows how to manipulate it.

The narrative, finally, relies upon magical features which are not treated satirically. The conception of the gem prince is treated seriously as is the curse of scabs invoked by his sister's sorcerer. The power of water to affect sorcery is characteristically paradoxical: Water can preserve the power of the charm from cancellation by another sorcerer; water can also cancel the powers of those sorcerers whom the king has thrown into the water. The sister apparently ran to retrieve the charm since she thought that the drowning of the sorcerers would in some way reverse the effect of the water on the charm and her brother would be cured. In doing so, she fell into the water and presumedly drowned. Her death by water corresponds to the conception of her brother through wine laced with the dust of gems.

VI. THE KING AND THE WISE MAN

The ironic, often bantering tone of "The King and the Wise Man" both betrays a nagging concern with the perennial problem of theodicy and enables the storyteller to present a fresh rendition of an age-old theme. The first king sends his wise man on a quest to bring back a portrait of a second king as proof of the attributes by which the latter is designated. The first king is puzzled by the second and third attributes: "a man of truth" and "a humble person." The second king is a thinly veiled reference to God; no one has his portrait "because he is hidden from men." It is no coincidence that the picture the wise man finally "draws" of the second king and brings back to his own master is blank: The second king is so humble that when the sage praises and exalts him he "became very humble and small, till he lost all substance."

Two passages in the middle of the story prepare the reader for the adventures of the wise man in the land of vicious jokes and lies, the land of the second king. In the first passage we learn that one can judge the essence of a certain country by its humor, whether it be vicious or benign. In the second we are informed that the country of the second king is, after all, symptomatic of all countries and what one finds there is true for the entire human race.

After gathering evidence concerning the corruption of the human race, the wise man confronts the king with two biting statements which lead, however, to an explanation of the king's withdrawal from this world. The king rules over a country full of lies; one might think the king is like his deceitful subjects if this is the type of kingdom over which he rules. The argument of theodicy, that is, that the king withdraws from his subjects because he cannot bear their lies, explains the first of the two titles which had puzzled the wise man's king—the second king designated as "a man of truth."

301

The second puzzling title, "a humble person," is explained by a novel narrative twist. As the wise man praises the king, the latter diminishes in size to the point where he loses all substance, since "this is the way of the humble person: The more one praises and exalts him, the smaller and humbler he becomes." If the identification of the second king as God is correct, the explanation for God's insubstantiality is daring since it makes this insubstantiality contingent upon human behavior, not upon God's will or his essence. Even the explanation of God's withdrawal is theologically problematic though by no means at odds with the temper of Bratslav ideology.

An identification of the second king as the hidden zadik, or, more specifically, with Rabbi Nahman himself would be less problematic theologically, but would not conform to the specifics of the narrative, which refer to the threefold title and the unavailable portrait. Though Bratslav tradition often speaks of Rabbi Nahman in hyperboles which transcend even the enthusiastic norms of standard Hasidic discourse concerning the zadik, the attributes here seem to be more appropriate to God than to Rabbi Nahman himself.

VII. THE KING WHO FOUGHT MANY WARS

The royal figure which appears in other Bratslav tales, immediately evoking tacit comparison between temporal kings and the King of the Universe, appears in this story as the central hero. Here, as in "The King Who Decreed Conversion," the external show of power and pomp is undermined by the king's fears that his power will be destroyed by his foes. In the present story, the focus is on the psychic life of the king, his dreams and spiritual evolution. In this sense, this story, more than any other story in the cycle, is like those Bratslav tales found in the "Sipurim Hadashim" section of *Hayye Muharan*. What we find here is a three-part narrative: a quasi-historical setting during which the king observes the spectacle of the spider and the fly; a dream sequence after which the king decides to convert to Judaism, the religion of the truth; and the king's quest for a precise interpretation of his dreams so that he might gain the wisdom to bring all his people to the truth. What he sees while enveloped in a cloud of incense is not a precise interpretation of the dreams we encounter in the second part of the story, but rather a vision of the descent of his soul from the supernal world where it had been to the lower world of human history.

The author skillfully prefaces the king's dream with a narrative sequence designed to motivate specific elements in the dream. The dream occurred on the anniversary of the king's great military victories, shortly after a ball during which comedies were produced satirizing the manners and customs of every nation, including the Jews. Eager to check the authenticity of these presentations, the king consults an encyclopedia of customs and manners. Again not coincidentally, it is on this encyclopedia that the king observes the fable-like spectacle involving the fly, the spider, and the leaf of the book. As the king begins to ponder the meaning of this spectacle, he dozes off and dreams his two-part dream.

The dream intensifies and distorts the conflict and terror of the spectacle. Of the three components of the spectacle, only the leaf is carried into the dream; the spider is replaced by the grotesque people who emerge from the diamond, and, instead of the fly, we find the king's portrait and crown. Again the leaf saves the victim from the aggressor. In the second part of the dream, the mountain assures the king that he has no need to fear those who rebel against him in the dream as long as the leaf protects him as it protects the mountain from its foes. The mountain seems to be a fanciful reflection of Mt. Sinai since on its peak there is a tablet inscribed with the customs also found on the protecting leaf. By this point in the story, it should be clear to the audience that the leaf is the Torah which was given to the Jews by the Lord on Mt. Sinai. The Lord also protects the mountain—and the tablet on its peak—from the menacing hordes below by planting a magical grass on the one path up the mountain, since it is written on the second tablet at the foot of the mountain that "whosoever had teeth could climb the mountain," but whoever trod or rode on the grass lost all his teeth. It appears that, in the ambience of the dream, the leaf is transformed into the two tablets, another standard symbol of the Torah. Calmed by the mountain's story, the king dreams that his portrait and crown were restored and repaired by the grotesque people who had emerged from the diamond.

It comes as no surprise to the reader that the king, upon awakening, discovers that the protecting leaf bore the customs and manners of the Jews and therefore converts to Judaism, the religion of the truth. It is a bit surprising, however, that the story does not end here but continues, in the next phase, with the king's quest for a way to bring all his people to the truth. To do so, the king understands that he must learn the truth about the essence of his soul as presented in the dream and therefore sets out to seek a wise man who would interpret the dream exactly as it appeared. He discovers, however, that no one can interpret his dreams, but that he can arrive at the same goal of self-knowledge through meditation assisted by a special mixture of incense prepared on a special day—perhaps the Day of Atonement.

The king's vision involved the origin and essence of his soul as evidenced in the trial scene in the supernal world before the soul's descent to our world. Samael's objection to the descent of the king's soul: "What will I do? Why did you [God] create me?" implies that the king had been destined to be a spiritual force, a zadik or even the messiah, powerful enough to cancel Samael's influence in history. Samael is allowed, however, to devise obstacles for the king's soul which he does with the help of the unnamed "hunched old man." It is thus due to Samael's influence that this soul descended into the world as a Gentile king rather than as a zadik or even the messiah.

Though the end of this story is admittedly garbled, the basic implication regarding the possible destiny of the king's soul is clear. The ending might, indeed, have been intentionally garbled since eschatological matters have often been treated obliquely or clandestinely by Bratslav Hasidim. The narrative makes it abundantly clear that the king is guided in his pneumatic development by a divine force since three different devices—a spectacle, a double dream, and a vision—are utilized to lead him to the same goal of self-knowledge. While it is intriguing to speculate regarding the possible identity of the king or the hunched old man, the edifying climax of the story is the anonymous king's discovery that though he was patently a victorious monarch, his perception of the truth had been distorted by Samael even before his soul descended into this world.

VIII. THE RABBI'S SON

Stories of the zadik's power to attract new followers are legion in Hasidic literature and served to spread the doctrines of the movement or of specific Hasidim. Ordinarily, the potential Hasid is initially skeptical and has to be won over to the belief in the zadik even though logic dictates the contrary. Usually the story climaxes in the Hasid's acceptance of the zadik as his spiritual master.

"The Rabbi's Son" is a variation on this motif in that the story ends in failure—the young man dies—and a necessary failure at that as we are told that had the young man united with the zadik, the messiah might have appeared. And since our experience of this world indicates that the messiah has not yet come, these two figures were not destined to be joined in master-disciple relationship. The actual cosmic dynamic is presented in Kabbalistic terms. The young man is described as being in the aspect of "the small light," that is, the moon or the sefirah *malkhut*, the lowest of the ten *sefirot* of the standard Kabbalistic system. The zadik is in the aspect of "the great light," that is, the sun and either the sefirah *tiferet* (the seventh) or *yesod* (the ninth) in the system. If *malkhut* joins with either *tiferet* or *yesod*, the messianic process can be set in motion.

Samael, naturally, does not want this to happen and does his best to prevent the fateful meeting. The story, then, is a working out in narrative terms—with great attention given to both psychological realism and divination—of Samael's will. The father, a traditional rabbi of esteemed family lineage, does not want his son to seek comfort for his malaise from the zadik, whom he regards as fallacious. Only repeated evidence of his son's unhappiness prompts him to make the trip which he assumes will fail, as he cannot imagine that the zadik is of any consequence. The father's skepticism is manifested, somewhat ironically, in the two tests he proposes as omens of God's will. In both cases, the carriage breaks down, interrupting the journey. What the father thinks is proof of God's will turns out to be the work of Samael. Ironically, again, it is the son, a potential Hasid, who rejects this type of divination while suggesting that only truly bizarre phenomena should be considered omens.

The third and final obstacle to their trip is not an omen but rumors spread by an ostensibly disinterested merchant (Samael disguised) whom they meet at the inn; the merchant tells them the zadik is frivolous and has committed a sin in his presence. (We are never told what the sin was, just as we are never told what commandment entitled the rabbi's son to be in the aspect of "the small light.") The seemingly frivolous act is not only the merchant's (Samael's) description of what might have been a true spiritual deed, but points to the different perception of reality presented by Hasidism, in general, and Bratslav Hasidism in particular. Thus "the frivolous act" which dissuades the rabbi from allowing his son to continue to the zadik is both a deliberate distortion by Samael and a possibly honest misunderstanding of a simple merchant. Significantly, the son dies after their return from the encounter with the merchant (Samael) at the inn.

The father does not realize that he has been duped all along by Samael until, on his son's request in a series of dreams, he makes the journey to the zadik alone and meets Samael in the inn. It is Samael who tells him how he, Samael, prevented the union of the two lights which might have brought the messiah. The zadik, apparently presenting the point of view of the author himself, gives voice to the depth of despair caused by this failure to bring the messiah. His statement reveals the full significance of the failure: "What a pity, what a pity! A pity on those who are lost and will never be found! May the Lord, blessed be He, return our exiles shortly, Amen!"

IX. THE *HAKHAM* AND THE *TAM* (THE CLEVER MAN AND THE ORDINARY MAN)

Since the matrix of this story is the obvious contrast between two character types, the *hakham* (the clever man) and the *tam* (the ordinary man), it is crucial to assess what Rabbi Nahman was actually referring to by these names. The terms are used consciously and become part of the proper names of the characters. Ordinarily in Jewish literature the *hakham* is a sage, a truly wise and pious person whose advice one would follow. Here, however, the term is used ironically, almost in its Yiddish sense, connoting a person who is endowed with certain superior talents, who often boasts of his wisdom, but makes foolish choices in the conduct of his life. In the story, the *hakham* is brilliant, ambitious, arrogant—and basically miserable. He is clever rather than wise. If wisdom is supposed to bring one happiness, he is certainly a fool. The *tam* is an ordinary man, not a simpleton or a fool, but a man who, in his guilelessness and simple perceptions, is ultimately wiser and certainly happier than the *hakham*. The *tam* is content to live the life of a poor cobbler in a provincial town, while the *hakham* is driven to wander the great cities of Europe where one wears fine clothing and dazzling jewelry and spouts philosophy. The *tam* has a devoted wife, while the *hakham* is a lonely bachelor; since he is so critical of others, he cannot tolerate their foibles or enjoy their company. He does not appreciate the loyalty of his childhood friend, the *tam*, and enjoys only the company of another *hakham*, shrewdly sent by the king to accompany him.

The story develops in three sequences; each presents the contrast between the two characters and advances the plot. While the religious aspect of the contrast is hardly evident in the first sequence (chapters 1-3),

309

it is patent in the second (chapter 4) and dominant in the third (chapter 5). In the first sequence, the *tam* lives the spiritual life of the pious Jew while his boyhood friend, the *hakham*, delights in the outward show of worldly brilliance and wealth. In the second sequence, the *tam* joyously accepts the invitation of the king to visit the capital, but the *hakham*, overcome by his skepticism, cannot even accept the fact of the king's existence. The *tam* is immediately rewarded by a meteoric rise in the service of the king while the *hakham* embarks upon a life of wandering and poverty.

Several allusions in the second sequence lead the reader to surmise that the king is probably an allegorical representation of God. The *tam*, for instance, joyously accepts the invitation to meet him, while the *hakham* denies his existence. In the same sequence, the *hakham* casts aspersions upon a *Baal Shem*. And in the last sequence, which actually complements the second sequence, a summons is sent to each of the main characters by Azazel, the devil, the counterpart of the king whom we have identified as God. We discover that the deftly drawn and often satirical characterizations of the first and second sequences are actually the preparation for a contrast between belief and skepticism.

The rejection of belief here is different from that in "The Rabbi's Son" in which the father who opposes the zadik is himself a rabbi. While the father opposed the zadik's particular type of religious belief and practice, the *hakham* denies the very existence of both the king and Azazel. In this sense he resembles the *Maskil*, the modern, westernized Jew who prided himself on his rationality and often rejected outright the basic tenets of Judaism which he mocked as benighted and foolish. Though the *hakham* bears some resemblance to the Faustian hero (he even claims that the messenger of the devil is really his brother), the archetype of the *Maskil*—which Rabbi Nahman knew firsthand—cannot be avoided. It is therefore logical that the author also derides the *hakham*'s secular self-reliance which fails him, and the corrupt, devious sophistication of urban life. The *hakham*'s scorn of the *tam*'s ignorance is the outrageous irony of the story: It is the *tam* with his "simple" faith and love who saves the *hakham* from the mire of Azazel.

X. THE BURGHER AND THE PAUPER

Like "The King and the Emperor," "The Burgher and the Pauper" utilizes a basic plot found in romances of all nations: A young man and woman, destined to be married, are prevented from doing so by one of their parents who refuses to honor the pledge made to join the children in marriage; through a series of intricate adventures involving intrigue, violence, deception, and escape, the lovers are joined in a happy ending often affirming some of the basic values the society cherishes.

Structurally, however, these two stories differ radically. In "The King and the Emperor," once the young couple has escaped and then become separated, the king's son is totally forgotten while the emperor's daughter acts aggressively and resourcefully in a series of episodes, always avoiding marriage and harm, until she rejoins and ultimately marries her beloved. At least two of these episodes could have been deleted with little change to the plot. "The Burgher and the Pauper," on the other hand, is so tightly contrived that no episode can be omitted, thus enhancing the sense of both divine and authorial control. Much attention, furthermore, is devoted to the wealthy man's son and to the parents of both children. The decisiveness of the daughter of the pauper (who becomes emperor) is balanced by the despair and resignation of the wealthy man's son. The struggle against all obstacles to the consummation of the predestined marriage is complicated by the young man's hesitant personality.

The central story is enriched by the events that precede it: the enigmatically identical dreams, the warm relationship between the two families, the kidnapping of the pauper's wife, and her rescue by the wealthy merchant. And while one expects in such a romance a reversal of fortunes—the impoverishment of the wealthy man and the enrichment of the pauper—the reprehensible behavior of the pauper/emperor is a bit surprising. His base character had never really improved and his rise to prominence was due not to his virtues but to the remarkable beauty and personality of his daughter. A series of parallel situations helps to shape the narrative: The promise made in the presence of the seven bodies of water is reinforced by the pledge made by the daughter of the pauper/ emperor and attested to by the document sent to the wealthy man's son; the seven bodies of water figure in the rescue of the pauper's wife and in the kidnapping of his daughter; both young lovers are spirited away in sacks. True to the pattern of the well-wrought romance, the suspense in this story is generated not by the happy ending itself—which we take for granted—but by the artful strategies used to reach that ending. Three of the protagonists meet mysteriously in an uninhabited place and live together for some time before revealing their identities to each other. The reader, of course, knows the truth all the time. Once they join forces in search of the lost document, which the wealthy man's son had sought for so long, it is discovered and the way is clear for the marriage of the young couple. Psychological behavior repeatedly echoes or manifests the designs of cosmic forces operating in the story.

Bratslav exegetes from Rabbi Nahman's period until today have insisted upon an allegorical reading of the story based on Kabbalistic principles. The story allegedly deals with the mystical secret of redemption and, more specifically, the development of the soul of the messiah, here the wealthy man's son. One of the Hebrew postscripts to the story tells us: "The Jews in Egypt had signs who the redeemer would be, and there are surely signs for the savior who will come." The parallel between the Exodus from Egypt and the final redemption, between Moses and the messiah, is, of course, traditional.

More recently, Adin Steinsalz has suggested an elaborate allegorical interpretation in which the son is, indeed, the messiah and the daughter is both Knesset Israel, the community of Israel perceived as an aspect of the Godhead, and the Shekhinah, the presence of God in the world or the lowest of the ten *sefirot*. The experiences of the parents represent the sojourn in Egypt and the Exodus therefrom, since the wealthy man portrays Moses, and the pauper's wife, the historical community of Israel. Impelled by his devotion to her, he tries to free her from the general who captured her, from her Egyptian bondage. This act of redemption has always been considered by Kabbalists to be both incomplete and an archetype of the future perfect redemption at the end of time. "The pledge the daughter grants [the wealthy man's son], the sign by which she will recognize him, is the memory of the first salvation; the final salvation is, in fact, the completion of the first." The seven sources of water in the story represent the seven watering places in the desert mentioned in the story of

Exodus and associated in the Kabbala with the seven lower sefirotic spheres. The document, then, would be the Torah which, to be acceptable to the Shekhinah, has to be studied and presented esoterically, hence the rejection of the three royal suitors who could sing certain parts but not all the formula on the document. Other features of the narrative are also standard Kabbalistic items: the exile of the messiah; the storm of evil winds; the residence of the messiah in a place of refuge until the time of redemption. The union of Knesset Israel with the messiah ushers in the final redemption.

If this allegorical interpretation is plausible, Rabbi Nahman presents here a remarkable psychological study of the agonies of the messiah confronted with constant frustration in his attempt to bring the final redemption. He is supported and inspired in this effort by the Shekhinah or Knesset Israel, each a different aspect of the same sefirotic phenomenon. The centrality of Israel in history manifest in "The King Who Decreed Conversion" is expanded into cosmic dimensions in the mythic word of the Kabbalah.

XI. THE KING'S SON AND THE MAIDSERVANT'S SON WHO WERE SWITCHED

Though this story seems, at first, to be a version of the "Prince and the Pauper" theme in which the displaced son struggles and finally regains his rightful patrimony, Rabbi Nahman's story is actually a study in the discovery or rediscovery of self. The true prince, switched at infancy with his mother's maidservant's son, must regain the sense of self he lost when he was forced to leave home by the maidservant's son, who had been erroneously reared as a prince in the royal palace. Despondent over the injustice of the situation and his loss of identity, the true prince abuses himself in drinking and whoring. When he is finally overcome by thoughts of repentance, supernatural forces lead him first to a fair, then to a forest where he meets the maidservant's son who had become king but had abdicated his throne when he realized that it was not rightly his.

One might expect the story to end happily at this point with the restoration of the true prince and the reward of the maidservant's son with a high position, but Rabbi Nahman has his hero proceed through a series of fantastic sequences, including two trials of his wisdom, to the final acceptance of the fact that he is, indeed, the royal personage he is supposed to be. Only when he earned this position by exorcising the bewitched garden and repairing the royal chamber does he accept his own identity as king.

The story is a fascinating meld of psychological insights and fantastic episodes. The true prince's despair, for instance, is carefully motivated and well drawn. The author captures the irony in the desire of the maidservant's son to ruin the wealthy man who, he must realize, is his own father. The fantastic appears in the form of the sun's laughter, the house floating in air, the magic instrument that can elicit wondrous music from all animals it touches. The fantastic is employed to externalize psychological states when, for instance, the true prince hears a message repeated in several dreams, or the man of the forest tells him that the animals he chases are really his sins, or when both the true prince and the usurper begin to discern marvelous music in the hitherto terrifying bellowing of the beasts, a change in audial perception induced by initiation of the process of role reestablishment: The maidservant's son has sold himself to the real prince and has informed his new master who he is. Beautiful music is associated with various steps in the restoration of the prince's sense of identity; the throne room, once restored, begins to play an exquisite melody. Terrible cacophony becomes ravishing harmony as the real prince gropes towards a rediscovery of his true self.

Bratslav exegesis holds that this story is a dramatization on a personal level of the process of *tikkun* whereby the cosmos is restored to the harmony it once had before the disruption of the proper structure of the sefirotic world. The ostensibly whimsical act of the midwife, therefore, is not an experiment in child psychology, but a cataclysm similar to the king's anger in "The Loss of the Princess."

Even the demonic forces are progressively neutralized throughout the story. At first, the midwife wantonly switched the children, a chaotic, heartless act. The cruel merchant for whom the true prince works is the personal agent who moves the prince from the city to the forest, the locus of adventure and change which would be impossible in the city. The bizarre "man of the forest," though greatly feared at first by the prince, turns out to be his major benefactor. He guides him; he gives him a sack of bread by which he gains mastery over the maidservant's son; he presents him with the magical instrument.

Wisdom, finally, is the salient character trait by which one demonstrates the right to rule. The true prince barters the musical instrument he received for the power of logical deduction. With this power, he has the confidence to undergo the two trials which will restore the original name of the kingdom—"The Foolish Country with the Wise Government"—decreed by the former king before his death. The true prince's superior wisdom is not so much a matter of birth as a divine gift, a reward for his rejection of the dissolute life and his payment (through his labors for the cruel merchant) for his sins—the two animals he searches for in the forest. The courage needed to undertake the two trials was born of his confidence in his newly gained power of reasoning. Repentance, thus, leads to wisdom which, in turn, leads to courage; these three qualities make him fit to be king.

XII. THE MASTER OF PRAYER

The opening description of the Master of Prayer (*Baal Tefilla*), who devotes all his efforts to the service of the Lord and the conversion of other men to the truth, invites comparison with the role of the zadik in Hasidism and Rabbi Nahman's relentless obsession with his own mission. The autobiographical echo, however, is only the initial situation in a lengthy cosmic epic which dramatizes some of the basic phases of the Lurianic myth of the world. The narrative seems, at first, to be limited to the efforts of the Master of Prayer to rescue the people of the Land of Riches from their absurd belief that money is the final purpose of life. The satire, so reminiscent of Swift (the scatological passage is deferred to the end of the story), derides the folly of an entire society structured according to financial worth. The pious faith of the Master of Prayer is contrasted here not with traditional rabbinic praxis, or with the secular, rationalistic spirit, or with Gentile society as a whole, but rather with bourgeois ideals reduced to their lowest common denominator: money. As the reader progresses, he discovers that the initial situation is vastly enriched and modified by two "framed stories," one told by the Master of Prayer and the other by one of the soldiers of the Warrior. These two stories present no less than a coherent history of civilization fancifully presented in line with Lurianic principles.

While the story of the Master of Prayer and the Land of Riches is told straightforwardly, the cosmic myth is told in fragments, retrospectively. The general outline is clear and the reference to the King and his court is not veiled; they are, in fact, called the "Holy Community" toward the end of the story. We learn that early in the history of this kingdom — obviously, the world — when the King had sent his ministers to various lands to obtain their specific powers, a tempest devastated the kingdom, and while it did not damage the palace itself, it scattered the royal family:

317

the King, the Queen, the Princess, and the Princess's remarkable son. In the second "frame story" we are told the effects of the tempest on human beings. Having lost their natural king, men had to elect a new ruler and, divided on what is the final purpose of life which the king should embody, they arrived at a variety of solutions, all satirized by Rabbi Nahman in a chain of nine comic sequences. In several of the cases, the chosen final purpose leads to an absurd choice: a crotchety beggar, a parricide, a mad Frenchman, a drunken Gentile. In other cases, the choice is not absurd in itself, but the chosen could not possibly serve as the new king of the universe: a rich man, a beautiful woman, a wise man, a muscular man, even a "master of prayer."

The link between the original Master of Prayer and his quest to save the Land of Riches, on the one hand, and the cosmic history, on the other, is provided by the Warrior, one of the original Holy Community, who decided to conquer the world not for personal gain but rather to find and restore the original King. The people of the Land of Riches fear the Warrior and send the Master of Prayer whom they had captured to intercede in their behalf with the Warrior. When the two meet, we discover that both were original members of the Holy Community. Though their individual quests seem to differ, they turn out to be different aspects of the same process. Though it is never specifically stated in the story, we are led to comprehend that the worship of money is one of the manifestations of the cataclysm at the dawn of civilization; the deluded people can be redeemed only when the Holy Community is reunited. Neither the Master of Prayer nor the Warrior (acting by himself) nor the Treasurer knows how to redeem these deluded people. Only the King knows, and once he is found by his former ministers, the Master of Prayer, the Warrior, and the Treasurer, he gives the proper instructions for the remedy. Not coincidentally, the locus of the act of remedy is the top of the mountain which the Warrior had climbed to obtain his magical sword at the beginning of history. The power emanating from that source both impelled the Warrior to find the King and feeds the fire which cooks the magic dishes that cure the money-mad people of their madness. In contrast with the sublime fragrance of the sacred food, the money stinks like feces and must be buried in the ground.

One must conclude from this story that mankind cannot properly perceive the truth unless aided by a figure such as the Master of Prayer who, though portrayed as a human being, is one of the original Holy Community. The human mistake that feces are gold or money is the cardinal example of misperception, but other examples are strewn throughout the story. As the Holy Community begins to reassemble to-

ward the end of the story, we discover that what men thought was the
blood of murdered people was actually the Queen's tears, or that what
they thought was a drunken Gentile was really the King's bosom friend.
Primarily preoccupied with the process of *tikkun* (remedy, redemption),
the story deals at length with the contact between the upper and lower
worlds.

XIII. THE SEVEN BEGGARS

In consonance with the paradoxicality of Nahman's spiritual temperament, the last of his stories, "The Seven Beggars," is both the most quoted and least understood of his narratives. The story is so complex, so richly allusive, so enigmatic, that no commentator, either traditional or modern, has dared to claim mastery of it. Most exegetes have argued that the story is incomplete, either because Nahman declined cloture here as in "The Loss of the Princess" for ideological reasons, or he was simply too feeble toward the end of his life to complete so demanding a work. Yosef Dan, who has produced the most coherent overview of the story, suggests that the story was to have eleven discrete units, but Nahman deliberately left out the last three.

Without delving into the detailed problematics of the tale—a task for an independent multivolume study—we can, nevertheless, present some of the undeniable narrative facts which have led Dan to his conclusions. The tale begins with a familiar episode regarding the transfer of power from a king to his son (a bit unusual here since the king decided to transfer the power during his own lifetime) and the son's misrule of the kingdom (cf. stories IV, VII, X, and XI. We then shift to a slightly sketched tale of a political upheaval in which a young couple is abandoned in a forest and succored by a series of beggars, implying some sort of providential intrusion into history (cf. stories II and X, both romances). We are thus not surprised that this young couple are married, entailing restoration of the harmony disturbed by the flight which had scattered the populace. The appearance of the beggars bearing wedding gifts and prepared to relate elaborate, often fantastic stories should not startle readers of the folktale. The assemblage of a group of master narrators is a standard technique, for example, *The Decameron* or *The Canterbury Tales*. Two outstanding questions come to mind: (a) What is the connection between the tale of the king who transferred his power and the main story of the two children who were first lost, then united in a festive marriage? (b) Why do only six of the seven beggars appear to tell their stories at the wedding?

Without citing or subscribing to all of Dan's explanations, plausible answers are, nevertheless, possible. The king's transfer of his power to his foolish son obviously precipitated the mass flight which left the children alone in the forest. The deletion of the seventh beggar does have ideological implications, that is, reticence concerning the coming of the day of redemption. Regarding the omission of the seventh beggar, one does not need to have recourse to the Kabbalistic, sefirotic structure. There are, for instance, seven days of wedding feasts at a traditional Jewish wedding and the introduction of the seventh beggar would be analogous to the completion of the feast, the total consummation of the wedding, an episode Nahman might not have cared to introduce. There are also seven days in the week crowned by the Sabbath, a day of joy — celebrated in Bratslav circles by song and dance (the last beggar had no legs and was probably a consummate dancer)—suggestive, therefore, of life in the next world.

Dan's comparison of the structure of "The Seven Beggars" with "The Loss of the Princess" is traditional and helpful in that both stories deal with an initial cataclysm and have a declined or incomplete cloture. In "The Loss of the Princess" the king's unexplained anger precipitates the daughter's exile and, in turn, the viceroy's search which is the focus of the story. In our notes on that story, we referred to the exegetical consensus that the king's anger is a short, veiled reference to the Kabbalistic act of *tzimtzum*. In "The Seven Beggars," the same phrase precipitated the action of the story, but the narrative details are far richer and comprise the entire first narrative sequence.

The transfer of power is first described as a political act culled from a royal chronicle. Only when the king makes his farewell address (he has no intention, incidentally, of leaving the kingdom) do we sense something strange. The king's testament to his son is enigmatic (cf. story III, "The Cripple"): You should always be joyous! This injunction is complicated by two remarks: If you are not joyous, you do not deserve to be king; if you are joyous, I shall also be joyous! The theme of joy is abruptly dropped and we learn that the son foolishly established (secular) wisdom as the criterion of virtue in his kingdom (cf. the criterion of wealth in "The Master of Prayer") which led to the heretical conduct of the kingdom. Only when he occasionally intuited that he had misruled his kingdom did he groan and feel sorrow.

COMMENTARIES

In a second seemingly abrupt shift, we learn about a mass flight and the loss of the two children in the forest. Dan has demonstrated that the entire first sequence, including the flight into the forest, is a vivid narrative account of the process of *tzimtzum* and *shevirat hakelim* in which the king who willingly transfers his power during his lifetime is the correlative of the *En-sof* (the infinite pure core of divinity devoid of all attributes and contamination by contact with this material world), and the son's abandonment of joy and espousal of secular wisdom (Nahman constantly preached against secular wisdom, but encouraged a life of naive religious joy) is the cataclytic era of *shevirah* and scattering. The act of *tikkun* actually begins when the children first meet the beggars in the forest.

Unlike "The Loss of the Princess," which is primarily devoted to the agonized struggle of the search that is never consummated, "The Seven Beggars" is mostly a celebration of the act of *tikkun*, a long wedding feast in which six of the seven beggars tell delightful stories as do guests or jesters at wedding banquets in all literatures. We should not forget that the story begins with Nahman's declaration (found only in the Hebrew version): "I will tell you how our people were once joyous."

The locale of the celebration, a shabby pit, clearly contrasts with the majestic ball scene of the opening sequence and we surmise from the contrast that the world of reality is a world of illusion—a standard Bratslav dictum. The grand ball was the focal point of *tzimtzum* and *shevirah* while the shabby pit is the continued locus of *tikkun* with its festivities. Just as in the case of the *tam* (in "The *Hakham* and the *Tam*"), taste is in the palate of the consumer: The *tam*, the king's true son ("The King's Son and the Maidservant's Son Who Were Switched"), and these children do quite well on bread.

The notion that there is a true world beyond this illusory world of our daily existence is the one guiding principle in the description of the beggars: Each has a defect which, when examined, turns out to be a virtue. The blind beggar, for instance, can *really* see since his vision antedates the vision necessary to perceive all material objects; it is a vision which requires no objects. The story of his life parallels the story of the creation of all life and, as such, proves that he is older than all his competitors at the wedding. In each case, the beggar—be he the deaf one, the stutterer, the one with the twisted neck, or the hunchback, or the one without hands—comes to bring his gift to the couple. The story which purports to explain his gift is complicated, delightful, enigmatic, virtually a gift in itself. Not every story told at the wedding has Kabbalistic implications (as does the story of the Source and the Mountain told by the stutterer); not all stories are terribly serious (the story of the hunchback is satiric); and not all seem to be related to the spiritual quest (as is that of the beggar without hands and the Water Castle). But all are well-wrought, artful miniatures of inventive fabulation.

With their deliberately wild logic they confound the rationality of the king's son; by their festive spirit they nullify his worries; and in their fantastic play of the imagination, they replace for the reader the missing dance of the seventh and last beggar who would have made the wedding feast complete.

BIBLIOGRAPHY
(Selected)

The literature on the areas touched upon in this volume—Hasidism, Kabbalah, East European Jewish history, and folklore—is vast and I shall suggest only those items which have been either indispensable or especially useful. Since much of the material is in Hebrew or in Yiddish, I shall stress English sources, but call attention to the most important Hebrew or Yiddish works. A list of bibliographies will also be supplied for more precise information and the reader's further study.

A. The Text and Its Traditional Commentaries

The Hebrew and Yiddish text I have used for my translation is the traditional Bratslav text, often reprinted and copied scrupulously from the first edition of 1815. Though the place of publication is usually cited as Ostrog, recent scholarship has argued that it was actually published in Moghilev. The traditional Bratslav exegetes consulted were Nathan Sternhartz of Nemirow, Nahman of Cheryn, and Abraham Hazan.

B. Studies of Nahman of Bratslav and Bratslav Hasidism

The only scholarly study in English of Nahman's life and spiritual ambience is Arthur Green's *Rabbi Nahman of Bratslav: A Critical Biography*. Originally a doctoral dissertation (Brandeis, 1975), it will soon be published by the University of Alabama Press. The *Encyclopaedia Judaica* article offers nothing not found in Green's book. Standard introductions—including that of Martin Buber—or chapters in histories are either incomplete or unreliable. Though available only in Hebrew, two scholarly volumes are indispensable to Bratslav research: Mendel Piekarz' *Bratslav Hasidism* (Jerusalem, 1972) and Josef Weiss' *Studies in Bratslav Hasidism* (Jerusalem, 1974). Acute insights into the motifs of each story may be found in Martin Mantel's unpublished doctoral dissertation *Nachman of Bratzlav* (Princeton, 1977). Three individual stories have been explained rather traditionally by Adin Steinsaltz in *Ariel 35* (1974), *Shefa* I/1 (Summer, 1977), and *Shefa* I/2 (Autumn, 1977). Available only in Hebrew are two of the most important and perceptive studies of the Hasidic tale in general, and the Bratslav tale in particular: Yosef Dan's *The Hasidic Story: Its History and Development* (Jerusalem, 1975) and Yoav Elstein's unpublished doctoral dissertation, *The Structure of the Hasidic Tale* (U.C.L.A., 1974).

Among the Hebrew and Yiddish authors listed in the bibliographies, the following are of particular significance: Charney (Niger), Dan, Horodoezky, Kook, I. Rabinovitz, Sadan, Schmeruk, Werses, M. Weiner, H. Zeitlin, S. Zetser.

C. Hasidism and Kabbalah; East European Background

There is, to date, no comprehensive scholarly work on Hasidism in English. Though Martin Buber's books have introduced Hasidism to a wide audience, his views are subjective and do not reflect the findings of historical, philological studies of the past fifty years. The standards for scholarship in Jewish mysticism and Hasidism have been set in the magisterial studies of Gershom Scholem, many of which, fortunately, are available in English: *Major Trends in Jewish Mysticism* (New York, 1941); *On the Kabbalah and Its Symbolism* (New York, 1965); *The Messianic Idea in Judaism* (New York, 1971); *Sabbetai Zevi: Mystical Messiah* (Princeton, 1973); *Kabbalah* (New York, 1974). Since these works do not deal comprehensively with Hasidism, the *Encyclopaedia Judaica* article on this subject will be of use. Valuable background material can be found in R.J.Z. Werblowsky's *Joseph Karo, Lawyer and Mystic* (Oxford, 1962) and Simon Dubnow's *History of the Jews in Russia and Poland* (Philadelphia, 1916). Significant articles by Josef Weiss and Alexander Altmann can be found in the bibliographies listed below. Among the Hebrew authors listed in the bibliographies, the following are of particular significance: Balaban, Dinur, Dubnow, Halpern, Horodezky, Mahler, Schatz-Uffenheimer, Schmeruk, Tishby, Weiss, Wilensky.

D. Folklore

Martin Mantel's unpublished doctoral thesis, *Nahman of Bratzlav* (Princeton, 1977) is the first attempt at a comprehensive analysis of the narrative sources of the various Bratslav tales. The thesis lacks a scholarly apparatus.

E. Bibliographies on Hasidism and Nahman of Bratslav

1. English. Appended to Arthur Green's *Nahman of Bratslav: A Critical Biography* (Alamaba, 1978 ?).

2. English. Appended to *In Praise of the Baal Shem Tov*, translated and edited by Dan Ben-Amos and Jerome Mintz (Bloomington, 1970).

3. English. Articles on "Hasidism" and "Nahman of Bratslav" in the *Encyclopaedia Judaica*.

4. Hebrew. Appended to volume 2 of Yoav Elstein's unpublished doctoral thesis, *The Structure of the Hasidic Tale* (U.C.L.A., 1974).

5. Hebrew. Article on "Hasidism" and "Nahman of Bratslav" in the *Encyclopaedia Hebraica*.

INDEX

Haifa, 18
Hakham, 141, 309, 310
"The Hakham and the Tam",
  323; date of, 44, 141, 191;
  discussion of, 141, 309–310
Hannukah, Sabbath of, 18
hasagah, 32
Ha Sefer Ha Nisraf, 24
Hasidim, and folktale, 29, 30;
  learning of, 16; meaning of, 13;
  relatedness to zadik, xiii, 13, 17,
  18, 20, 25, 36, 302, 307
Hasidism, and the Baal Shem Tov,
  13, 14–15; and Bratslav
  Hasidism, 308; description of, 9;
  of Faith, 21, 22; literature of,
  xiii, xiv; and messianic claims,
  12; origins and spread of, 10, 13,
  14, 15; research into, 48; and
  traditional rabbinic leadership,
  10, 14, 141; typology of, 21
Hasidut of Mysticism, 21, 22
Hayye Muharan, 303
Hebrew literature, 30, 43, 45
Hellenistic period, 289
Holy Land, 16, 18
Holy Sparks, 33
Holy Tongue, 35
Horodetzki, S.A., xiv
Hosea, 290
Hurwitz family, 24

Idra Rabba, 33
Illumination, 34, 36
Irony, 115, 301, 308, 309, 315
Israel, in history, 313; Lord of,
  300; people of, 11, 53, 286, 291,
  298, 312

Jerusalem, 48
Jews, attitude towards tales, 30; in
  Egypt, 312; enlightened, 24, 97,
  141, 191, 310; exile of, 97;
  history of, 297, 304; literature of,
  xiii, xvi, 290, 297, 309; and
  mysticism, xiv, xvi, 10, 14, 48;
  restrictions on, 18; sources of
  tales, 33; spiritual life of, xiii, 9,
  10, 12, 97, 293, 297, 298; in
  Tales, 123, 295, 297, 298, 303,
  304; traditional life of, 10, 16,
  290, 322
Judaism, 123, 303, 304, 310

Kabbalah, and Adam, 286; and
  biblical exegesis, xiii, 11; and
  "The Burgher and the Pauper",
  312, 313; and "The King and the
  Emperor", 291; and "The Loss of
  the Princess", 285; Lurianic, xvii,
  xix, 11, 20; and "The Master of
  Prayer", 213; and Nahman's
  journey, 19; and "The Rabbi's
  Son", 307; and "The Seven
  Beggars", 322, 323; and Tales,
  xiv, xv, 3, 43, 45, 46, 47, 48; and
  Zohar, 11, 14
Kamenetz-Podolsk, 18, 23
Karo, Joseph, 14
Kassel, 29
Kermode, Frank, 38
Kinder und Hausmaerchen, 29
"The King and the Emperor",
  165, 311; date of, 44; discussion
  of, 65, 289–291
"The King and the Spider", cf.
  "The King Who Fought Many
  Wars"
"The King and the Wise Man",
  date of, 44; discussion of, 115,
  301–302
King of the Universe, 298, 303
"The King Who Decreed
  Conversion", 115, 123, 303,
  313; date of, 44; discussion of,
  97, 297–298
"The King Who Fought Many
  Wars", date of, 44; discussion of,

Weiss, Yosef, xv, xvi, 16, 21, 22, 35, 38, 48
Wiesel, Elie, 43
Wisdom, 303, 316, 322, 323

Ya'ari, Yehudah, 43
Yesod, 307
Yiddish literature, 45, 309

Zadik, cf. also Nahman; Baal Shem Tov, 13; and cosmic restoration, 12, 14; *emet*, 38; of the generation, cf. *Zadik Hador*; and Hasidim, 13, 17, 18, 20, 25, 36, 107; hidden, 299, 302; learning of, 16, 17; and Messiah, 20; and mysticism, 10; role of, xiii, 9, 22, 35, 317; in the *Tales*, 53, 107, 123, 133, 141, 213, 299, 300, 302, 304, 305, 307, 308, 310; as true, 20, 34, 53
Zadik hador, list of, 15; motif of, 15; Nahman as, 15, 20, 21, 35; need for, 22; and tales, 38, 39; in *Tales*, 286
Zaslow, 24
The Zeide, cf. Aryeh Leib of Shpole; 19, 20
Zemer, 36
Zlatopol, 19
Zohar, xvii, 11, 14, 16, 31, 33

INDEX TO THE TALES